The Cost of Belonging

ISSUES OF GLOBALIZATION
Case Studies in Contemporary Anthropology
Series Editors: Carla Freeman and Li Zhang

Global Nomads: Migration, Insecurity, and Belonging in West Africa
Susanna Fioratta

*Indebted: An Ethnography of Despair and Resilience
in Greece's Second City*
Kathryn A. Kozaitis

*Burning at Europe's Borders: An Ethnography on the
African Migrant Experience in Morocco*
Isabella Alexander-Nathani

Labor and Legality: An Ethnography of a Mexican Immigrant Network,
Tenth Anniversary Edition
Ruth Gomberg-Muñoz

*Marriage After Migration: An Ethnography of Money, Romance,
and Gender in Globalizing Mexico*
Nora Haenn

*Serious Youth in Sierra Leone:
An Ethnography of Performance and Global Connection*
Catherine E. Bolten

*Low Wage in High Tech: An Ethnography of Service Workers
in Global India*
Kiran Mirchandani, Sanjukta Mukherjee, and Shruti Tambe

*Care for Sale: An Ethnography of Latin American Domestic
and Sex Workers in London*
Ana P. Gutiérrez Garza

The Cost of Belonging

An Ethnography of Solidarity and Mobility in Beijing's Koreatown

SHARON J. YOON

New York   Oxford
OXFORD UNIVERSITY PRESS

Oxford University Press is a department of the University of Oxford.

It furthers the University's objective of excellence in research, scholarship, and education by publishing worldwide. Oxford is a registered trade mark of Oxford University Press in the UK and certain other countries.

Published in the United States of America by Oxford University Press 198 Madison Avenue, New York, NY 10016, United States of America.

Library of Congress Cataloging-in-Publication Data

Names: Yoon, Sharon J., author.
Title: The cost of belonging : an ethnography of solidarity and mobility in Beijing's Koreatown / Sharon J. Yoon.
Description: New York, NY : Oxford University Press, [2021] | Includes bibliographical references and index.
Identifiers: LCCN 2020025280 | ISBN 9780197517901 (paperback) | ISBN 9780197517925 (ebook)
Subjects: LCSH: Koreans—China—Beijing—Social conditions. | Koreans—China—Beijing—Economic conditions. | Belonging (Social psychology)—China—Beijing. | Wangjing (Beijing, China)—Social conditions. | Wangjing (Beijing, China)—Economic conditions. | China—Foreign economic relations—Korea (South) | Korea (South)—Foreign economic relations—China.
Classification: LCC DS795.9.K67 Y66 2021 | DDC 305.8957/051156—dc23
LC record available at https://lccn.loc.gov/2020025280

Printing number: 9 8 7 6 5 4 3 2 1
Printed by LSC Communications, Inc.,
United States of America

For my parents, Barnabas and Evelyn Yoon

TABLE OF CONTENTS

....

ACKNOWLEDGMENTS

....

My interest in the Korean diaspora was sparked during my undergraduate years at Dartmouth College. More than fifteen years later, my advisors—Steven Ericson, James Dorsey, and Dennis Washburn—have continued to support my growth as an academic. With their encouragement, I started my graduate training at Princeton University, where I met Gilbert Rozman. I am grateful to Gil for allowing me to chart my own path as a researcher, even if it meant diverging from his own interests at times, and for cultivating within me a thirst for going into the field and connecting with locals on their own terms. I can only hope that I will be able to return the favor, by being the mentor he has been to me to my own students someday.

At Princeton I was also lucky to meet King-to Yeung, who spent many hours reading earlier drafts with a fine-tooth comb, and Douglas Massey, who took me under his wing during a critical time in my career. Even many years after I left Princeton, I remain influenced by scholars who mentored me, such as Amy Borovoy, Paul DiMaggio, and Mitchell Duneier, as well as friends who later became colleagues, such as Rachel Ferguson, Rene Flores, Denia Garcia, Laura Berzak Hopkins, Becky Yang Hsu, Jennifer Huynh, Jaeeun Kim, Akito Kusaka, Tina Lee, Carol Ann MacGregor, Alex Murphy and Naomi Sugie.

My fieldwork in Beijing was made possible through funding from the Princeton Institute for International and Regional Studies' (PIIRS) Global

Network for Inequality, the National Science Foundation Dissertation Improvement Grant (DDRI #1131006), and the National Science Foundation Graduate Research Fellowship. The Chinese Academy for the Social Sciences provided institutional sponsorship while I was in Beijing, and the Yanbian University of Science and Technology provided access to archival resources and research support when I traveled to the Korean Autonomous Prefecture in 2006.

During the early phases of this project, I relied heavily on my research assistant, Young-me Piao, a third-generation Korean Chinese minority. With her support as my right-hand woman, I was able to establish rapport with many Korean Chinese minorities, who were otherwise suspicious of my presence in the field. Young-me vouched for me, helped me translate important documents, distributed survey questionnaires, and provided key insights when I was out in the field. Though she was a wide-eyed college student when I first met her, she is now happily married and the mother of a beautiful little girl in Seoul.

While I was in China, my Korean Chinese Bible study group treated me like I was a member of their family. Their warm presence provided me with the emotional sustenance I needed to finish my field research. I am also grateful to my South Korean fellowship group for introducing me to their friends and helping distribute surveys. A South Korean missionary, who will remain anonymous, connected me to several different South Korean and Korean Chinese pastors in and around the enclave. He treated my project as if it were his own and did his very best to make sure that I was well-integrated within the Korean Christian community in Beijing.

I continued to work on my manuscript as a Korea Foundation Postdoctoral Fellow (#C201300323) at the James Joo-Jin Kim Center for Korean Studies at the University of Pennsylvania, where I met Eugene Park. With external funding from the Northeast Asia Council, Gene and I organized a symposium on the Koreans in China while I was at Penn. I thank Gene for his kindness, as well as the participants of the symposium for sharing their research with me.

A year later, I moved to Osaka to start a two-year position as a Japan Society for the Promotion of Sciences Postdoctoral Fellow (P13725). Without any professional contacts in Kansai, I sent an email out of the blue to Scott North, the sole American sociologist at Osaka University, asking him to be my sponsor. Scott made time in his hectic schedule to meet with me regularly, and I found myself continuously touched by his selflessness and compassion toward others in need. I spent many days during the week writing at a coworking space located in the heart of Osaka's financial district. The friends I met there—and in particular Hiroko Osaki, Yukihiro Sada, and Mai Teramoto—became my family in Japan.

During the summer of 2014, I was fortunate to participate in the Korean Studies Junior Faculty Workshop, which was sponsored by the Korea Foundation and the Social Science Research Council in Monterey, California. My manuscript benefited immensely from the detailed feedback I received from the faculty advisors that year, including the late Nancy Abelmann, Nicole Constable, and Nicholas Harkness.

In 2015, I moved from Osaka to Seoul to take on a position at Ewha Womans University. My colleagues at Ewha were endlessly patient as I tried to finish my book while juggling my new duties as an assistant professor. I am indebted to the faculty in my department—Joon-sik Choi, Young Hoon Kim, Youngkyu Kim, Kyongmi Kwon, Haiyoung Lee, and Sunny Park—who took on a heavier administrative load so that I could carve out time to write. Throughout my time at Ewha, I depended heavily on my long-time friend Sangho Ro who helped me overcome various personal and professional roadblocks that came my way. I was also fortunate to make new friends like Harris Kim, who humored me with witty conversation when I felt discouraged and offered honest, incisive feedback on several drafts when I was in need of a critical perspective. Numerous other faculty and aspiring scholars helped my project come to fruition, including Sei-jeong Chin, Jasmine Healey, Thomas Kalinowski, Eun Mee Kim, Jennifer Oh, Rita Udor, and Heather Willoughby.

During my five years in Seoul, I was surrounded by an intellectually stimulating community of researchers devoted to the study of Korea, including scholars based in the city, such as Jinkyung Park, Jee-Eun Song, and Jaeyoun Won, as well as Korean studies faculty from North America who visited during the summer to conduct fieldwork, such as Hae Yeon Choo, Todd Henry, Jiyeon Kang, Hagen Koo, Yoonkyung Lee, Alyssa Park, Stephen Suh, and Myungji Yang. I feel lucky to have crossed paths with scholars like Peggy Levitt, who provided warm words of encouragement and feedback during a particularly low point in my journey, and Jennifer Chun, who took precious time during her sabbatical to help develop many of the theoretical ideas I present in this book. The sincerity with which Jennifer approaches her research has continued to inspire me to reflect upon the type of writer and researcher I want to be, and I am deeply grateful that she has taken the time to mentor me as a junior scholar—I know that I would not be where I am today without her support.

As a Korean American returnee, I found a home away from home in Itaewon, the so-called American military ghetto in Seoul, and I spent countless hours marking up revisions in the bars, restaurants, and coffee shops in my neighborhood. My friends, who were often owners of these establishments, brought me complimentary drinks and appetizers as I worked and periodically asked about how my revisions were going. I am particularly grateful to Charles Chun, Kenny Hirata, and Justin Sasaki of California Kitchen and Craft Pub; Ki Na and Thomas Buckley of Le Chien Blanc; Linus Kim of the Linus BBQ franchise in Itaewon and HBC; Philip Abowd, Bobby Kim, and Robbie Nguyen of Southside Parlor and the Pocket; and Wendell Louie of Pussyfoot Saloon and Mix & Malt. I would also like to express my appreciation to Haeryong Ahn, Eun-hae Go, Katie Lawrence, Takaaki Kawakami, and Kwanghyun Oh.

Sherith Pankratz of Oxford University Press, as well as my series editors, Carla Freeman and Li Zhang, took a chance on me, a first-time author, and helped transform my manuscript into a book. Earlier versions of my book benefited from in-depth comments of several anonymous reviewers. Petrice Flowers, a colleague who revealed her identity after my book was awarded a contract, sacrificed time she could have spent working on her own book to review my manuscript, all while taking care of two toddlers and acting as director of an exchange program.

I don't think that I could have completed this project without a partner who was personally invested in helping me realize my professional goals. Throughout the course of my work on this project, Hiroshi Shirakawa, who is himself a third-generation Korean minority from Japan, made sure I was in an ideal environment to focus on writing, never once speaking of the many sacrifices he made in the process. I am also indebted to my brother, Joe, and his wife, Jane, as well as my extended family in Seoul—namely, Joon-Hee Woo, Yoon-hee Yoon, Yeo-gook Yoon, Kyung-sook Shin, Ayeon Sun, and Joong-Tae Kim—for their support.

This book is dedicated to my parents, who experienced their own bouts of entrepreneurial failure as Korean immigrants in the United

States. When I was in the field, I thought about my parents when I interviewed struggling South Korean entrepreneurs who faced bankruptcy. I felt pangs of guilt when I interviewed elderly Korean Chinese couples who faced unemployment and lived with their adult children who financially supported them. I was not able to provide my parents with financial or even emotional support during the many years of hardship they endured due to my various weaknesses and shortcomings. Initially, by writing this book, I wanted to prove to myself that the many years of precariousness that my family had experienced had been for a greater purpose. As this book approaches publication, I feel deeply appreciative to my parents, who patiently believed that my research would help others understand the plight of Korean migrant entrepreneurs even when I was full of doubt. I know that no work I produce could ever make their past suffering worthwhile, but I hope that in spite of its flaws, this book will impart some sense of meaning and gratification to them.

The author and OUP wish to thank the following reviewers who provided helpful commentary on this manuscript prior to publication:

Mark Anthony Arceño, The Ohio State University
Jennifer Jihye Chun, University of Toronto
Robin DeLugan, University of California-Merced
Adam Dunstan, University of North Texas
Petrice R. Flowers, University of Hawai'i Mānoa
Sue-Je Lee Gage, Ithaca College
Heather Hindman, University of Texas
Ares Kalandides, New York University, Berlin
Kyeyoung Park, University of California, Los Angeles
Audrey Ricke, Indiana University-Purdue University, Indianapolis
Anne Schiller, George Mason University

As well as several reviewers who wished to remain anonymous.

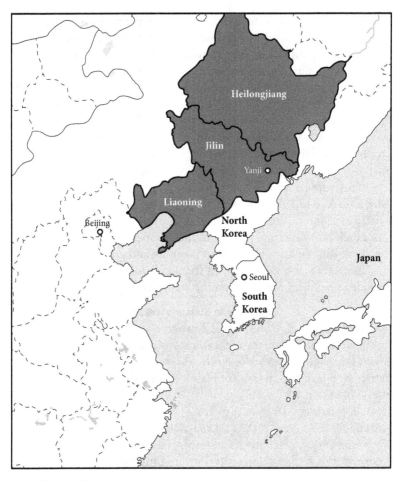

MAP 1 China and the Korean Peninsula

NOTE TO THE READER

....

Korean-ness is a socially constructed term and the process of demarcating and negotiating what "Korean" denotes is precisely what this book is about. In this book, I use the term "Korean" liberally, in spite of its deeply complicated and politicized nature, primarily to enhance readability. "Korean" is used to generally refer to all peoples of Korean ancestry, including diasporic Koreans (such as ethnic Koreans of Chinese, American, Russian, or Japanese citizenship) as well as ethnic Koreans of North or South Korean citizenship. Similarly, by labelling an ethnic business or culture as "Korean," I intend to emphasize ties to a broader cultural heritage connected to the Korean peninsula. At times, I explicitly state that someone or something is "South Korean" or "Korean Chinese" to refer to a more specific manifestation of Korean-ness tied to a particular historical and geopolitical context.

The Cost of Belonging

CHAPTER 1

Introduction

When the Asian financial crisis triggered economic upheaval in South Korea in 1997, South Korean multinational corporations (otherwise known as the *chaebol*) saw expansion into Chinese markets as a way to revitalize their businesses. Wangjing— a district in Beijing designed by the Chinese government to attract foreign investment—reached new heights of economic growth as flows of capital and labor poured in from Seoul. The *chaebol* not only set up offices and factories in and around Wangjing, but they also created a lucrative captive market for Korean goods and services by sending expatriate workers (commonly referred to as "expats") to supervise operations overseas. The expats started to live clustered together in expensive apartment complexes in the area, planting the seeds for what would become a Korean enclave. Though only about 500 Korean households lived in the district in 2001, by the time I started to conduct fieldwork in 2010, the majority of the 200,000 Koreans who lived in Beijing resided in the district of Wangjing (Spencer, Flowers, and Seo 2012). Today, Beijing's Koreatown represents one of the largest overseas Korean communities in the world.

At first glance, Wangjing looks like a typical ethnic enclave where Korean is the lingua franca and *kimchee* is sold at the local store. Insiders know, however, that the enclave is a highly stratified space where Koreans consort within clearly defined social and spatial zones according to their socioeconomic and cultural backgrounds. Three different types of Koreans live in Koreatown: South Korean expats, who are dispatched by the *chaebol* on short-term assignments; South Korean grassroots migrants, who arrive with plans to open small mom-and-pop businesses in the enclave; and third- and fourth-generation Chinese citizens of Korean ancestry (known as *joseonjok* in Korean or *chaoxianzu* in Chinese), who have left the Chinese countryside in search of better job opportunities in the city.

Even casual passersby will notice that the Korean enclave is rife with tension. A series of grassroots surveys conducted by South Korean journalists and civic leaders document a surge of gang violence, robbery, and kidnapping between South Koreans and Korean Chinese minorities in Beijing since the mid-1990s (Yoon 2020). But in spite of these conflicts, Koreans from various backgrounds have continued to live and work together because they needed one another. The enclave thrived on a delicately balanced ecosystem. The expats, though resented for driving up living costs, played an important role as wealthy consumers who paid a premium for Korean language and cultural goods. South Korean grassroots migrants, in spite of their distrust toward the Korean Chinese, relied on their bilingual managers to communicate with Chinese workers and clientele. And though Korean Chinese minorities were equally suspicious of their South Korean employers, they depended on the South Koreans to gain the know-how and seed money they needed to start their own businesses.

This book argues that the growing dominance of global capital and neoliberal restructuring has caused ethnic communities to become increasingly stratified spaces where coethnic migrants compete over scarce emotional and material resources. Rather than benefitting from a collective conscious as coethnic migrants, the Koreans in Wangjing engaged in ethnic boundary-making processes, where conflicting notions of class and morality justified who deserved to belong. In the chapters to follow, I weave together original survey data of nearly 800 Korean migrants in Beijing with intimate stories of everyday life I gathered as a participant observer at a South Korean conglomerate, a small Korean Chinese mom-and-pop store, a Korean Chinese underground church, and a South Korean megachurch in the enclave.

The day we met for our interview, Nam-soo Park[1] wore freshly pressed khaki slacks, a crisp white button-down, wire-rimmed spectacles, and a gold wristwatch. His hair was neatly combed to the side, and

---

1. All names of people, companies, and organizations mentioned in this book have been changed to protect anonymity.

he carried himself with an air of confidence. Mr. Park had graduated from a prestigious university in Seoul and had worked his way up the corporate ladder at a major South Korean firm. After he was promoted to department chief [*bujang*], he grew restless. The South Korean economy had fallen into a state of crisis, and he became apprehensive of his future as he watched his colleagues get laid off, or in slightly more fortuitous cases, "encouraged" to retire early. All the while, in the early 2000s, business circles in Seoul were abuzz with anticipation over China's future stature as the world's next economic superpower.

Eager to take advantage of the lower costs of labor and living in Beijing, South Korean migrants like Mr. Park used their retirement savings to open small businesses—Korean restaurants, cafes, hair salons, and travel agencies—in the enclave. Some were middle-level managers who had been laid off as a result of corporate downsizing. Others were entrepreneurs whose businesses had been hit by economic downturn in Seoul. Most entered as "tourists" and led semipermanent lives flitting back and forth between Seoul and Beijing. While the expats led lives of luxury in the enclave, these grassroots migrants represented the casualties of the 1997 Asian financial crisis and the 2008 global financial crisis.

As he reflected on his past, Mr. Park grew uncharacteristically sentimental. Having depleted his personal savings after many attempts to salvage his business, he repeatedly explained how his sacrifices had not been in vain because he had raised his children to speak fluent Chinese. He wanted to believe that his children's language abilities would protect them from the difficulties he endured in Beijing. "They will have a leg up when they look for jobs as adults," he explained to me.

As my involvement in the field deepened, I started to come across troubling numbers of South Korean migrants who, like Mr. Park, confessed that they were leaving the enclave after having lost everything to a failed business. I frequently overheard whispered rumors of South Korean entrepreneurs who suddenly disappeared because they were unable to pay their workers several months of back wages. There was even a phrase for this phenomenon in Korean: *yaban doju* or running away by night. According to a report by the Chinese Academy for Social Sciences, one in three South Koreans, or about 20,000 to 30,000 migrants, had left Beijing in 2009 because of economic hardship (Park 2009).

As South Korean investors started entering China, they drew an influx of bilingual Korean Chinese migrants from the countryside. Mr. Park put it this way:

> For South Koreans, the Korean Chinese acted as our "hands and feet" when we first arrived in China. They acted as your translator when you needed to negotiate with Han Chinese bureaucrats. They introduced you to the appropriate vendors in the area. They led you around the vicinity, showing you the lay of the land, teaching you where you can go buy certain things, where the foreign hotels were, when you can go eat Korean food.

Like the South Korean entrepreneurs, Korean Chinese migrants also arrived with middle class aspirations. The vast majority had grown up in Korean agricultural communes near the Sino–North Korean border, where their ancestors had tilled rice paddies since Japan overtook Manchuria in 1932. But while their South Korean counterparts struggled to maintain their businesses, many Korean Chinese minorities eventually grew entrepreneurial firms that quickly out-performed those of their former employers.

One objective of this book is to understand why Korean Chinese entrepreneurs thrived in the enclave, while South Koreans did not. Compared to the Korean Chinese, South Koreans had better access to material resources, schooling, and job experience.[1] Eighty-three percent of the South Korean entrepreneurs I surveyed, for instance, had college degrees, and of this number 17.8 percent had graduate degrees.[2] Nearly half (or 48.6 percent) had past entrepreneurial experience, as well as access to considerable savings and loans from friends and family in South Korea.

Many assume that the Korean Chinese were able to achieve upward mobility because of the various advantages they enjoyed as locals. But such reasoning overlooks the fact that Korean Chinese minorities, as Chinese rural migrants, also faced significant structural barriers in the city. Despite *hukou* [household registration] reform in the late 1970s, past research on China's so-called floating population demonstrates that the livelihoods of Chinese rural migrants have, if anything, worsened over the years (Whyte 2012).[3] Many continue to lack adequate healthcare, job security, public housing, or subsidized food services in urban areas. And while a minority have been able to open small restaurants, produce stands, bicycle repair shops, and recycling centers (see Ma and

Xiang 1998), most lead lives as China's underclass, filling 3-D (dirty, dangerous, difficult) jobs in the city (Solinger 1995 1999; Wong, Chang, and He 2007).

Unlike other rural migrants in the People's Republic of China (PRC), Korean Chinese minorities were able to benefit from Wangjing's rich transnational resources. Early works show that during the 1980s, most Korean Chinese migrants in Beijing subsisted as street peddlers selling *kimchee* and other ethnic foods. They only started to amass significant wealth after Sino–South Korean normalization of ties in 1992. As transnational migrants, the Korean Chinese took advantage of their peripheral positions as cultural brokers, flexibly moving back and forth between Seoul and Beijing to effectively tap into niche market opportunities.

Contemporary theories on transnational entrepreneurship fail to account for the downward mobility of South Korean grassroots migrants, however. Despite the growing prevalence of transnational entrepreneurs in recent years, theories remain surprisingly limited in scope. The vast majority of scholarship in the field has focused on Latin American (and to a lesser extent, Caribbean) migration to the United States—a less than ideal case study as migrants from developing countries tend to fill menial jobs and lack the resources to engage in entrepreneurship (see Levitt and Jaworsky 2007).

In part because of these methodological shortcomings, the existing literature continues to project a relatively optimistic image of transnational migration. Whereas globalization is generally criticized for perpetuating the concentration of wealth, transnational migration is valorized as a "countervailing" force, a "globalization-from-below" (Portes 1997: 2). Transnational migrants are believed to "by-pass the menial dead-end jobs that the host society assigns them" (7) by creating "communities that sit astride political borders and that, in a very real sense, are 'neither here nor there' but in both places simultaneously" (3).

This book reveals a darker side of transnational communities. Although the disadvantages of the transnational enclave may seem more obvious when examining the case of South Korean entrepreneurs who fall deeper into poverty in Wangjing, I argue that the potential harms of the transnational enclave extend to the seemingly prosperous Korean Chinese as well. Though Korean Chinese entrepreneurs are able to amass significant material wealth in Wangjing, many of my Korean Chinese interviewees expressed regret and a deep sense of longing for the rural villages they had left behind.

Initially, when I heard the Korean Chinese minorities yearn for their premigration past, I dismissed the gravity of their sentiments. What was more important, I thought, was the fact that the material conditions of their lives had dramatically improved: Korean Chinese minorities now lived in nicer homes, had become owners of profitable businesses, and could even afford to take vacations overseas. Clearly, their story was one of success. I later realized that for the Korean Chinese the very source of their economic prowess—as cultural hybrid minorities who fit neither here nor there—was also the source of considerable emotional angst. Though their economic lives had improved since coming to Beijing, many wondered whether their departure had been worth the psychological and emotional costs—the feeling of alienation and homelessness—that ensued.

Ultimately, I argue that neither South Korean entrepreneurs nor Korean Chinese migrants were able to achieve the middle class dream in Wangjing. Particularly during times of economic crisis, migrants who venture overseas to open small businesses have taken fate into their own hands. They arrive not only with dreams of material wealth, but also with hopes of acquiring the immaterial benefits—feelings of belonging, inclusion, and legitimacy—associated with the middle class. Along these lines, the second objective of this book is to illuminate how the changing contours of the spaces where migrants live and work have affected how they were able to achieve the emotional aspirations of the middle class.

Diasporic Return

I became acquainted with Jong-suk Shin, a third-generation Korean Chinese man in his late thirties, at a volleyball club organized by a Korean Chinese "underground" church in Beijing. Mr. Shin had a complicated relationship with South Korea and South Koreans. As a boy growing up in a small Korean village in rural China, he had always been fascinated by South Korea—a mysterious country where, he was told, everyone looked and spoke like he did. Under Mao Zedong's rule (1949–1976) travel to South Korea was prohibited, but he often dreamed about what it might be like to visit. He asked his grandparents to tell him stories about the small village in the southern part of the Korean peninsula where they had grown up. At first, he didn't believe the stories he was told: "I wondered if there could really be a place like South Korea [*hanguk*]. Could there really be a place where everyone speaks Korean?" But the more he heard, the more his curiosity grew. His grandparents, who at first happily obliged him with stories of their homeland, later grew annoyed by his incessant pestering and often shooed him away, telling him to go play with his friends instead.

In 1985, seven years before sanctions to travel from China to South Korea were lifted, Mr. Shin's father took his mother (Mr. Shin's grandmother) to visit Seoul. They were among some 150 Koreans who were granted special permission to cross the 38th parallel to meet family members with whom they had lost contact during the Korean War. Mr. Shin recalled that his father received a letter from the Korean Broadcasting System (KBS) one day, stating that his mother's younger sister had been searching for her sister.

While his father and grandmother flew to Seoul, Mr. Shin hovered over a small transistor radio with friends and kin in his village, listening to live broadcasts of Koreans who shed tears of joy as they embraced their brothers, sisters, parents, and even former wives and husbands—family they assumed had died during the war. Only a few months after their emotional reunion, Mr. Shin's grandmother passed away. Two years later, during the 1988 Seoul Olympics, Mr. Shin's father was given a temporary visa to reconnect with her mother's side of the family. He returned to China with a brand new 21-inch Sony TV and exciting stories of how modern and clean Seoul was. Two years later, he also passed away.

Mr. Shin was able to see Seoul with his own eyes in the late 1990s, after China and South Korea established diplomatic relations. As a young man in his early twenties, he found a job working as a translator for the Beijing branch of Samsung, and was periodically sent to the headquarters in Seoul for training. To this day, he can still remember his first visit like it was yesterday: "When my plane landed in the airport, I felt so excited. I said to myself, 'Wow! There really *is* a place where everyone speaks in Korean and all the signs are in Korean!' I was so, so happy. I thought to myself to that this really *is* my country."

Though Mr. Shin continues to live in Beijing, ever since the barriers to trade and travel with Seoul opened in 1992, his everyday life is viscerally shaped by even mundane shifts in South Korea's political economy. In a span of three decades, China went from being completely cut off from contact with South Korea to becoming its most favored destination for both foreign direct investment (FDI) and international travel.

In addition to attracting more than four million South Korean travelers in 2013, according to statistics from the Korea Export-Import Bank, South Korean FDI to China the same year surpassed five billion USD, accounting for 20 percent of total FDI from the country.

Moreover, since the 1990s, Korean Chinese minorities have left their villages to migrate en masse to South Korea. As visas to South Korea became more accessible, the number of people crossing the border also surged. Data from the Korean Statistical Information Service demonstrates that nearly 700,000 Korean Chinese minorities of a total population of about 2.3 million lived in South Korea as of 2017, representing by far the largest group of "foreigners" in the country.

Mr. Shin told me with pride that several years after his father passed away, his mother, who was a skilled cook and seamstress, had found a job working as the head housekeeper for a prominent South Korean family in Seoul. A few years earlier she even naturalized, giving up her Chinese passport to take on a South Korean one. Ironically, however, greater exposure to South Koreans and South Korea has tarnished the emotional attachment that Mr. Shin once felt toward his country of ancestral origin. Should you ask him how he feels about South Korea now, nearly thirty years after the doors of travel opened, the mystery and longing that Mr. Shin had once felt is all but gone.

Scholars of diaspora have spilled much ink writing about the nostalgia and longing so intrinsic to the experience of leaving the homeland. The term "diaspora" first appeared in a Greek translation of the Hebrew Bible in the third century BC (Dufoix 2008). For the Jews, the suffering that was induced by the fall of Jerusalem in 586 BC was in part assuaged by dreams of one day returning to the territorial homeland. The soothing prospect of return also resonated with early pan-African intellectuals. As the trans-Saharan slave trade reached unprecedented heights, "men and women were uprooted from the African soil and separated from their families and communities for centuries, deprived of institutions, and condemned to an existence that the sociologist Orlando Patterns qualifies as 'social death'" (Dufoix 2008:14). Sonia Ryang, an anthropologist who is herself an overseas Korean born and raised in Japan, asserts that for the "people in diaspora," who are "dispersed and displaced, uprooted and homeless . . . the lost homeland symbolizes the loss of, say, meaningful life, or indeed, humanity" (2008: xix).

Benedict Anderson argues that the concept of the nation has come to command such profound emotional legitimacy because it provides people with a cosmic sense of time immemorial. As members of a nation, people feel a sense of immortality—they are able to connect themselves to a lineage that can be traced back to the beginning of humanity, and a legacy that they presume will persist long after their death. An emotional connection to this so-called imagined community has become a defining quality of human existence in the modern era (Anderson 1991: 4).

For members of the diaspora, however, "returning" is no simple matter. Societies are constantly in the process of evolution—linguistically, culturally, politically, and economically. The magnitude of these changes often goes unnoticed because they occur incrementally, and people make incremental adjustments in their everyday lives. Incremental changes, however, accumulate over time, and in their aggregate can seem jarring. As Korean Chinese journalist Hae-sun Lee (2003: 15) writes in her book *The Korean Dream*:

> It was my first trip to the ancestral homeland [*goguk*], and I was feeling deeply sentimental. How lonely I felt when I became aware of the immense cultural barriers that separated me from a homeland, that had over the years, become so alien and unfamiliar. I realized how different our political regimes, our economy, and our cultures had become, that I felt hurt by even the trivial act of bumping into someone on the streets of Seoul. In China, we walk on the rightside of the street, while in South Korea, people walk on the leftside. The pain and loneliness I felt every time I collided into someone on the streets was overwhelming. For members of the diaspora, coming into contact with the country of our ancestral roots is at once, an experience of joy, as well as one of suffering.

For even first-generation migrants then, repatriation is an illusory dream. Mr. Shin's sense of alienation is linked to his realization that his imagined community does not exist. Instead, what was once an agrarian society has split into two ideological regimes—one taken over by modern-day capitalism and neoliberalism, and the other by *juche*, an indigenous version of Communism. North and South Koreans have evolved to speak mutually incomprehensible versions of Korean. Sociologist John Lie even goes so far as to argue that North and South Koreans have become so physiologically distinct that "by the early 2000s, the average height of South Korean men was 13 centimeters taller than that of their North Korean counterparts: a difference that would be tantamount to a 'racial distinction'" (2014: 2).

But how is return experienced for ethnic minorities who live in a transnational enclave? By analyzing a transnational community, my book argues that the experience of return is not limited to diasporic Koreans who venture back to the physical territory of their ancestors. Even Korean Chinese minorities who themselves have never set foot in South Korea experience feelings of alienation in Wangjing because the enclave has become a liminal space where the social, economic, and political vicissitudes of everyday life in Seoul have reverberating effects on the Koreans overseas.

In South Korea, Korean Chinese return-migrants are commonly perceived as the nation's underclass. Along with the long hours and physical strain of their jobs in the 3-D market, Korean Chinese minorities tolerate sexual harassment, verbal abuse, and humiliation from their bigoted employers. On the one hand, the power dynamics and labor relations between the Korean Chinese and South Koreans are indeed different in China. In the PRC, Han Chinese rural migrants occupy low-wage positions while Korean Chinese minorities are hired to fill semiskilled managerial positions thanks to their bilingual skills. But on the other hand, while the Korean Chinese in China do not endure the explicit discrimination they do in Seoul, they are not unaffected by the abuses that occur abroad. Negative feelings formed in Seoul continue to affect mutual perceptions in Beijing.

Given the sheer number of Korean Chinese minorities working in South Korea, Korean Chinese minorities in Wangjing are regularly exposed to discrimination whether vicariously, through the experiences of a family member or close friend, or through their own experiences moving back and forth across the border. According to the survey I conducted, 88 percent of over four hundred Korean Chinese respondents had family members living in South Korea and 73 percent of individuals over twenty-five years old had been to South Korea before.

In addition, stratified labor relations in the enclave perpetuated misleading perceptions of privilege and disadvantage in Beijing. Even though South Korean migrants were in fact more financially precarious, Korean Chinese minorities were rarely in a position of power when interacting with South Koreans in the enclave. South Koreans who had lost their savings in foreclosed businesses often left the enclave, and few, no matter how desperate they were for a job, deigned to work for Korean Chinese entrepreneurs. The South Koreans who remained in the enclave were thus a selective group of people who overwhelmingly occupied higher status positions as employers, managers, or customers. Their positions of power subsequently projected an image of socioeconomic advantage, in spite of their precarious legal and financial circumstances in Beijing.

The Transnational Enclave

The sociologist Alejandro Portes first came up with the concept of the enclave in the 1980s (Portes 1987). A Cuban immigrant himself, he pointed to Little Havana, the Cuban enclave in Miami, as an example of how immigrants of the same ancestry could bond over a sense of common fate in a foreign country. To Portes, this bonding was important because it allowed the enclave to function as a haven sheltering disadvantaged minorities from discrimination, and providing them with the know-how and social networks critical to building small businesses. As a graduate student, I read about Cuban migrants, who had left everything behind in the 1960s as political exiles, sharing what little they had to rebuild their lives as petty entrepreneurs in America. Portes argued that the enclave—which he defined as a space where coethnic civic organizations, places of work and commerce, and residential neighborhoods were clustered together—was key to their economic success. By living and working together in the same neighborhood, enclave residents were "structurally embedded"—they were enmeshed in dense, overlapping relationships that bolstered mutual reliance and accountability, and subsequently perceived their fates as individuals as intertwined with the welfare of their community at large.

This way of looking at the enclave made a splash in sociology because it painted a picture of poor immigrant neighborhoods not as ghettos, but as places of opportunity. As a second-generation Korean American, I found myself resonating with this theoretical perspective. All throughout my childhood, I had watched Korean immigrants of my parents' generation build profitable dry cleaners and liquor stores from nearly nothing.

When I entered the field to study Beijing's Koreatown, I was full of optimism. Wangjing, with its beautiful high-rise buildings and perfect grid-like streets, seemed like the Promised Land for Korean migrants of diverse backgrounds. While I had to stretch my imagination to envision how the Korean enclave in Flushing, New York might actually, despite its run-down appearance, provide its inhabitants with resources for securing a middle class lifestyle, such was not the case for Wangjing. It was obvious from the outset that Wangjing was a well-to-do neighborhood desirable even to China's urban elite, and that Korean migrants enjoyed a special edge in finding jobs and opening shops in this district, by virtue of simply being Korean.

I later discovered that Beijing's Koreatown was different from enclaves like Little Havana in the extent to which it was interconnected—socially, institutionally, and economically—to South Korea, the country of origin. One important impetus for this growing connectivity includes the changing migratory patterns of people. People are able to travel more frequently back to their "home" country, as well as to a second or third destination. And this has changed how people form collective identities, how comfortable they feel in trusting one another, and how culturally complex their backgrounds have become.

Earlier works on the ethnic enclave are based on the experiences of immigrants,[4] who, because of the high costs of overseas travel and communication even as recently as the 1980s, were by and large cut off from their home countries. These immigrants did not consider repatriation a viable option and channeled their efforts into making it in the so-called new world. They were, to put it colloquially, "all in." And because they had no safety net, they were able to forge new identities in the host society that became so strong that they were able to bond with even others who came from different class and regional backgrounds. In Nathan Glazer's (1954) account of Polish immigrants, for instance, peasants and rural lords who had little in common in the homeland bonded over the common obstacles they faced as discriminated minorities in America.

By contrast, transnational enclaves like Wangjing represent a liminal space where enhanced geographic mobility has made the enclave's social structure more porous (see Coleman 1998). Although people are more interconnected with friends and family across national borders, their frequent back-and-forth movement has led to looser relationships. People in transnational spaces thus struggle to cultivate a strong sense of community because of a heightened sense of uncertainty. South Korean migrants in Wangjing, for instance, were reluctant to trust members of their community because people left suddenly, on a moment's notice. While many returned, others did not. Rumors of people who borrowed large sums of money only to flee frequently circulated social circles. Such increasingly precarious ways of relating have caused transnational migrants to face new challenges in sustaining networks of trust and solidarity spanning national boundaries.

Moreover, some argue that immigrants of the past were able to overcome differences in class precisely because the gaps that separated them were not so big to begin with. Research on immigrants who arrived in the United States prior to the 1990s, for instance, shows that people were often clustered by class and education according to their country of origin (see Portes and Rumbaut 2001). The immigrants who left their home countries were often prompted by a specific set of circumstances that affected a certain type of person. To return to the example of Koreans in the United States, Kyeyoung Park's ethnographic account shows how New York's Koreatown in the 1980s and 1990s was inhabited by a relatively homogenous group of Koreans. Those who left South Korea following the Immigration and Nationality Act of 1965 were by and large middle class professionals, including "medical professionals—doctors, dentists, pharmacists, nurses, medical technicians—and scientists, engineers, and other skilled professionals"—who were frustrated by the rigid social hierarchies and lack of opportunities in their home country (1997: 14–15).

Though migrants still leave and settle together in waves, laws on travel and immigration have become less restrictive and overseas travel has become more affordable to a wider range of people in recent years. Nowadays, a growing number of migrant enclaves are inhabited by people who share little else but language or ancestry. On the one hand, increasing diversity has led to increasing stratification and social divisions among enclave inhabitants. But on the other hand, the growing complexity of migratory patterns today has also led to the emergence of culturally hybrid migrants who flexibly bridge otherwise isolated groups of people with unprecedented ease.

Steven Masami Ropp's (2000: 220) research, for instance, sheds light on the so-called phenomenon of secondary migration among Asian Latinos—"Chinese from Cuba, Peru, or Brazil; Japanese from Peru, Brazil, or Argentina; Koreans from Brazil or Argentina"—in Los Angeles. Asian Latinos, he argues, elide "easy categoric ordering" because their very existence challenges assumptions about ethnicity and culture (225). Ropp tells us the story of Jorge Kim, who was born in Mexico City and appointed as "'a Spanish-language spokesman' for the Los Angeles Unified School District." Jorge's grandparents migrated from the Korean Peninsula to the Yucatan in 1905, and as someone who identified as both Korean and Mexican, Jorge felt a sense of responsibility to help lessen the prejudices that South Koreans held toward Mexicans: "Mexican immigrants are productive and contribute to this country. My father always told me that I'm Mexican and owe my success to Mexico and the education that I got in Mexico" (226).

With the influx of transnational migration in recent years, ethnic enclaves like Wangjing have taken on the form of transnational "social fields"—such that even those who lead relatively sedentary lives are influenced by the "dense, thick and widespread" circulation of people, money and "social remittances" (ideas, norms, practices, and identities) within these spaces (Levitt and Jaworsky 2007: 132). Transnational enclaves are distinct in that they are self-sustaining microcosms—migrants are able to satisfy all of their economic, organizational, and social needs within its borders. Wangjing, for instance, is not merely a neighborhood of Korean migrants or a Korean commercial district; it is a miniature Seoul within Beijing, so insulated and replete that many South Koreans I interviewed could not speak a word of Mandarin even after having lived in China for more than ten years because they rarely left its confines. It offers a wide range of businesses that cater specifically to the linguistic and cultural needs of Korean migrants; civic organizations such as nongovernmental organizations (NGOs) and ethnic churches help cultivate a thriving social life; and financial institutions, such as banks, multinational corporations, and chambers of commerce.

The insulated nature of everyday life in the transnational enclave has a cumulative effect on migrants. I argue that the influence of the transnational enclave is potent precisely because the different types of space within the enclave work together to reinforce and legitimize a specific set of perceptions and behaviors—an entire worldview. My study is designed to analyze more explicitly how these different contexts of interaction within the enclave, according to their respective institutional and spatial arrangements, helped shape coethnic conflict and solidarity.

Neoliberal Restructuring and the Makings of Global Inequality

The Cost of Belonging captures a critical moment in Korean history, when the weakening of Cold War politics and the liberalization of laws governing migration and commerce transformed the ways Koreans lived and worked. Until recently, South Korea was primarily a country of emigration. In the 1930s, millions of Koreans left the Korean penin-sula forcibly and otherwise to China, Japan, and the Russian Far East as part of Japanese colonial projects for imperial expansion. The second mass wave of Korean migration was triggered by South Korea's "Miracle on the Han River" in the 1970s and 1980s, when numerous middle class Koreans migrated to more distant destinations in the West to pursue economic opportunities (Yoon 2012).

The tides reversed from emigration to "return-migration," however, when the South Korean economy plummeted from its rapid ascent in the late 1990s. Following the Asian financial crisis of 1997, a series of new policies were launched to lure back "meritorious" Koreans over-seas in an attempt to facilitate the circulation of transnational capital to galvanize economic recovery (E. J. Kim 2010: 179). President Kim Young Sam, who saw *segyehwa* [globalization] as the pathway to eco-nomic growth, implemented the first of these initiatives. Kim sought to attract the some 5.3 million Koreans abroad by establishing the Overseas Koreans Foundation (OKF), a nonprofit organization affili-ated with the Ministry of Foreign Affairs and Trade, which provided educational and cultural programs for members of the diaspora (S. Kim 2000). His successor Kim Dae Jung expanded the scope of the OKF in 1999 by establishing the Overseas Korean Act (OKA), which granted overseas Koreans special privileges such as property ownership rights, work permits, healthcare, pensions, and flexible entry into the ancestral homeland (Park and Chang 2005).

The expansion of the OKA led to a surge of transnational migra-tion. New waves of diasporic Koreans, many of whom were descendants of colonial labor migrants cut off during the Cold War, traveled to South Korea for the first time in an attempt to (re)connect with their ancestral heritage. The influx of these return-migrants stimulated an outpouring of research on the diaspora in Korean studies (Lie 2008; E. J. Kim 2010; Kim 2016; Park 2015; Jo 2017; Lee 2018; Park 2019). Scholars in the field analyzed the implications that changing state attitudes toward diasporic Koreans had on notions of nationhood. Many brought to light the con-tradictions between the new policies that included overseas Koreans as part of the primordial ethno-nation, on the one hand, and the alienating experiences of Korean returnees living in Seoul, on the other (E. Kim 2010; Lee 2018; Jo 2017).

While I share with my contemporaries an interest in understand-ing the diasporic quest for belonging, I diverge in my approach to studying how these sentiments of belonging are negotiated and con-tested. Rather than focus on the state, I analyze how global capital has influenced boundary-making processes of class and a sense of "ethnic morality" within overseas communities. Although the state remains in-fluential in its role as gatekeeper, I argue that with neoliberal restruc-turing, the powers of the state have considerably weakened (Lim and Jang 2006).[5] State policies in recent years are arguably more reflective of *chaebol*, as opposed to state, interests (though the two share a symbiotic relationship).

This book thus shifts our focus to studying how corporate interests and neoliberal restructuring have transformed coethnic labor relations within overseas communities. I argue that diasporic identity politics are increasingly enmeshed in class conflict and market competition, and notions of nationhood and feelings of belonging are utilized to legitimate and perpetuate processes of stratification—both inside and outside the geopolitical territory of the nation-state. In other words, as migratory patterns become more diversified, feelings of belonging and worthiness have become a quintessential emotional privilege of the global middle class.

Around the world, the acceleration of globalization and neoliberal reform has irrevocably changed the structure of the middle class in recent years. As Heiman et al. (2012: 14) argue, "declining rates of ac-cumulation during the 1970s triggered new policies of systematic dein-dustrialization in Western industrialized nations (that is, the 'offshoring' of industrial labor) with a matched industrialization in nations such as India and China, along with the privatization of state functions (such as health, education, and security) around the globe." These large struc-tural changes, the authors argue, have made it difficult for the "tradi-tional middle classes" to find social and economic security, while the "new (neoliberal) middle class" have clustered around centers of global finance, "where they are best situated to feed off the 'trickle down' lar-gess of the neoliberal economic boom" (14).

In South Korea's case, market deregulation following the Asian fi-nancial crisis led to sharp cleavages within the middle class. While the nation was in a state of chaos and suicide rates climbed to an all-time high, South Korean elite expanded their wealth by purchasing stock and real estate properties below market value (Koo forthcoming). According to sociologist Hagen Koo (2016: 450), the global middle class is distinct from the Korean middle class of the precrisis era in the transnational and cosmopolitan nature of their consumption patterns and strategies for upward mobility. They represent the top 10 percent of the income bracket, and are mainly comprised of elite managers employed by South Korean conglomerates (Koo forthcoming). Furthermore, though the differences in wealth between the top 1 percent and the global middle class are significant, Koo points out that both have a shared interest in legitimating the expansion of a global capitalist system from which they both benefit.

The experiences delineated in the chapters to follow illustrate how the privilege of the global middle class surpassed national boundaries, pointing to the beginnings of a new social order. I show how the global middle class have not only secluded themselves within the gated communities of Seoul's Gangnam district (see Gelézeau 2008), but also in exclusive luxury apartments in transnational Korean communities like Wangjing. Chinese real estate agents I interviewed in the enclave, for instance, noted how the South Korean expats by and large congregated in a select few apartment complexes where the rent was nearly seven times as high as those of surrounding areas. One real estate agent remarked:

> Those South Korean [expats] are really rich. They all get housing stipends from the companies they work at. It's a fixed amount and sometimes the housing units are actually a little cheaper than their stipends. So we will tack on things like a Korean Chinese housekeeper, a full set of luxury furniture, a personal driver and so on to compensate for the gap in price. I like working with these clients because they don't really haggle. They also know that we know how much they usually get, so it's relatively easy. We know what type of place they want.

While the gaps in income and lifestyle distinguishing the global middle class from the rest of the population are staggering in Seoul, the story of the Koreans in Beijing demonstrates how these vast differences grow even exponentially larger within the transnational enclave. In Wangjing, expats were paid nearly double their salaries in Seoul, in addition to extra stipends covering their children's private school tuition, housing, domestic help, and transportation overseas. When adjusting for the lower living costs in Beijing at the time, these elite Koreans were able to afford a lifestyle that was outside the reach of other Korean migrants in the enclave.

Moreover, my book stresses that it is short-sighted to only focus on the material wealth of the expats. Rather, the full extent of their privilege extends to the emotional realm as well. In Beijing, the microcosm of the enclave buffered the inconveniences—both emotional and practical—typically associated with life overseas. Instead of experiencing feelings of alienation and discrimination as foreigners in China, South Korean expats remained confident in their identities as Koreans—like members of the global middle class in other parts of the world, they had a "globalized mind but remained firmly rooted in their local urban environments," where they were protected by a "dense networks of friends and family" and a "local social and political sphere" that prioritized their interests (Andreotti, Le Gales, and Moreno-Fuentes 2015: 3). Along these lines, this book brings to light how major institutions within the enclave—the South Korea media, the multinational firm, and the ethnic church—worked in tandem to perpetuate, legitimate, and sustain the dominance of the expats in Beijing's Koreatown.

Despite the enormous advantages they were privy to, the expats largely felt entitled to their wealth because they believed a "meritocratic" system of free markets had rewarded their industriousness and technical training. Many of my interviewees explained that they had been promoted to their managerial positions because of their superior work ethic. Boasting degrees from highly selective universities in Seoul and the United States, they spoke of the sacrifices their parents had made to educate them overseas and the many grueling hours they had spent studying to ultimately gain admission to the schools of their choice.

The South Korean expats' sense of entitlement must be understood within the context of the changing systems of labor market stratification in South Korea following the Asian financial crisis. Economic decline upended the *chaebol's* organizational culture from one stressing loyalty to the firm to one that stressed individual talent. During the years of rapid economic development, for instance, South Korean youth who were hired to work for the *chaebol* enjoyed considerable job security. The so-called lifetime employment system promoted workers as they gained experience with age, and teamwork was prioritized over individual talent. This system of hiring and promotion was criticized as dysfunctional when the South Korean economy collapsed in 1997, however. Along with major reform of the South Korean financial system, the International Monetary Fund (IMF) demanded reform of the *chaebol's* organizational culture. In addition to globalizing their operations and increasing foreign ownership shares, the *chaebol* replaced their paternalistic management styles with a market-driven one that prioritized performance (Yoon 2019). Past studies document the many changes implemented in Korean management styles in the late 1990s (Bae and Rowley 2003). In the case of Samsung, for instance, rather than recruit new graduates en masse, the company started to streamline its hiring process by using "structured tools and methods" such as problem-solving, case analysis, and simulation task assignments to evaluate the "core competencies" (defined as professionalism, creativity, leadership, and humanity) of potential hires (Bae and Rowley 2003: 86).

As I note in chapter 4, economic spheres of interaction like the workplace are important sites of ethnic boundary-making where notions of morality and market competence help validate existing patterns of stratification and inequality. New corporate policies were interpreted and implemented in a way that justified the interests of those already in power. Notions of competence and hard work were shaped not by workers' performance, but rather by deeply ingrained stereotypes of gender, class, and ethnicity privileging South Korean middle-aged men at the top of the workplace hierarchy, while marginalizing Korean Chinese young women at the bottom. Most notably, even though Korean Chinese minorities were recruited from prestigious universities in Beijing, their complete absence in upper-level management positions was legitimated through the feminization of their labor. South Korean managers hired large numbers of young Korean Chinese women every year and restricted their roles to "soft" interpersonal tasks. In a catch-22, Korean Chinese workers' response to a lackluster incentive structure was interpreted as "laziness" by South Korean managers.

Such processes bring to light the contradictory tendency to view positions of advantage and disadvantage as controlled by "rational" free markets, whereby workers are awarded according to "objective" measures. Compared to precrisis South Korea when the exploitative labor practices of the authoritarian regime were arguably more clear, the mechanisms perpetuating labor market stratification in the neoliberal era have become less visible.

In a world where migration is often treated as a last-resort strategy for circumventing stunted mobility at home, the precarious lives of South Korean grassroots migrants in Wangjing demonstrate the extent to which class boundaries have become hardened with globalization. Although working conditions between white-collar and blue-collar workers were highly unequal throughout the 1970s and 1980s, mobility within classes had still been relatively fluid under Park Chung-hee's military dictatorship (Koo forthcoming). Many South Koreans were able to join the ranks of the middle class through speculative real estate investment and self-employment (Yang 2018). These channels of mobility have largely disappeared following market deregulation.

While entrepreneurship had previously provided South Koreans with an alternative pathway into the middle class during the earlier years of economic boom, after neoliberal reforms, the self-employed have become part of South Korea's insecure class. In Seoul, more than half of South Korean entrepreneurs fail within three years (Lee 2015). The influx of small businesses in the late 1990s made competition for a rapidly dwindling consumer population fierce. This trend has only increased in recent years as South Korea continues to have a self-employed population that ranks fourth highest in the Organization for Economic Cooperation and Development (OECD). In 2014, nearly one-third— or 27 percent of the employed population—were self-employed (Koo forthcoming). With average monthly incomes just 60 percent of those of regular workers, about 74 percent of the self-employed were small businesses where the owner was the only employee (Lee 2015).

This book provides readers with a window into what happened to the thousands of South Koreans who decided to migrate to developing countries, emboldened by the lower costs of living, cheaper costs of labor, and growing levels of consumerism overseas. As foreigners, many arrive on tourist visas and become undocumented migrants without access to public welfare. Afraid to face their friends and family back home in South Korea, South Korean migrants like Namsoo Park isolated themselves in a foreign land where they were linguistically, culturally, and institutionally handicapped. In spite of the prolific sociological research on undocumented migrants, we are rarely exposed to people like Mr. Park, who on the surface may appear privileged. In North America, undocumented migrants are typically associated with images of Mexican factory workers or Filipina nannies working for affluent white families, for instance. With growing rates of globalization, however, patterns of migration and inequality are becoming more complex, such that displaced peoples encompass highly skilled labor from wealthy nations who migrate to developing countries where their foreign capital and training are expected to give them a competitive edge.

In contrast to the global middle class, for the traditional middle class, competition over scarce resources has led to the heightening of tensions and as Heiman et al. (2012: 14) put it, the intensification of "moral politics, pitting against each other new and old economies, nationalists and trans- (or even post-) nationalists, religious conservatives and progressives, social collectivists and 'self-made' entrepreneurs, and many others." Masculinized notions of worthiness and morality during the height of economic downturn shaped the ways Korean migrants in Beijing interpreted their precariousness. South Korean news outlets portrayed South Korean men who lost their jobs and homes because of corporate restructuring as faultless victims who were "deserving" of public sympathy and state aid (J. Song 2009). The *chaebol* mobilized age-old ideologies of "the good wife, wise mother" to encourage women to soothe their husbands' egos, as seen in the Chaeil Bank's "Boost your husband's spirit!" campaign (Kim and Finch 2002: 130). Television dramas and popular talk shows offered advice on how wives could support their husbands during a period of financial hardship (Kim and Finch 2002: 130).

While South Korean men were at the forefront of national sympathy, media portrayals of Korean Chinese minorities in the late 1990s were colored by moralistic narratives of greed and deceit. Korean Chinese women who wed South Korean farmers were depicted as seductresses who used their feminine wiles to swindle innocent South Korean farmer bachelors, and Korean Chinese men who provided their manual labor in Seoul were hypermasculinized as violent criminals who went to extreme lengths—even going so far as killing their South Korean "brothers"—to make an extra buck.

Many South Koreans in the enclave, including Mr. Park, believed that opportunistic Korean Chinese middlemen were responsible for the downward mobility of South Korean entrepreneurs in Beijing. They frequently warned me to keep my distance from money-grubbing Korean Chinese minorities. I was told stories of how so-and-so had hired a Korean Chinese manager who later turned out to be a con artist, who "stole" the ideas and resources from his South Korean boss to grow a more successful, similar business in Wangjing.

The concept of status anxiety helps explain why so many South Korean entrepreneurs in the enclave alluded to narratives of "dirty money" and "coethnic betrayal" in explaining why their businesses had failed. They clung to whatever moral and cultural resources were at their disposal as their economic statuses became increasingly precarious. Erving Goffman helps clarify the ways in which status anxiety incites boundary-making activities. He argues that during times of instability, status symbols work to retard the rise of the nouveau riche:

A time is reached when social decline accelerates with a spiral effect: members of a declining class are forced to rely more and more upon symbols which do not involve a current outlay, while at the same time their association with these symbols lowers the value of these signs in the eyes of others. (Goffman 1951: 303)

By donning symbols of wealth and engaging in conspicuous consumption, many Korean Chinese minorities attempted to not only outwardly prove that they were middle class, but some attempted to pass as South Korean by masking their Korean Chinese accents, buying clothes that were imported from Seoul, and otherwise flaunting their wealth. As marginalized minorities, the Korean Chinese lacked the moral and cultural resources to construct an alternative narrative of their identities that invoked pride and self-esteem outside the confines of their in-group. As Sayer (2005: 947) writes:

The poor are not disadvantaged primarily because others fail to value their identity and misrecognize and undervalue their cultural goods, or indeed because they are stigmatized, though all these things make their situation worse; rather they are disadvantaged primarily because they lack the means to live in ways which they as well as others value.

What did it mean to be a member of the middle class? Did the Korean Chinese really achieve the middle class dream? Our first inclination, when viewing the disadvantaged, may be to assume that "the means" that Sayer refers to point to economic and material means. This book demonstrates the importance of moral and cultural means—the means over legitimacy and feelings of belonging—that remain within the hands of the global elite.

Getting in

I first learned about Wangjing the summer of 2006, when I worked alongside a team of Korean American college students and young professionals teaching English at the Yanbian University of Science and Technology (YUST) in the Korean Autonomous Prefecture. I taught two hours of intermediate-level conversational English each morning to a class of over sixty students. Up until the early 1990s, Yanbian was home to over 50 percent of the ethnic Korean population in China. In my entire class, for instance, only three students were not Korean Chinese. Over the years, YUST became an important feeder institution for prominent South Korean firms in China because of the strong networks between the faculty and South Korean business executives. Many of my students dreamed of finding well-paying positions working for Samsung in Beijing or Shanghai. They told me stories of their friends who led luxurious middle class lifestyles in the booming Koreatowns in these cities.

To get to know my students better, I lived in a tiny dormitory room, jam-packed with four bunk beds, two on each side of the wall, and eight lockers, where my seven roommates and I stored our clothes, books, and personal items. We shared bathroom facilities with more than fifty other girls on our floor. Living conditions resembled those of other Chinese university dormitories in the countryside. Electricity in our building was shut off promptly at eleven in the evening, and we were woken up by the bright fluorescent lights that automatically turned back on at six every morning. Hot water for showers was available only three times a week for two-hour windows at a time. Laundry was done by hand with ice-cold water in the bathroom, and we hung our clothes on makeshift twine in our rooms to dry.

My experiences in Yanbian were formative in helping me conduct fieldwork in Beijing. I got a taste of what life was like for a Korean Chinese minority in the remote corners of northeast China. When the Korean Chinese minorities I later interviewed during my fieldwork in Beijing spoke of the ethnic villages where they came from, I could relate their depictions to my own experiences living in Yanbian. By the time I arrived in Beijing, I knew what the center of Yanji looked like, had shopped before in the commercial districts, understood the acquired taste of Yanbian cold noodles, and had walked by the KTV rooms that my interviewees frequently spoke of.

In 2010, I moved into a small studio apartment in the middle of the enclave to start my dissertation field research and lived in the enclave on and off for more than a year. I strategically located several different sites to conduct participant observation. For several months at a time, I worked as an intern at a major South Korean multinational firm, a volunteer as a pianist at a South Korean megachurch, an English teacher at a Korean Chinese underground church, and a sales clerk at a small Korean boutique.

In spite of my efforts to be a helpful presence to the people I encountered in the field, I struggled to establish rapport with the Korean migrants who lived and worked nearby. Most of the Korean Chinese minorities I met in Beijing were suspicious of my intentions because the ways I spoke and dressed marked me as South Korean. Those who recognized me as a diasporic Korean associated me with the privileged status of Korean Americans in South Korea.[6] Nearly all my solicitations—including innocuous coffee dates and dinner invitations—were declined.

My breakthrough came accidentally, when I decided to attend daybreak prayer service [*saebyeoggido*] at First Presbyterian, a Korean Chinese underground church I attended.[7] After weeks of sitting alone in the back of the pews every Sunday, I had become emotionally exhausted. Unable to sleep, I hopped inside a cab on a whim and headed to First Presbyterian early in the morning. As the daughter of a Korean immigrant pastor in the United States, the cultural practice of praying before sunrise carried special symbolic currency to me. I remembered how my father placed his hands on the backs of people who came to church early in the morning in search of answers and solace.

When Pastor Kim at First Presbyterian turned down the lights to commence prayer time, I felt moved by the familiar notes of "How Great Thou Art" playing in the background and to my embarrassment, tears started streaming uncontrollably down my face. In truth, I had come to Beijing with a heavy heart. The church that my father had served for the better part of a decade had recently split after several years of tense conflict, and my father, unable to find a new church to lead at his age, used his retirement savings to open a small pet supply store in a wealthy suburb. The store was unprofitable and closed within a year, however, and my parents lost everything. I felt guilty that they had to work a series of odd jobs at minimum wage, barely making ends meet, while I read about inequality in the comforts of the Ivory Tower. I ran away to the other side of the world to distance myself from the problems I faced back home, only to find myself surrounded by people like my parents in the field. As I sat crying in the sanctuary that day, I felt a woman quietly place her hand on mine.

Vulnerable Ethnography as a Methodological Approach

When I talk about my emotional involvement in the field, my words invariably cause some of my colleagues to shift uncomfortably in their seats. Some ask how I maintained enough distance to ensure my findings were credible. Others gingerly ask whether the details of my family background and upbringing are topics I need to bring up.

What did it mean to be too close to the people in the field? What was I putting at stake by making myself vulnerable? Why were academics so wary of ethnographers who became overly involved? Howard Becker notes that some writers intentionally overwhelm readers with a "barrage of detailed knowledge," including "dates, names, and places only a specialist will recognize," to prove the validity of their claims: "How could someone who knows all that be wrong?" (1986: 45). Or, as Matthew Desmond notes, some use the first-person to establish a sense of legitimacy: "I was there. I saw it happen. And because I saw it happen, you can believe it happened" (2016: 334). Desmond, in his intimate account of people on the brink of homelessness, even goes so far as to abandon the first-person narrative, arguing that the "I" so prominent in typical ethnographic accounts shouldn't matter. "There is bigger game afoot," he explains. "I hope that when you talk about this book, you talk first about Sherrena and Tobin, Arleen and Jori, Larraine and Scott and Pam, Crystal and Vanetta—and the fact that somewhere in your city, a family has just been evicted from their home, their things piled high on the sidewalk" (Desmond 2016: 335).

For me, vulnerable writing is an act of respect toward the reader—without it, the reader is left to his own devices in piecing together how the author's emotional baggage perpetually filtered the information encountered. How else can we be transparent to our readership, than to narrate in our own voice what we saw and how we made sense of these encounters? Ruth Behar (1996: 14) put it best when she asserted that "the exposure of the self . . . [can] take us somewhere we couldn't otherwise get to."

In order to understand why people behave in the ways that they do, I believe that they must let us inside their inner worlds. As an ethnographer, I wanted to create an environment where people, who otherwise may have lost any semblance of faith in the system, felt safe enough to share the full extent of their experiences. I believed that it was imperative to behave in a matter that clearly demonstrated that my intentions to observe and write were sincere. Vulnerable observation, to me, is therefore a necessary condition for empirical rigor—without it, I believe that ethnographers are only shown a selective slice (oftentimes, the less embarrassing slice) of disadvantage.

This is not to say that vulnerable ethnographies do not come with their own set of risks. Though I attempted to blur the boundaries between friend and researcher, I grew increasingly aware that I could not be a true friend—I could not be transparent about my own beliefs for fear of influencing what they felt safe about expressing and what they would be more inclined to filter. I could not deny the fact that I was spending time with them to further an agenda as a professional academic. I also knew that when it came time to leave the field I would return to my privileged life in America, and our friendship would over time slowly wither over the vast distance that separated our worlds.[8]

As my relationships in the field grew more intimate, I also became concerned that my personal baggage might make me more receptive to certain stories, and more oblivious to others. I wanted to be at once emotionally invested in the people I was meeting, while doing my due diligence to find the equally disadvantaged people who I was less inclined to meet. And in an effort to cover my blind spots, I traveled around the enclave to major churches, commercial districts, and public parks, and distributed survey questionnaires with a team of local college students.[9] The surveys not only helped me understand broader demographic and attitudinal trends that expanded beyond the reach of my personal networks, but they also gave me a better understanding of the lay of the land.

In my survey questionnaire, I included a blurb offering an honorarium of 50 RMB (or about 7 USD) for at least an hour of interview time. Those who were interested were asked to check a box and write down their contact information. After collecting all the questionnaires, I strategically selected interviewees who were coded according to their demographic backgrounds as well as attitudes. I was particularly interested in people who had extreme views—both exceptionally negative and positive—to get a sense of what the full range of experiences and attitudes were. The interviews I conducted were scattered over a period of two years, and were used periodically as a reference point to check whether the problems that people in my intimate network of friends spoke of were also happening elsewhere. By the end of my time in the field, I had collected nearly eight hundred questionnaires and more than eighty in-depth interviews. Although the thrust of my findings was based on participant observations, my survey and interview data served as important supplementary data that helped me discern what was idiosyncratic from generalizable.

The Journey Ahead

The next two chapters contextualize how the Korean transnational enclave in Beijing emerged. Chapter 2 follows the story of Young-me, a Korean Chinese woman who struggles with feelings of nostalgia for the

Korean village in the rural Liaoning Province she left behind. I explain the significance of these early Korean enclaves in the Korean Chinese imagination and how they are connected to feelings of attachment and belonging. Chapter 3 explains the social and political context shaping Wangjing's emergence and the impact that dense transnational linkages with South Korea have had on identity politics.

Chapters 4 and 5 focus on the impact of transnational organizations. Chapter 4 links how workplace stratification has justified the wealth and privilege of the expats and the disadvantage of Korean Chinese youth along gendered lines. In chapter 5, we see how stark class divisions within the South Korean megachurch further solidify the privilege of the global middle class. The South Korean entrepreneurs who are in dire need of institutional support largely feel alienated in the process. By contrast, Korean Chinese underground churches, though outwardly spartan and modest, help cultivate a sense of pride and collective consciousness. As ethnic minorities who are dually marginalized from both South Korean and Han Chinese societies, the Korean Chinese feel a strong sense of solidarity and provide one another with both material and emotional support. Korean Chinese entrepreneurs thus have access to important collective resources to help sustain their businesses that their South Korean counterparts are not privy to.

Chapter 6 compares how South Korean and Korean Chinese migrants are able to attain access to upward mobility by managing small businesses. In particular, I explain how the Korean Chinese, unlike the South Koreans, are able to achieve economic success by mobilizing their cultural skills and ability to establish emotional rapport, as cultural brokers. In the final chapter, I write about the implications that neoliberal restructuring has had on the future of South Korean youth in Wangjing.

Endnotes

1. According to the Chinese government's *Ethnic Statistical Yearbook*, in 2005, 8.38 percent of Korean Chinese minorities had completed college, compared to 3.73 percent of the national population and 0.009 percent of the minority population. Rates of illiteracy among the Korean Chinese were also the lowest at 2.86 percent, compared to 9.08 percent of the national population and 14.54 of the minority population (National Bureau of Statistics of China, 2005). Data from my own survey also demonstrates that in an absolute sense, levels of schooling among the Korean Chinese in Beijing are quite

high. Of 383 Korean Chinese respondents, 61.9 percent had attained either a two-year or four-year college degree, and 20.6 percent had finished high school. Still, due to restrictions on private enterprise under the Mao regime, previous entrepreneurial experience, and any type of work experience in the private sector for that matter, was virtually unheard of in the Chinese countryside. Although it is difficult to make any detailed comparisons due to different sampling procedures, data on the Korean Chinese population from the Chinese Census Bureau shows that a significant proportion of the Korean Chinese had held low-wage, low-skilled positions prior to their mass wave of urban migration in the 1990s. According to this data set, of the 918,673 Korean Chinese minorities who were employed in 1982, 59.7 percent were employed in the agricultural sector and 17.3 percent were employed in manufacturing. Only a small fraction had held white-collar jobs: 2.5 percent were employed in the public sector, 4.7 percent in education and the arts, 0.4 percent in finance, and 0.4 percent in scientific research. These statistics correspond to existing descriptive accounts of the Korean Chinese that claim that the vast majority were farmers who lived in agricultural communes prior to Deng Xiaoping's economic reforms in the late 1970s and 1980s.

2. Of the 376 South Koreans I surveyed, 10.4 percent were entrepreneurs. This is admittedly a small sample size; however, ethnographic observations and interviews provide corroborating evidence of my findings that despite the high levels of education among South Korean entrepreneurs, the vast majority were susceptible to downward mobility.

3. Since the implementation of economic reforms under Deng Xiaoping, sociologists have produced numerous works examining the effect of market reforms on socioeconomic mobility and inequality in the PRC (Bian 2002). The economic reforms did away with strict regulations in commerce and domestic migration that had blocked opportunities for upward mobility during the pre-reform era. Under Mao Zedong, Chinese class structure was largely bifurcated between the urban elite and poor farmers, and poverty was primarily concentrated in rural areas (Davis 1995; Whyte 2012). According to Davis and Feng (2009), in the 1970s, average city incomes were triple those in the countryside. This pattern of social stratification was rigidly kept in place through China's *hukou* system, which strictly controlled movement and settlement patterns of Chinese citizens. Furthermore, because *hukou* status was passed on intergenerationally and is virtually immutable in one's lifetime, opportunities for mobility were extremely rare. With economic reforms since 1978, however, Deng did away with the regulations of Mao's redistributive state privatizing the agricultural sector

and encouraging foreign investment. In addition, the *hukou* system, which had once sustained wealth in the hands of the urban elite, underwent significant modifications such that migration to the cities among poor farmers became feasible. These dramatic series of structural changes in the economy unleashed a tidal wave of rural migration to urban areas. But despite *hukou* reform and mass rural-to-urban migration, subsequent studies have found evidence of lingering legal, structural, and institutional barriers that rural migrants faced in pursuing upward mobility in urban areas.

4. Migration scholars are careful in distinguishing "immigrants" in their trajectories of movement and attitudes toward the host society. Whereas "migrants" are people whose patterns of movement are broadly and loosely defined, and "transnational migrants" exhibit more circular patterns of movement back and forth between the host and home societies (as explained later), "immigrants" see the host society as their final destination and as a place where they want to settle more or less permanently.

5. Lim and Jang (2006: 445) summarize the shifting balance of power between the *chaebol* and South Korean government in the following excerpt: "The Chun Doo Hwan government (1980–87) could be characterized by the military government's authoritarian supremacy over *chaebols*. For example, in 1985, the government was able to bring a disobedient *chaebol* group (the Kukje group, then seventh-largest *chaebol*) to heel, eventually dissolving it by having state-controlled banks coordinate an announcement of the group's bankruptcy, allegedly due to reckless management. In the period of the Roh Tae Woo government (1988–91), the power of *chaebols* grew significantly against the state, ironically, due to the 'effects of democratization' during the late 1980s, which saw the weakening of authoritarian state power. During this period, the term 'Chaebol Republic' was often heard in the news media. Under the Kim Young Sam government (1992–1997) which defined itself as the 'civilian government' being a post-military regime, the power of *chaebol* in generals was biggest, while differentiation among the *chaebols* became more visible than ever in terms of their relational closeness to the government. For example, Hyundai chairman Chung Ju Yung created his own political party capitalizing on his business group and became a Presidential candidate himself, challenging Kim Young Sam in the 1992 elections."

6. I would later learn that their resentment was rooted in discriminatory laws like the 1999 Law on the Entry/Exit and Status of Overseas Koreans, which quickly garnered controversy for defining "overseas Korean" as ethnic Koreans who left the peninsula after 1948, thereby excluding Korean

Chinese and Soviet Koreans. After much protest from Korean Chinese activists and South Korean NGOs, the law was modified in 2003 to include all overseas Koreans. Discriminatory laws such as the Overseas Korea Act undoubtedly affected the nature of responses I received from the Korean Chinese when I first reached out to them.

7. I write about this experience in more detail in chapter 5.

8. For a more thorough discussion of the "relational ethics" for ethnographic research, please refer to Carolyn Ellis's (2007) work.

9. About 62 percent of the Korean Chinese survey participants (n=417) were recruited at one of six churches I visited. Eighteen percent (74 people) were recruited at restaurants and clothing stores owned by Korean Chinese minorities. The remaining members of the sampling population were located via public venues and friendship networks. Despite the strong bias in recruiting methods, the different attitudes and demographic traits of the Korean Chinese who were located through church networks and those who were not were minimal. The quality of the survey data for the Korean Chinese population, however, was far from perfect as we encountered two significant problems in administering the survey. First, perhaps because the respondents were not provided with an incentive, many did not fill out the questionnaires entirely, sometimes leaving entire pages empty. Second, people with low levels of education did not know how to read or fill out the questionnaires by themselves. My research assistants and I read the questions out loud to these people and helped fill out the answers for them one by one, but this was time consuming. Many of the people we weren't able to help grew frustrated waiting for our assistance and left before we had a chance to approach them. I conducted an additional survey targeting the South Korean population (n=379) toward the end of my time in Beijing. Although I used similar sampling techniques to recruit participants, the quality of the survey data was much higher than that of the Korean Chinese population. Using funding from the National Science Foundation Doctoral Dissertation Research Improvement Grant (NSF DDRI #1131006), I purchased 330 USB ports for 30 RMB (5 USD) each and handed out the USB ports as an incentive to fill out the questionnaires. In addition, none of the South Koreans I approached seemed to experience the same types of difficulties that the Korean Chinese participants did, in filling out the questionnaires. South Koreans seemed much more accustomed to filling out surveys, given higher literacy rates and levels of education. Fifteen percent were recruited at public venues, while the remaining 85 percent were recruited through church networks.

CHAPTER 2

Mourning the Loss of *Gohyang,* a Place of Belonging

Young-me, a third-generation Korean ethnic minority of Chinese nationality, grew up in a remote village in the outskirts of Shenyang. When she speaks about her childhood, she fondly refers to her village as her *gohyang,* a sentimental Korean word for one's hometown.

The last time Young-me visited her hometown was in 2005, when she was still in high school. She returned with her father that day because they had arranged to sell their house to a Han Chinese peasant. By then, nearly all her Korean Chinese neighbors who had occupied the thatch-roofed houses nearby had left to work in Seoul. She explained the calculus that went into their decision to leave:

> From the perspective of a Korean Chinese minority, we think, "Is abandoning my *gohyang* worth the money I can make if I leave my village?" Then, even 1,000 RMB [about 150 USD] isn't enough for me to consider throwing that away, so we would decide not to leave. But Seoul is different. I could make ten times more than what I could make in my village.

Young-me knew that her village had become a ghost town, but as she stood in the fields with her father in front of the home where she grew up, she found herself heartbroken. She thought back to how as a little girl, she and her friends had run across the fields without a care in the world. She thought about the relationships that she left behind—of how her life had been so intimately intertwined with the villagers who lived nearby and how they had supported and depended on one another. The house where she had spent her entire childhood had become so run-down due to neglect that when she cautiously stepped inside to inspect her old room, she worried the roof would collapse on top of her. They sold off the house quickly for the cheap price of about 10,000 RMB (about 1,470 USD), assuming that the new owner would tear down what remained and build a new house in its place.

That Young-me defines her *gohyang* as the agricultural village she left behind in China is noteworthy, particularly in light of the fact that the Korean term for "hometown" also denotes one's place of ancestral origin—the Korean peninsula. In Korean popular culture, *gohyang* is often used to signify more than just a geographic locale, but rather a spiritual and existential space where one feels a sense of complete belonging. In Yong-kyu Yoon's 1949 film *Hometown of My Heart* [*maeum ui gohyang*], for instance, Yoon utilizes a mother figure as a powerful metaphor to represent the ultimate *gohyang*, a place where one can find unconditional acceptance.

Over the years, these three overlapping dimensions of *gohyang*—as a place of ancestral origin, regional hometown, and existential belonging—have come to lead many to believe that members of the Korean diaspora were in many ways sojourners who were bound by an unbreakable, metaphysical connection to the Korean peninsula, regardless of the number of generations that had passed since their departure. Notions that Koreans were inextricably bound together by blood first crystallized under Japanese colonial rule, when speaking Korean was strictly prohibited and asserting one's identity and pride as a Korean could mean imprisonment. The first mass exodus—and the birth of the contemporary Korean diaspora—was also instigated by the Japanese. As I detail later in this chapter, thousands of Korean farmers were forced to relocate to Manchuria and the Russian Far East as part of Japanese land reform projects since 1910, while others were shipped to Japan to work as cheap laborers in factories. When civil wars broke out in after World War II in both China and the Korean peninsula, many overseas Koreans found themselves stranded. They yearned to reunite with their families and return to their hometowns, but were unable to.

It was within this historical context that the concept of *gohyang* first permeated the Korean imagination. Korean independence fighters, many of whom were in exile, referred to their hometowns in poems to express their longing for freedom from the Japanese imperial regime and love for their *joguk* [ancestral homeland] (Kim 2005). Those who were imprisoned for their activism reminisced about the vast fields they had run across as children and the beautiful natural landscape of the Korean peninsula as they wrote within the cramped confines of their prison cells. They yearned for the better, simpler days of their childhood when Korea had been free and autonomous (Kim 2005). And because of these circumstances, for many Koreans the term *gohyang* has continued to evoke sentiments of loss (of independence and autonomy), nostalgia (for a time of unadulterated innocence), and perhaps most importantly, yearning (for a place of belonging).

In this chapter and the next, I analyze Young-me's longing for her *gohyang* to better understand how feelings of belonging and notions of ethnic identity among Korean Chinese have been shaped by the rise of global capitalism and the emergence of transnational communities in the PRC. Since the 1990s the vast majority of Korean villages in the Chinese countryside have disappeared, as Korean Chinese peasants left the agricultural communes where they had tilled the rice paddies for over three generations to pursue better economic opportunities elsewhere. Many Korean Chinese migrants flew to Seoul to fill the demand for cheap labor in the 1990s. But as restrictions on foreign trade and travel continued to liberalize in the 2000s, China became a major destination for South Korean foreign direct investment (FDI), and increasing numbers of Korean Chinese minorities started to travel to major cities within the PRC, such as Beijing—the site of my study—to find jobs as interpreters and cultural intermediaries within South Korean companies. Over the past two decades, the new Korean transnational enclaves that have formed in the cities have eclipsed the Korean villages of the Mao era, profoundly changing the ways Koreans in China understand notions of self and form communities.

Cultural Islands and *Gohyang* as a Place of Belonging

I was introduced to Young-me in 2008, through a friend of a friend. She was a college student in Beijing looking to earn some pocket money. Incidentally, I had been trying to find a bilingual research assistant to help me conduct interviews and surveys. During our initial interview, I learned that she came from a poor peasant family and that her father had warned her early on that he wouldn't be able to provide her with tuition for college. If she wanted to attend, she would have to obtain a full scholarship at Minzu University, a government-sponsored university known for providing generous financial support to ethnic minorities. Minzu, though prestigious in its own right, was a safe bet for her; she had always easily earned exam scores that placed her at the top of her class. Had she more emotional or financial support from her parents, she would have aimed higher—for Peking or Qinghua University. But she quickly cut her losses, knowing that there was no way she would be able to convince her father otherwise, and in 2006 she moved to Beijing to matriculate.

I remember feeling struck by Young-me's self-assuredness. I was working under a tight budget as a graduate student and expected to pay her the same rate I paid my Han Chinese language tutor. Young-me however, suggested double the amount I was prepared to offer, citing wages that were more typical of hourly rates in South Korea. After a few rounds of going back and forth, we reached a compromise—I would pay her a base salary of 30 RMB (about 5 USD) an hour and compensate her an additional fee for each interview she helped conduct. She seemed satisfied with the final deal. Even as a sophomore in college, Young-me had already had several experiences working with South Koreans as a tour guide, a translator, and a Chinese language tutor for international students and businessmen. Though she herself had never set foot in South Korea at the time, she spoke with surprising specificity about how to negotiate with South Koreans and the nature of everyday life in Seoul.

Nearly ten years after conducting fieldwork in Beijing, I reconnected with Young-me in Seoul. Somehow, we both found ourselves living and working in the country of our ancestors despite having sworn to ourselves that we would never return. Young-me's trajectory from Benxi (the outskirts of Shenyang, where she grew up) to Beijing, then Shenyang, and later to Seoul, is by no means considered extraordinary in her community. Most of Young-me's friends and family members have spent significant periods living in various cities across South Korea and China. The constant movement to-and-from these different locales has led to the increasing prevalence of transnational families and transnational lifestyles among Korean Chinese minorities.

This was precisely the case for Young-me and her family. Her estranged mother, who divorced her father many years ago, lived with her boyfriend in Mokpo, a small port city located on the southernmost tip of the Korean peninsula. Her brother, who earned a living as a construction worker in Seoul, spent seven months out of the year living with Young-me and the rest of the year in Shenyang with his Han Chinese wife and young son. Even her father, who lived in a hospice in Benxi due to his failing health, had worked in the 3-D (dirty, difficult, dangerous) industry in Seoul in the early 1990s when the borders between South Korea and China first opened. Her extended family—her aunts, uncles, and cousins—were similarly dispersed across the Sino–South Korean border.

Still, although Young-me leads a cosmopolitan lifestyle now, traveling back and forth between China and South Korea at a moment's notice, her upbringing was anything but. When Young-me was young, her whole world was contained within the bounds of a small agricultural commune in China, secluded from any semblance of urban life.

Young-me's parochial upbringing is quite typical for a Korean Chinese minority. Until the end of the Mao Zedong regime in 1976, the vast majority of Korean Chinese minorities lived in Korean enclaves so isolated from the surrounding Han Chinese society that they were dubbed "cultural islands" by historians and geographers (S. J. Kim 2003). These tightly knit, insular villages resembled a time capsule of sorts, enabling the Korean Chinese to preserve the language and customs of their ancestors for many generations. Until the 1990s, of the 1.1 million Korean Chinese minorities in China, 99.2 percent of the population was concentrated in a region known by local Chinese as *dongbei* or the northeast, spanning across the Liaoning, Jilin, and Heilongjiang Provinces. Within the northeastern provinces, the Korean Chinese further isolated themselves by living in ethnic enclaves—the largest of which was located in the southern Manchurian region known as "Kando" by Koreans or "Jiandao" by the Chinese during the prewar era. This border region later became known as the Yanbian Korean Autonomous Prefecture after the founding of the Communist regime, and accounted for 42.5 percent of the entire Korean Chinese population throughout the Mao era (1949–1976) according to Chinese Census data.

Historical records demonstrate that the early Korean sojourners were rice farmers who relied on collective labor to build irrigation systems and cultivate rice paddies. They thus migrated in groups with their kin and fellow villagers (Lee 1986; Lee 1932). Korean migrants who ventured across the border into Manchuria fled a series of natural disasters that caused famine and poverty in agricultural villages within the

Korean peninsula in the 1860s (Piao 1990). Prior to this wave of migration, the Qing state had closely patrolled the border area. As the grip of the Manchus weakened following the Taiping Rebellion (1850–1864), increasing numbers of sojourners left Korea (known as Chosŏn between 1392–1897) for Kando. In 1870, there were over 20,000 Koreans spread across 30 villages north of the Yalu River. By 1894, this population nearly doubled to 37,000 Koreans (Piao 1990). Throughout the early 1900s, over 75 percent of the population in Kando was ethnically Korean.

Migration across the border accelerated after Japanese annexation of Korea in 1910. Between 1910 and 1918, the Japanese colonial regime conducted a large-scale land survey, displacing an unprecedented number of Korean farmers to Kando. Japan invaded this region in 1931, establishing a puppet regime known as "Manchukuo" to help prepare the colonial government for full-scale war with China. To expedite their infiltration of Manchuria, the Japanese implemented a fifteen-year plan to transfer 300,000 Korean rural households, or 1.5 million Koreans, across the Sino–Korean border (Lee 1986). Although the fifteen-year plan was never fully executed, the Korean population surged from 460,000 in 1920 to 607,000 in 1930, and to 1.45 million in 1940. According to a Korean geographer who visited the region in the early 1930s, the cities in Kando became so "Korean in their outward appearance in their content" that a stranger would "feel that he is no longer in Chinese territory but in Korea" (Lee 1932: 201).

Following the end of World War II in 1945 many returned to the Korean peninsula, but about 1.4 million Koreans stayed behind (Lee 1986). Those who remained continued to live in the prewar Korean enclaves that had formed across the northeast. Young-me's grandparents decided not to return to their *gohyang* in the Korean peninsula after the war ended. Her grandfather passed away in 1983, six years before Young-me was born. The reasons for his death remain a family secret, and to this day none of her family members will tell her why or how he passed away. She suspects that he did not die of natural causes.

Young-me's grandmother, for her part, continued to struggle to come to terms with the fact that she could no longer return to the Korean peninsula even in her old age. Her grandmother dealt with her feelings of loss by blaming Young-me's father. For every misfortune or hardship, she could be heard muttering under her breath that had she not been pregnant with Young-me's father, they would have been able to return. She spoke so often of her *gohyang* that even many years after her grandmother's death, Young-me could still recite the exact address in Northern Chungcheon Province where her grandparents had lived prior to migrating to China. Her grandmother was from a small village called Tanjiri in the district of Hansu-myeon in Jecheon city, located about 170 kilometers southeast of Seoul. "My grandmother wanted me to visit her *gohyang* if I ever had the opportunity to visit South Korea. Every chance she had, she would mention where her tiny village was located. Stories of her *gohyang* seemed to perpetually hang from her lips," she said. The elderly women in her village often gathered together to share stories of their youth, and in reminiscing about their past, they found solace in talking about the hometowns they had left behind.

Ironically, though Young-me would ultimately relocate to South Korea several years after her grandmother's death, she had never once expressed interest in visiting Tanjiri in the four years since moving to Seoul. As my relationship with Young-me grew more intimate, I learned that she had been abandoned by her parents as a child and had grown up solely under her grandmother's care. After her parents' divorce, her mother disappeared from her life and her father quickly wed another Korean Chinese woman from a neighboring village who had a daughter of her own only a few years older than Young-me. The couple decided to make a new family together, each bringing only one child from their former marriages. Subsequently, Young-me's father, in choosing his son, abandoned his daughter. Young-me was six years old at the time.

Having grown up in the absence of a traditional family, for Young-me, the small farming village of her childhood served as her surrogate, extended family. I heard about her childhood village over a generous bowl of *bingsu* [a Korean dessert made of shaved ice with red bean, fruit, and rice cakes] at a local Paris Baguette, a well-known South Korean bakery chain, on a hot summer day in the enclave. The agricultural commune was located atop a small mountain in the outskirts of Shenyang. She and her neighbors lived along small dirt paths branching off from the large road that ran from the base of the mountain to the peak. Their mud-thatched houses were built in an L-shape, typical of traditional Korean houses, with a *madang* [front porch] facing the main road. The villagers cultivated rice and vegetables in plots of arable land at the foot of the mountain, and every thirty years, the plots were rotated among members of the community.

Throughout the Mao era, agricultural communes were sheltered from external influence as people were tied to the area where they were officially registered. Under the *hukou* [household registration] system, the district where someone was registered at birth was intertwined with access to grain rations, employment, housing, education, and healthcare. Consequently, outsiders were precluded from penetrating the Korean agricultural villages, and Korean minorities were largely blocked off from experiencing life outside the provincial confines of their village.

Because Young-me's village was demarcated as a Korean autonomous district by the Communist regime, she grew up in an environment that promoted the preservation of their ethnic language, education, and culture as part of protectionist policies for ethnic minorities (Jin 1990). After the Chinese civil war came to a close in 1952, the Mao regime recognized a prefecture, in addition to one county and forty-three townships with high concentrations of Korean minorities, across the three Northeastern provinces as special autonomous districts. Korean Chinese children in these zones by and large attended Korean schools; public announcements and documents were available in both Korean and Mandarin; and both languages were spoken freely on the streets, in government offices, and in their homes.

In Young-me's case, more than 90 percent of her village was ethnically Korean, and many first-generation migrants had spent their entire lives in the village never having had to learn Mandarin. Young-me's grandmother, for instance, had gone about her daily life speaking only her ancestral tongue. Even the two or three Han Chinese households that resided in Young-me's agricultural commune were conversant in Korean.

When Young-me was seven years old, she started attending the local ethnic Korean elementary school located half a kilometer up the road from her home. As a little girl, she walked up a dimly lit dirt path every day, frightened to death of the possible wild animals she might run into on her way as her grandmother stood at the foot of their *madang*, watching from afar. Young-me's school, like most elementary schools in the Chinese countryside, was small and humble. About thirty Korean Chinese children studied together in four cramped classrooms inside a run-down building. As she described it:

> Sometimes because of the limited number of students and classrooms, if there weren't enough students in one grade, they would just eliminate that grade level for that year. So when I was in sixth grade, we didn't have a second grade or a fifth grade. We didn't have

enough teachers in our village . . . When I was in elementary school, my cousin taught my math class. She was scary and would beat us with a wooden stick if we didn't listen.

There was no money for repairs and the broken glass in the windows of the school had been taped over with paper. During the winter the classrooms were heated by a wooden furnace set in the middle of the room, and Young-me and her classmates arranged their desks around the furnace to keep warm. Their metal lunchboxes, which were placed at the foot of the furnace, would burn on the bottom, and when the students opened them up to eat the classroom filled with the scent of rancid *kimchee.*

Despite their material lack, Young-me claims that she was happiest when she lived in her *gohyang.* Her eyes sparkled as she recalled stories of climbing up the mountains and playing outside with her friends. They foraged for *gosari* [wild herbs] to eat—mostly, ferns and dandelions—and made a game of trying to see who could collect the most. In the fall, she and the village children gathered branches and twigs that fell off the trees to bring back home and burn in the furnace.

During major holidays, like the Lunar New Year, the whole village congregated together to make rice cakes. The grown-ups took turns pounding the sticky rice with heavy wooden hammers as others relaxed from the sidelines, drinking homemade rice wine and playing card games. Young-me and her friends ate bits and pieces of rice cake as they ran around the *madang,* chasing one another and playing with the chickens and pigs that were kept as livestock. As she reminisced back to her childhood, she said, "It was as if our whole neighborhood [*dongnae*] was part of one big happy family, but now those villages are gone."

There were no doors on the houses in her village, but rather open *madang* where her neighbors would enter and leave one another's residences seamlessly, oftentimes stopping by to lounge and chat. When I asked her if they didn't get into any fights, she chuckled:

> Sure, but the fights that we had were like trivial quarrels that you might have with your family. One *halmoni* [literally "grandma," often used as an affectionate term referring to elderly women in general] would gossip about one of her neighbors behind her back, and then that person would find out and snub her. But then, the next day, their fight would blow over and they would make up and forget it ever happened.

Other Korean Chinese minorities I interviewed, particularly those who grew up in rural communities like Young-me, expressed a strong emotional attachment to their *gohyang*. Yoon-ho, for instance, expressed similar sentiments. A third-generation Korean Chinese minority who attended the same university as Young-me, Yoon-ho migrated to Beijing from a small Korean village that consisted of about one hundred households. Like his neighbors, he lived in a small thatch-roofed house with his family. A river ran behind the village, and in front of the houses there was a dirt road, and rice fields on the other side of the road. The Korean Chinese families lived in the western part of the large plain, while the Han Chinese farmers and their families lived in the eastern part; there was a clear emotional and physical divide that separated the two villages.

The Korean families in Yoon-ho's village worked in the fields every day, and in the fall, everyone helped gather the crops and sold them in the marketplace in town. "We had a stable life. I mean it wasn't as if we were wealthy or anything, but we weren't poor either. We didn't ever worry about money," he explained. After working in the fields together, in the evenings, everyone went home to eat dinner and afterward, gathered together in the *madang* of one of their houses to chat and relax. At around eight or nine, when their favorite television programs came on, they went back to their respective homes to watch TV. The next day, the whole cycle would repeat.

Special occasions—holidays, weddings, funerals, even birthdays—were celebrated together as a community. When a grandmother in the village turned sixty years old, for instance, everyone prepared a huge feast in her honor. When Yoon-ho's neighbor got married, the whole village gathered to attend the wedding festivities. Yoon-ho noted that their celebrations were in some ways exclusive: "We didn't include the Han Chinese [in the neighboring village] in our gatherings. We just ate, drank, and celebrated together amongst ourselves."

Ghost Villages

In 2001, Young-me left her village to attend middle school in Benxi, a nearby town. There was only one ethnic Korean school in the area, and all the Korean children her age from nearby districts left their villages and moved into the student dormitories. Unlike Han Chinese children who attended public schools near where they lived, the Korean Chinese traveled vast distances to attend school because only larger townships had the resources to construct the facilities and provide the staff needed. These ethnic schools, in turn, depended on Korean Chinese families from more remote areas to send their children as students so that the schools could sustain operations.

Young-me periodically visited her village during the holidays, but each time she returned, she noticed significant changes. There were fewer young couples who settled in the village to start families. Although she had played with many of the neighborhood children as a little girl, as Young-me grew older, the sight of young children became increasingly rare. Instead, the village became mostly inhabited by the elderly, as the more able-bodied left, one by one, to work in South Korea. While the Korean Chinese minorities in Young-me's parents' generation met and married people from within their district, after the mid- to late-1990s young Korean Chinese singles started meeting their prospective spouses in Seoul. Among those who left to work in Seoul, few returned.

Certainly, in retrospect, Young-me's yearning for the village where she grew up is magnified by the fact that it has since disappeared. When I asked if we could go visit the area where she grew up, she explained that all of the homes had been either abandoned or taken over by Han Chinese peasants: "Every time I went back to visit, I would notice, 'Oh, that family moved out. And that house over there is now empty, and that house has a new, Han Chinese family.'"

Such has been the fate for the majority of Korean villages across northeast China. While about 398 Korean villages thrived as agricultural communities during the Mao era, by 2011 only about 150 remained (Paik and Ham 2011). Even in the Korean Autonomous Prefecture in Yanbian, Korean minorities, who once dominated as the majority, accounting for 63 percent of the population in 1949, had since fallen to minority status, representing 33 percent of the total population in 2007. According to an interview that Paik and Ham conducted with a Korean Chinese pastor:

> My hometown consisted of four Korean and eight Han Chinese brigades. Each brigade had four or five villages with thirty to sixty households. We had Korean elementary and middle schools and excelled in collective rice farming until the early 1990s. However, as migration to Korea and other cities began, our village lost 53 of 60 [ethnic Korean]

households, as did the three other neighboring Korean villages. . . .
When I visited in 2007, our brigade and villages had been reduced to
complete ruin. (Paik and Ham 2011)

With the disappearance of Korean villages throughout the rural
northeast, Korean schools have also started closing doors at alarming
rates (H. Kim 2010; S. J. Kim 2003). In Yanbian, Korean elementary
schools dropped from 419 to 177 between 1985 and 1995, and Korean
secondary schools similarly decreased from 118 to 49 during the same
time period. In Heilongjiang, only 51 Korean elementary schools remained in 1997, compared to 382 in 1990, and 15 secondary schools,
compared to 77 in 1990 (Huang 2002). According to *Asia Times*, between 1990 and 2000, 53 percent (or 4,200 Korean teachers) lost their
jobs due to school closures (*Asia Times*, August 16, 2007). Because the
Korean Chinese do not have the resources or proper institutional support from the Chinese government to set up Korean schools in the cities
they migrate to, Korean Chinese children in Beijing mostly attend Han
Chinese schools and have little opportunity to learn their ancestral
language. Korean Chinese leaders have thus lamented the loss of their
community. The schools had served as their institutional core, providing the Korean Chinese with the means to maintain fluency in their
ancestral language, form relationships with other Korean Chinese minorities, and preserve their cultural customs for nearly four generations
since the end of the war.

The exodus of Korean minorities from the agricultural communes
was, in many ways, part of a broader, nationwide trend of rural-to-
urban migration in China. When Mao fell from power, his successor,
Deng Xiaoping, instituted a series of market reforms in the late 1970s
and 1980s. Specifically, the *hukou* system, which had once bound people
to the land where they and their ancestors were born, was significantly
modified so that life outside of the countryside became possible for the
first time in many generations. By the close of the 1980s the government
abolished the ration-coupon system regulating food and other goods,
so that prices were now set by the market (Alexander and Chan 2004).
In addition, collective agricultural communes, like the rice farms where
Young-me had spent her childhood, became privatized, and jobs in general were no longer exclusively allocated by the state.

Reform of the *hukou* system led to a mass wave of urban migration throughout the country, as peasants sought better employment

opportunities in the cities.[1] But life in the city was by no means easy for rural migrants, who, because of their geographic volatility, became known as the "floating population" by China scholars and media outlets. Although the *hukou* legislation went through significant reform, it remained difficult for people who were born in the countryside to change their *hukou* status from rural to urban.[2] Without urban *hukous*, rural migrants experience difficulty gaining access to employment protection, healthcare, and public education, as well as a host of other welfare benefits (Alexander and Chan 2004).

Moreover, in the eyes of the Han Chinese middle class, rural migrants were perceived as second-class citizens and social pariahs. While the majority are Han Chinese, rural migrants continue to endure racialization by Chinese urbanites. The police patrolled the streets in search of these "undocumented" migrants, identifying them by their "shabby clothing, untidy hair, bad personal hygiene, and unrefined dialect" (Han 2010: 602). Dorothy Solinger (1999: 5) has even likened them to black people who underwent severe discrimination in South Africa during apartheid, and racial minorities in the United States. Others have drawn parallels between the structural position of Chinese rural migrants and that of undocumented foreign migrants in other countries. But in spite of these various disadvantages, by 1982, according to Chinese Census statistics, nearly 6.5 million Chinese rural migrants had left their hometowns to meet the growing demand for cheap labor in the cities.

Although Korean Chinese rural migrants can be broadly classified as members of this floating population, they are distinct in one important regard. Exodus from the countryside, for the Korean Chinese, was primarily prompted by job opportunities created by the South Koreans. In the years following Sino–South Korean normalization in 1992, Korean Chinese migrants by and large set their sights on Seoul and rural-to-urban migration within the PRC remained limited. Data on population shifts among Korean Chinese migrants provides evidence of these patterns (H. Kim 2010). The few Korean Chinese rural migrants who did live in Beijing in the 1980s and early 1990s typically earned a living selling *kimchee* in the markets or on the streets, because they did not have the capital to start larger-scale entrepreneurial businesses. Thus throughout the 1990s, Beijing's Koreatown consisted of only a small cluster of Korean restaurants, grocery stores, and K-POP stores located near the dormitories of Beijing Language and Culture University where many South Korean international students lived.

For Love or Money? Gendered Morality and the Decision to Leave

Korean Chinese migrants started to enter South Korea in the 1990s, as channels for travel between Seoul and Beijing finally opened after many decades of severed contact. In the early years of migration, many of the Korean Chinese women who left their families behind to cross the border filled a gap created by South Korean girls, who had similarly left their rural hometowns in mass numbers to work in urban factories in the 1970s. In South Korea, during the years of rapid economic development, young women between the ages of eighteen and twenty-two, who had only primary school education, were especially sought after as low-wage workers (Koo 2001; Cumings 1997). They were perceived as docile and unaware of their rights—and thus highly exploitable. In the 1970s, for instance, 30 percent of workers in the manufacturing sector, and 83 percent of all textile workers, were women (Cumings 1997).

Workers' diaries also demonstrate how many of these young girls sacrificed their health to work under dire conditions to support their sick parents or younger (often male) sibling's education. In Hagen Koo's (2001) account of their experiences, he writes how Korean factory girls persevered without complaint because of the deep devotion they felt toward their families. One woman endured the physical strains of her job by reminding herself of how much she loved her family: "When I get sleepy I think of my father who is sick in bed, and when my body gets too tired and my hands become numb, I crunch my hands thinking of my younger brothers and sisters" (61). Another wrote: "Because overnight work is so hard and painful, I hesitate to take it, but thinking of my mother and younger siblings in our rural hometown, I realize I must bear with it however hard it is for me" (61).

Unlike their female counterparts, rural bachelors in South Korea were bound by patrilineal duties to tend the farmland they had inherited. And the departure of these peasant girls led to a disproportionate number of South Korean farmers who were left behind without partners to marry, bear their children, and look after their aging parents. For these men, whose masculine identities were so tightly intertwined with marriage and starting families of their own, the prospect of staying single in their old age led to panic and depression. Even as early as the 1970s, the bride shortage in the countryside had become so severe that sixty farmer bachelors committed suicide as an act of protest. At the height of their agitation, slogans such as "Farmers are people too! Let's get married!" hung on banners in rural villages (Freeman 2011: 37).

The need to appease these South Korean farmer bachelors coincided with the opening up of the Sino–South Korean borders and an equally strong yearning among Korean Chinese minorities to enter South Korea after many years of severed contact. In light of the formidable obstacles in securing proper visas in the 1990s, "paper marriages" with South Korean farmer bachelors provided an alternative route— a legal loophole—that allowed Korean Chinese women to gain entry. According to data from the Korea National Statistical Office, by 2002, of 32,900 South Korean men who had married foreign women, nearly 43 percent (or 14,040) were married to Korean Chinese wives (Lee 2013).

During the early years of migration, the South Korean government welcomed Korean Chinese women, who they saw as "unspoiled by the urban prejudices" (unlike tainted South Korean women, who betrayed the good of the nation in pursuit of their self-interests), as the perfect means to appease the farmers' demands (Freeman 2011: 42). The Marriage Aid Program, as well as the Research Association for the Welfare of Korean Farm and Fishing Villages (RWFFV), two government programs that were established in response to the bride shortage, were praised in the media for "restoring the ethnic homogeneity" of the nation by matching Korean Chinese women with South Korean bachelors. According to Freeman's ethnography, government officials saw themselves as part of a greater, moral mission to reunite Korean Chinese minorities—involuntary exiles from colonization and the war—with their long lost homeland through holy matrimony (46).

Life in South Korea for these Korean Chinese women was far from the paradise they envisioned, however. Shortly after the implementation of the program, the South Korean media ran amok with stories of countless Korean Chinese wives who ran away from their husbands. And as the number of runaway brides increased, public perceptions of the Korean Chinese also soured. Media outlets started to depict them as "women obsessed with material wealth who are willing to transgress all moral principles and threaten the very basis of Korean identity" (Park 1996: 222). Blog posts of South Korean men who expressed interest in marrying Korean Chinese women were warned to check their bank accounts frequently, to report their wives as "runaways" to the police every time they left home for extended periods of time, to never give their wives any control over household finances, and to be cautious of possible extramarital affairs given alleged tendencies among Korean Chinese women to be promiscuous. In the eyes of the media, Korean Chinese women were increasingly viewed with suspicion—as conniving thieves who swindled naïve South Korean farmer bachelors, robbing them of their savings and dignity.

Freeman (2011) posits that many Korean Chinese wives were prompted to run away because they were unable to handle the many burdens placed on their shoulders. She reasons that it is no wonder so many would opt to leave given the physical demands of working in the fields every day, the pressure to dutifully submit to their in-laws, and the social isolation of the remote areas where their husbands lived. Interestingly, she also does not dismiss completely the notion that some in her case study might have intentionally arranged "faked marriages" to obtain visas. Freeman notes, however, that these women, though arraigned as criminals and swindlers by the South Korean media, were perceived as selfless mothers and wives within the Korean Chinese community:

> Men in Creek Road Village whose wives had migrated to South Korea by arranging a fake marriage were deemed worthy of pity by their fellow villagers. One stay-at-home husband . . . an affable, benevolent-looking man in his early forties, Kyuyong's father lived off the remittances his "fake ex-wife" sent regularly from South Korea. This income allowed the family of three—Kyuyong, her teenage brother, and her father—to relocate to an apartment in Mudanjiang City where the schooling was better for her brother. Kyuyong's father's primary occupation was the upkeep of their apartment, including cooking, laundry, routine housecleaning, and the supervision of his son's studies, which he appeared to handle efficiently and without complaint. (Freeman 2011: 216)

From the perspective of Korean Chinese minorities, migrant women who deceived unknowing South Korean farmers by entering fake marriages were still virtuous because the ends justified the means; the crime of these migrant women was committed as an act of love and sacrifice. They are perceived as willingly putting themselves in harm's way—even risking deportation and incarceration—not to lead a more luxurious lifestyle, but to sacrificially provide for their families.

These two contrasting interpretations of the same situation demonstrate how money and perceptions of morality are deeply embedded in relational contexts. As Viviana Zelizer (2011: 89) argues, "people employ money as a means of creating, transforming, and differentiating their social relations." Money, then, is not "a seamlessly fungible medium" that exists in the neutral sphere of the marketplace separate from the unpredictable volatility of human emotions, but rather the perceived value of money—and the ways in which we acquire and spend money— is inextricably shaped by the ways we view ourselves and others, form and maintain trust, and motivate and retroactively justify behavior in our everyday lives.

It is striking to note, for instance, the many parallels in how South Korean factory girls in the 1970s and Korean Chinese migrant women some twenty years later articulated their motivations for leaving their rural hometowns. We can see how, as migrant women, they are burdened by a particular "gendered morality" to behave as "sacrificial mothers and dutiful daughters" (Katigbak 2015: 527). They are expected to swallow the psychological and physical hardships of migration for the sake of their loved ones. And accordingly, "sacrificing one's self (including one's desires and aspirations) in the name of familial love" is essentialized as a distinctively feminine act. By earmarking the bulk of their earnings to be sent as remittances and gifts to family members, migrant women were able to demonstrate their selfless love and continuing devotion—they were able to engage in transnational caretaking. For the Korean Chinese women who ran away from their South Korean husbands, they were able to "'launder' their dubious earnings" by engaging in this "morally cleansing" practice (Zelizer 2011: 90).

As more and more Korean Chinese migrated—both as marriage migrants and low-wage labor—to South Korea,[3] questions of whether the Korean Chinese migrated for materialistic reasons or emotional ones became at the forefront of South Korean media coverage. For many of the Korean Chinese minorities I encountered in the field, there was much self-flagellation over their true motivations for leaving. Specifically, my interviewees grappled with a sense of shame and guilt in wondering whether leaving their families and communities behind had been worth the money they had been able to accumulate. As mentioned briefly in the beginning of this chapter, Young-me commented that many of her fellow villagers had decided to migrate to Seoul in the 1990s as the result of a simple cost-benefit analysis. Unlike Han Chinese rural migrants, Korean Chinese minorities felt a deep emotional bond for their *gohyang* and had much to lose by leaving:

> In the 1990s, no one in my village was interested in going to cities like Shenyang, or even Beijing. You can think of it this way: If I can make 500 RMB [75 USD] in my village, then I might be able to make about 700 or 800 RMB [100 or 120 USD] if I migrate and work in a nearby city. The amount that we could make would only slightly increase. If I went to a bigger city, like Shanghai or Beijing, maybe I could make 1,000 RMB [150 USD] . . . In the 1990s, if I could make 500 RMB [73 USD] in my village, I could make maybe 5,000 [730 USD] RMB in Seoul. That's ten times more than what I could make if I stayed. Then, that difference is so big, that it makes it worth leaving [laughs]. That's why. That's the difference. I think it's different for Han Chinese rural migrants. Even if they can only make slightly more money by migrating to a nearby city, it might be worth it to them, because maybe they hope to eventually settle and retire in that city rather than living in poverty in the countryside. But Korean Chinese are different. We like to live clustered together. We are emotionally attached to our *gohyang*. We would never consider giving up something as precious as that to make slightly more money. We just wouldn't leave. But the difference was so great in the case of South Korea.

The guilt in weighing the costs of migration is undoubtedly shaped by the emotionally heavy, priceless value of the losses they suffered. Could they have been so "immoral" as to have sacrificed their village communities (their *gohyang*) and their families for the sake of making more money? Was the money they earned, then, "dirty" money?

It was certainly true that most of the Korean Chinese young adults I encountered in the field had been raised in a household where one or both parents were absent. Most grew up with scant memories of their parents, who left to work under difficult conditions in South Korea and to fund their children's education. Among Young-me's forty-some high school classmates, for instance, more than half of their parents had divorced due to the strains caused by overseas separations. "You can think of this way," she explained. "If I find out that one of my [Korean Chinese] friends' parents are still together, I'm really surprised." According to a study conducted in Yanbian, 54 percent of Korean Chinese students lived with only one of their parents (*Heungyongang Shinmun*, May 19, 2004). Another survey of an elementary school in Yanji found that 71.4 percent of Korean Chinese were living in single-parent households (*Chosun Ilbo*, December 7, 2001).

While remittances and gifts were on the one hand interpreted as symbols of "sacred love," there was also an unspoken perception that these material gifts were, on the other hand, tainted by the fact that Young-me's generation had grown up alone. Some chastised the older generation of Korean Chinese minorities for thinking that money could atone for abandoning their children. Young-me recalled that when she was younger she watched her friends receive presents—beautiful stationery, mechanical pencils, and notebooks—from their parents who had left to work in Seoul. Particularly compared to the types of things that they were used to in China, everything from Seoul seemed so much nicer. Whenever someone got a new package from Seoul everyone gathered around, watching them unwrap their gifts in envy.

Morality and the Media

People are exposed to multiple different ways of interpreting the same types of phenomena in our everyday lives. As I argued in the preceding section, the same act of deception can be deemed as moral or immoral depending on how intent is framed. Along similar lines, for migrant women, remittances sent back to their loved ones can be interpreted as tainted by greed—if their act of migration is portrayed as prioritizing materialism over human relationships—or purified by sacrifice—if the hardships that the women experienced as migrants for the sake of their family are stressed.

Indeed, the Korean Chinese themselves are pulled in different directions in attempting to make sense of their decision to migrate. But for South Koreans, who are isolated from any meaningful contact with Korean Chinese minorities in their everyday lives, media narratives play a dominant role in shaping their perceptions of the group. By the late 1990s, negative stereotypes of the Korean Chinese had permeated mainstream South Korean media. One of the most notorious news events depicting the Korean Chinese as money-hungry criminals became known as the "Peskama Incident." On August 24, 1996, at ten in the morning, just four years after the Sino–South Korean normalization of ties, six Korean Chinese workers aboard the Peskama 15, a South Korean deep-sea fishing vessel in the South Pacific, brutally murdered eleven of the crew, including seven South Koreans. The tragedy occurred during a time when the number of undocumented Korean Chinese workers had reached significant heights in Seoul.

Graphic stories of how the Korean Chinese ganged up on their South Korean superiors to mercilessly murder them at sea circulated through the headlines of major South Korean media outlets, inciting waves of shock, fear, and horror across the nation. Even five years after the incident, *Chosun Monthly* (February 2001) published a lengthy editorial entitled:

> Six Korean Chinese engage in a gruesome killing of eleven South Korean, Korean Chinese and Indonesian crewmembers using knives, axes, and steel pipes after a tragic fishing trip for tuna in the South Pacific.

The article began with the following short excerpt summarizing the incident:

> Hatred, conflicts, and misunderstandings that festered between the South Korean captain and his Korean Chinese crew led to a bloody massacre among people of the same ethnicity. Six Korean Chinese workers seized control of the ship when they feared a life embroiled in debt after the captain threatened to force them to disembark, and [they] started to engage in a savage massacre in the middle of the night. They even threw a patient who was ill with appendicitis overboard, into the sea. The only South Korean they spared was shipmate Lee, who steered the hijacked ship for 22 days before he was able to lure and then lock the murderers inside the refrigerating unit. He cried for help and they [the Korean Chinese] were arrested by the Japanese Coast Guard. (*Chosun Monthly*, February 2001)

Although details of the physical and emotional abuse that the Korean Chinese workers suffered in the days and weeks leading up to the tragedy were detailed later in the editorial, mainstream South Korean journalists framed the homicide as primarily driven by economic motives. The Korean Chinese feared the insurmountable debts they would incur by leaving their livelihoods on the ship. They were presumably so frustrated by their economic losses that they were incited to stealthily engage in a bloody massacre, killing even their coethnic brothers. Such narratives played on latent stereotypes depicting Korean Chinese minorities as untrustworthy, savage, and money-hungry.

The editorial depicted Jeon, the alleged ringleader of the homicide who was sentenced to death in 1997, as a cunning man who lied about his age to get onboard the Peskama:

Jeon, Jae-Cheon, a Korean Chinese of Chinese nationality, was born in 1958 according to his [Korean] household registry. His actual year of birth is 1952. He claims to have adjusted the year of his birth to meet the requirements of working on the fishing vessel.

In its characterization of Jeon, this article continued to emphasize his deceptive tendencies. Though he claimed to feel contrite about his actions and begged forgiveness from the victims' families, the author stressed how Jeon shifted from taking full responsibility for organizing the killings to denying his role in the incident:

> The reason why Mr. Jeon was the only person to have been charged with the death penalty is simple. It is because Mr. Jeon was discovered to have acted as the ringleader, leading the others into action, during trial investigations. Even Mr. Jeon himself, when he was examined by the prosecution and during court hearings, admitted to having acted as the leader in the crime. However, Mr. Jeon argues, "I am not the leader of this incident." At the Busan detention center, Mr. Jeon claims, "I was swept up by the surrounding circumstances," and furthermore, "I felt that if I didn't act, I would have been killed by them."

Local Korean Chinese newspapers portrayed Jeon quite differently, however. Jeon was described as a hard-working and well-educated man who was respected by his peers. One article printed in the *Gilim Newspaper* (May 1, 2006) based in Yanbian, for instance, noted that Jeon had graduated from a local teaching college at the age of twenty-two. Prior to leaving for South Korea, he had spent thirteen years leading a quiet life as a teacher at a Korean junior high school in a small Korean village located in Huinan County, Jilin Province, close to the Sino–North Korean border.

Moreover, local Korean Chinese newspapers detailed the series of events leading up to the mass homicide, including an incident on June 27 when the South Korean captain lashed out at Lee, a Korean Chinese worker onboard, and attempted to strike him on the head with a steel pipe. When the captain saw Lee charging at him in retaliation, he grew incensed by Lee's defiance and asked another crewmember to bring him an ax. The Korean Chinese workers were able to protect themselves from the wrath of the captain by locking themselves inside a small room on the top floor of the ship. As they huddled inside the room in fear of their lives, they discussed committing collective suicide to escape their miserable lives onboard.

Newspapers and the media at large play an important role in creating dominant frames through which people make sense of their everyday surroundings. In this sense, they are, as Bourdieu (1993: 95) puts it, part of a "field of cultural production," which "give[s] rise to categories of perception which structure the perception and appreciation of its products." Not all sites of cultural production have the "power to convince" their audience, however. They must have the moral and cultural resources to make claims that appear legitimate. And in this case, the local Korean Chinese newspapers that provided an alternative narrative for the tragedy that happened on the Peskama 15 fell on deaf ears not only because they lacked direct access to a mainstream South Korean readership, but also because their interpretation of the incident was not in line with dominant perceptions of the Korean Chinese as violent and money-grubbing. Or to put it in Bourdieu's words:

> In accordance with the law that one only ever preaches to the converted, a critic can only "influence" his readers in so far as they extend him this power because they are structurally attuned to him in their view of the social world, their tastes and their whole habitus. (Bourdieu 1993: 96)

Since the 1990s, negative stereotypes of the Korean Chinese have become increasingly commonplace in South Korean news highlighting recent crimes committed by the Korean Chinese. Discursive analysis of newspaper articles on Korean Chinese minorities published between 1992 and 2004 by the *Chosun Ilbo*, a prominent South Korean newspaper with a daily circulation of 1.8 million readers, demonstrates that Korean Chinese minorities are portrayed as people with "hostility towards South Korea," due to the harsh discrimination that they encounter working 3-D jobs (Yang 2010). In addition, newspaper articles, by and large, portray Korean Chinese minorities as having come to their country of ancestral origin not due to an emotional attachment they felt toward South Korea, but as a means to make "dirty money" using unethical and illegal methods (Yang 2010).

Such frames overlook the emotional dimension motivating many Korean Chinese's decision to choose Seoul over other cities, however. Indeed, particularly for first- and second-generation Korean Chinese minorities—Young-me's grandparents' and parents' generation—South Korea was considered the ancestral homeland. Many of my interviewees spoke of the pride and yearning they felt when scenes of Seoul flashed onto their televised screens for the first time since the war, during broadcasts of the '88 Seoul Olympics. Reverend Hwang, a second-generation Korean Chinese man who ran an underground church in Beijing, found himself welling up with tears when he saw the Han River on TV:

> I remember my friend excitedly pointing to the TV, exclaiming, "Look! It's the Han River!" When I turned to see the image of the river on the television set, tears started flowing down my face. As a child, I had sung songs about the beauty of the Han River, so when I saw the river with my own eyes . . . that feeling was just inexplicable. When I realized how economically developed Seoul had become by the scenes that were shown on TV, I felt so moved . . . Up until then, China had favored the North [Korea], but the '88 Olympics marked a distinct turning point when our lives became decisively and inextricably linked to the South [Korea].

Analyses of South Korean movies and TV shows further embellish upon the negative stereotypes stressing the lengths to which Korean Chinese migrants will go to make money, however. The striking resonance of narratives criminalizing Korean Chinese minorities between fictive and nonfictive sources exacerbated fears that the Korean Chinese were intrinsically violent and immoral. Changzoo Song (2009), for instance, in examining the growth of discrimination against the Korean Chinese in South Korea, analyzes the film *Namnam Pungnyo* [*Southern Man and Northern Woman*] (1998), in which a Korean Chinese man from Yanbian is portrayed as a "street-smart, money grubbing, shameless" man who "cheats an innocent South Korean boy." Numerous recent South Korean movies that contain Korean Chinese characters, such as *Yellow Sea* (2010), *Missing* (2016), *Midnight Runners* (2017), and *Outlaws* (2017), similarly play upon South Korean perceptions of fear toward the Korean Chinese.

Midnight Runners, which was released in August of 2017, sparked controversy within the Korean Chinese community for portraying Daelim-dong—a neighborhood in Seoul where the Korean Chinese enclave is located—as a dangerous criminal den. The protagonists of the story are two handsome, naïve South Korean policemen-in-training who happen to discover a group of helpless young South Korean girls kidnapped by a Korean Chinese mafia. The girls are locked in a dark cement room where their ovum are forcibly extracted for trafficking in the black market. The movie follows the journey of the policemen as they embark upon a crusade to rescue these girls from the "evil" Korean Chinese. When the police officers ask the taxi driver to take them to Daelim-dong, the driver responds:

> This [Daelim-dong] is a place where only the Korean Chinese live and its full of undocumented Chinese as well. A lot of knife-fights take place there. Even the police do not go there often. I don't think it's a good idea for you to go there at night.

A recent study of right-wing internet communities demonstrates remarkable similarities in the fears of South Korean netizens and exaggerated stereotypes of Korean Chinese minorities portrayed in these films (Yi and Jung 2015). On one of the sites with the most registered users, Anti-Multicultural Policy, netizens referenced a notorious case whereby Oh Wonchoon, a Korean Chinese man, raped, murdered, and chopped a South Korean woman's body into 365 pieces on April 1, 2012. Many wondered whether the South Korean government was conspiring in covering up incidences of Korean Chinese "migrant gangs kidnapping thousands of [South] Koreans and stealing their organs" (Yi and Jung 2015: 998):

> Due to Oh Wonchoon, other *joseonjoks* [Korean Chinese] are blamed as well. When he came to Korea, he should have worked hard and returned home with money . . . why should he commit murder?
>
> This prejudice showed when I worked in a company, and I was very conscious of it . . . People said that *joseonjok* [Korean Chinese] eat human flesh and they are so brutal. (Yi and Jung 2015: 1004)

Ultimately, the authors of the study conclude that the Korean Chinese were deemed even more dangerous precisely because they shared genetic ancestry with the South Koreans—"they bore Korean names, spoke the Korean language, and traced their ancestry to specific family lineages and hometowns in the Korean peninsula" (Yi and Jung 2015: 1008). They further argue that "their ability to 'pass' physically and linguistically allowed dangerous, criminal elements, such as organ traders or abusive nannies, to infiltrate an unsuspecting, host population," whereas other more "foreign" migrants from Africa or Southeast Asia were physically and culturally distinct and thus "less likely to pose a threat" (1008).

Korean Chinese minorities were, on their part, acutely aware of the demeaning perceptions that South Koreans hold toward them as unflattering perceptions of the Korean Chinese have also permeated their social networks in Beijing. The consumption of South Korean popular culture, for one, is an integral part of the daily lives of the Korean Chinese in Beijing. According to my survey, 65.3 percent of Korean Chinese respondents reported that they watched at least three hours of South Korean television each week.

Moreover, not only did the Korean Chinese in Beijing regularly consume South Korean news, TV shows, and films, but they also vicariously experienced the suffering of their friends and kin who had traveled to South Korea to work. Complaints about discriminatory South Koreans were frequently shared in their social circles. Korean Chinese minorities in Beijing are by and large in regular contact with friends, parents, aunts, and uncles who work in Seoul: 88 percent of the Korean Chinese minorities who took part in my survey had immediate family members in South Korea, and an additional 73 percent of respondents over the age of twenty-five had traveled to South Korea before. The sheer mass of overlapping social networks between the Korean Chinese communities in Seoul and Beijing have led the Korean Chinese in Beijing to become regularly exposed to stories of exploitation and discrimination in South Korean society. Mi-hwa Yoon, a Korean Chinese woman in her mid-twenties, for example, spoke to her mother who worked in Seoul as a waitress at a restaurant in Seoul nearly daily:

> A lot of Korean Chinese mothers go to South Korea to work as manual laborers. Whether to work as housekeepers or as hospital janitors. There are a lot of people like that and it was hard for me to deal with this fact when I was young. [I thought to myself] why do Korean Chinese minorities have to live like this even though we are of the same ethnicity [as South Koreans]? My mother and my friends' parents would tell me how South Koreans would mistreat the Korean Chinese and how they would mistreat us.

I met Ms. Yoon at a Korean Chinese underground church in Beijing. She was always impeccably dressed according to the latest South Korean fashion trends. When we went shopping together in Koreatown, South Korean boutique owners were often surprised to learn that she was actually a Korean Chinese minority. They commented on how she looked and acted like a South Korean as if they were imparting a compliment. Unlike many Korean Chinese minorities who spoke Korean with a strong Korean Chinese accent, Ms. Yoon had learned to mask her speech patterns.

She told me that she had spent numerous hours painstakingly mimicking the ways that people talked in popular South Korean soap operas. She recorded herself and repeated certain phrases until she felt she had perfected the subtle nuances and intonations of contemporary South Korean speech. At times, I noticed that Ms. Yoon concealed her Korean Chinese identity. When South Korean store clerks assumed that we were both from South Korea, Ms. Yoon often played along, never stopping to correct them. Once, she commented that she worried that South Koreans would treat her differently if they could hear from her accent that she was Korean Chinese. She didn't want to feel inferior to South Koreans and found herself obsessed with shopping. She felt that if she had nice things, perhaps the South Korean store clerks wouldn't look down on her, because she knew that Korean Chinese minorities were often marked by the ways they spoke and dressed. She said during our interview:

> I wondered why I had to be poorer than they did. Why did I have to live amidst numerous Korean Chinese mothers who were looked down upon by South Koreans? I desperately wanted to prove to them [South Koreans] that there were Korean Chinese who were kind and smart, too.

Ironically, the only way for Ms. Yoon to escape the discrimination she experienced in her everyday life as a Korean Chinese minority was by acquiring access to material resources, but the very act of doing so caused the South Koreans to denigrate them as morally depraved for prioritizing money over other more "noble" pursuits.

From Heroes to Thieves

When Young-me yearns for her *gohyang*, she mourns for a place of belonging in both the physical and symbolic sense of the word. The loss of Young-me's *gohyang* points to the disappearance of Korean villages that had once covered the landscape of the rural northeast. She mourns because she can no longer return. But perhaps more significantly, Young-me's sense of loss is acutely tied to the dramatic shift in discursive portrayals of Korean Chinese minorities within the South Korean popular imagination. With the influx of transnational migration since the 1990s, friends and family who had once been revered as the descendants of independence fighters and patriots forced into exile during the Mao era were now perceived and treated as money-hungry con artists and untrustworthy thieves.

There used to be a time when their lives and sense of worth had not been so enmeshed in money, Young-me lamented. They were poor, but back then they didn't know what it meant to be poor. Her words make me think that perhaps, in yearning for her *gohyang*, she yearns to return not only to the physical space of her childhood but also to a *time* of innocence, when she and her loved ones had been content in dreaming about the possibility of an ideal place of complete acceptance that lay beyond the Manchurian border.

Endnotes

1. Mao China was essentially characterized by a "dual-class" system, whereby the elites were concentrated in the urban areas while the poor were stuck in the rural areas (Chan and Zhang 1999; Wang 2004). The state aimed to utilize agricultural villages for the sole purpose of providing an abundant supply of inexpensive food for urban workers. As a result, rural farmers were only permitted to sell produce at low prices fixed by the state and were prohibited from engaging in private trade or pursuing jobs in the industrial sector. Rural residents also did not have access to the high-quality public facilities under the redistributive economy that urbanites, who were largely employees of state enterprises, could access. Studies demonstrate average city incomes were triple those of the countryside (Davis 2000; Parish 1984; Walder 1986). The dramatic income gaps between urban and rural dwellers were thus a result of asymmetrical state policies that prioritized the development of the cities over the countryside.

2. In the past decade, *hukou* legislation has undergone major reform to improve the welfare of rural migrants (see Wang 2004). First, the PRC relaxed restrictions on internal migration of select groups, such as the elderly, children, and highly skilled workers, and streamlined local registration for temporary or permanent migration. Second, the government is progressively eliminating the rural-to-urban migration quota in small cities and towns. Third, individuals with at least a college degree who are hired by local employers can now easily obtain a local *hukou* in most Chinese cities, and it has become possible to purchase an urban *hukou* for a high price or by ownership of local property. Finally, from 2001 to 2002, some provinces began a national movement to "erase" the rural/urban distinctions in the *hukou* system, but this movement was discontinued by the national government within a year of its inception.

3. Labor standards for low-wage workers in South Korea started to improve as workers and students engaged in bloody protests in the 1980s. But as wages increased for the native population, South Korean business

owners started looking for ways to outsource menial work to foreigners. To help facilitate the recruitment of foreign workers, the South Korean government established the Industrial Technical Training Program (ITTP) in 1991, attracting thousands of Korean Chinese minorities who flooded the factories, construction sites, and restaurants in South Korea. Since the induction of the program, the Korean Chinese have represented the largest group of foreign workers (Seol and Skrentny 2009). Studies show that policymakers explicitly encouraged the recruitment of Korean Chinese workers, providing employers with a separate quota for the Korean Chinese and offering coethnic Koreans higher wages (Seol and Skrentny 2009). Though the Korean Chinese were favored over other foreigners as ethnic Koreans, their shared ancestral heritage did not shield them from many of the abuses commonly associated with labor migration. Soon after its inception, the ITTP program became notorious for perpetuating the surge of undocumented migrant workers. By defining workers as "trainees," employers were able to ignore labor laws guaranteeing the minimum level rights and conditions of their employees. Moreover, as trainees, Korean Chinese workers who were hired under this program were paid only a fraction of normal wages for the job. Thus in the early years of the program, more than 60 percent of trainees opted to leave the program, giving up their visa privileges, to find higher paying work elsewhere (Lim 2002: 17). The continuing demand for jobs in South Korea, combined with tightening restrictions for entry, "led to the proliferation of counterfeit documents, increased use of brokers and human smugglers, and a greater tendency to overstay visa limits" (Freeman 2011: 185).

CHAPTER 3

Everyday Life in Wangjing

Between Appearance and Reality

During my time in the field, I was frequently told by locals that Beijing's Koreatown had been relatively nonexistent until recently. Though nearly 150,000 Koreans lived in Wangjing in 2012, the district had been covered in farmland just a decade earlier. In the 1990s, according to Chinese census data, the number of Korean Chinese minorities in major cities outside of the three northeastern provinces—Liaoning, Jilin, and Heilongjiang—was still less than 1 percent. In Beijing for instance, there were only 3,734 Korean Chinese minorities in 1982—and the majority of this population were not rural migrants, but elite government bureaucrats hired to work in the city. While this number grew to 7,375 in 1990, the Korean population in Beijing was still too scattered and small to form a substantial enclave community.

The Korean enclave's sudden growth owes to the Chinese government's concerted efforts in drawing foreign investment into the district in the 1990s. Wangjing's location—between the city center and the Beijing international airport—was ideal for foreign investors. Bordered by four major highways (the Fifth Ring Road, the Fourth Ring Road, the Airport Expressway, and the Daguang Expressway), travel between the financial district and the outskirts of the city was swift and expedient. In the early 2000s, major South Korean conglomerates such as Samsung Electronics, Hyundai, Naver, LG, POSCO, and Pohang Iron Steel, as well as well-known Japanese enterprises such as Sony and Panasonic and Western companies such as Siemens, Motorola, Nortel Networks, Microsoft, Daimler, and Agilent Technologies, set up offices in the state-sponsored Wangjing Science and Technology Park. In 2005 the technology park, which spanned 70,000 square meters, hosted 228 foreign enterprises, accounting for a total registered capital of 256 million USD. South Korean financial enterprises such as Korea Trade-Investment Promotion Agency, Korea Trade Insurance Corporation, Woori Bank, and Korea EximBank also established regional headquarters in the district. Within a matter of years, Wangjing established a reputation as a wealthy, cosmopolitan district, with a booming transnational economy and high-rise buildings lining its perfectly straight streets.

Though the cost of rent was relatively expensive in Wangjing, many ethnic Koreans chose to live in the district not only because of its convenience, but also because of the sense of comfort they felt in the enclave. On the surface, Wangjing in many ways resembled an urban version of the tightly knit Korean villages that had once graced the Chinese countryside. Korean is regularly heard on the streets, and signs on the storefronts and billboards are written in both Korean and Mandarin. For ethnic Korean residents—whether South Korean or Korean Chinese—there was a sense of community and small-town familiarity in Wangjing.

This quaint image of Koreatown poses a stark contrast to Han Chinese perceptions of Wangjing. Friederike Fleischer's (2007) ethnographic study of Wangjing, for instance, finds that young, upwardly mobile Chinese residents were drawn to the anonymous lifestyles of the high-rise apartment complexes in the district. Many of the Han Chinese residents he interviewed actually welcomed the fact that they had little interaction with their neighbors: "I have no idea of others [neighbors]. I don't think people like to associate with each other. It's not like living in a *siheyuan* [traditional courtyard house]. People don't know each other very well here" (294). In fact, Han Chinese residents in Wangjing perceived the communal lifestyles of the Maoist era as oppressive:

> My old neighbors worked in the same company as my husband. We cooked and ate together. Your home was mine, mine was yours. . . . But now we are far from our neighbors, we are no longer just one big family. . . . We were happy to be with friends [in the old apartment], but whenever friends came to ask you to eat with them you couldn't refuse, even if you actually wanted to read something, for example.

You couldn't refuse even if you felt tired or wanted to study. Now I can do everything I want; I have plenty of time of my own. We knew each other when we lived in the old place, there were no strangers. We knew each of our neighbors. You were afraid to be seen if you were doing something wrong. But now, nobody knows us here, people can do whatever they want. (Fleischer 2007: 295)

For the Han Chinese, Wangjing represented a marker of wealth and prestige. The new housing complexes symbolized the lifestyle of the urban middle class, and the Han Chinese residents relished in exercising ownership and control over their own space, decorating and furnishing their apartment according to their liking. Such luxuries were all the more appreciated given the spartan living spaces—the "bare cement floors, wooden bed, wooden chairs and tables"—of the Mao era (Fleischer 2007: 296).

By contrast, for the ethnic Koreans who lived in Wangjing, the neighborhood retained a distinct feeling of intimacy somewhat uncharacteristic of city life. It was not uncommon, for instance, to spontaneously run into people from church or work or school. The frequency of these unplanned meetings was amplified by the fact that the possible routes that people took in going about their daily routines were limited. Korean residents of the enclave, including myself, frequented the same set of Korean grocery stores, hair salons, and restaurants (see Figures 3.1 and 3.2). Our schedules were also, in many ways, synchronized. I often ran into friends from church when I walked outside my apartment to catch a cab on Sunday mornings. On the weekdays, I crossed paths with other Koreans going to daily morning prayer at 5:00 a.m. In the evenings, after work, I found myself gravitating to the same coffee shops frequented by Koreans who lived in nearby apartment complexes. In addition, throughout the week, I bumped into people I knew at beloved hang-out spots within the enclave, like the Kentucky Fried Chicken near the entryway of the Wangjing New City Apartments, or the Paris Baguette where Young-me and I had our initial interview.

In spite of Wangjing's small-town charm, Korean Chinese migrants in the enclave were also aware that the enclave was different from the tightly-knit prewar villages where they grew up. This chapter analyzes how the changing spaces of interaction within the transnational enclave affected coethnic relations, and how these interactions in turn affected the ways Korean migrants constructed and negotiated their ethnic identities in everyday life. Along these lines, if the previous chapter focused

FIGURE **3.1** A Korean sign for beef in the middle of the Wangjing New City apartments. Photo courtesy of the author.

on "fields of cultural production," this chapter examines more closely the physical space of the enclave and how pre-existing perceptions influenced daily behaviors. Specifically, I will show how practice in everyday life represents processes by which concepts that were once abstract become experienced as reality. I argue that stereotypes become internalized as real when they seem supported by concrete encounters, and that the Korean migrants in the enclave are predisposed to selectively interpret their surroundings in ways that support their pre-existing views.

The Rise of Wangjing

I met Joon Lee, a South Korean man in his early sixties, while serving as a member of the praise band at a South Korean church in Beijing. Mr. Lee played the guitar, while I played the keyboard, and we met every Saturday morning for practice and Bible study.

Mr. Lee had lived in China since the early 1990s and had witnessed how the enclave had evolved over the years. He was one of the few

FIGURE **3.2** A small Korean shopping complex near the entrance of the Wangjing New City apartments.
Photo courtesy of the author.

South Koreans who had started traveling to China on a series of short business trips even before channels between the two countries had officially opened. At the time, Mr. Lee was a purchasing representative for a medium-sized South Korean export company that had business ties with a manufacturing firm based in Hong Kong. The Hong Kong firm had factories in Fujian that were struggling to produce goods that met their quality-control standards. After two years of trying to fix the problem remotely, the company sent Mr. Lee to resolve the issue in person. He explained that travel to China had been difficult and costly in the early 1990s:

> In the early years there were not many routes [from Seoul] to Beijing or China, for that matter. I had to take a charter plane from Tianjin. And from Tianjin, I had to transfer to Shanghai, and then from Shanghai, I traveled to Fujian . . . A train between Shanghai and Fujian at the time took twenty-two hours.

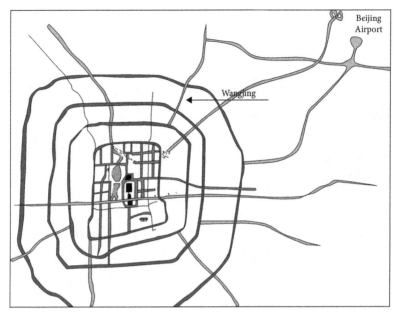

MAP 2 The City of Beijing

Two years later, the company decided to move operations to a factory in northeastern China instead, and in the winter of 1996 Mr. Lee was dispatched to set up a branch office in Beijing. Back-and-forth travel between Seoul and Beijing was complicated by various legal restrictions on foreign residents in China at the time. The state still tightly regulated housing under the socialist housing system and foreigners were only permitted to live in one of three districts in Beijing: East Chang-An, the Asian Games Village, and the Third Embassy Area (Wu and Webber 2004). Mr. Lee lived in government-approved housing in the district of Yayuncun, near the Asian Games Village, where rent was exorbitant. For a small apartment unit, foreign residents were expected to pay an estimated 5,000 USD a month, and subsequently only the wealthiest South Korean dignitaries and business executives could afford staying in these residences for extended periods of time.

Because of the high costs of travel and housing, in the early 1990s most of the South Koreans who traveled to Beijing were elite *chaebol* executives who worked with Chinese politicians and business leaders

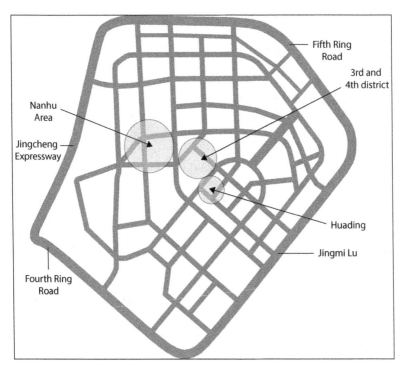

MAP 3 The District of Wangjing

to set up an institutional infrastructure that would help facilitate the flow of transnational resources between Beijing and Seoul. Most notably, in the days following Sino–South Korean normalization in 1992, Kim Sang Ha, the president of the Korean Chamber of Commerce and Industry, helped establish the Korea-China Economic Council, which included CEOs from all major *chaebol* firms and representatives from the Federation of Korean Industries, the Korean Foreign Trade Association, the Korea Federation of Small Business, and the Korea Employers Federation (Lee 1996). As a result of these efforts, by 1994 China had become South Korea's primary destination for foreign direct investment.

South Koreans of more diverse socioeconomic backgrounds started to migrate to Beijing after China liberalized its regulations on foreigners and foreign investments following its accession into the World Trade

Organization (WTO) in 2001. As laws on private landownership became more relaxed in the early 2000s, wealthy Chinese landlords started to rent out newly constructed apartment units in the district of Wangjing to South Korean migrants. Constructed in 1999, Wangjing New City was the first major apartment complex in the district and the third private real estate property in Beijing. Units sold for an average unit price of 3,500 RMB (514 USD) per square meter (Seo 2007).

Within the district of Wangjing, the New City apartment complex formed the hub of Koreatown, and Korean residents were by and large concentrated in the area surrounding the complex. Whereas Korean shops and businesses in Koreatowns in other parts of the world are typically clustered along specific streets, Wangjing's Korean enclave is more sprawling and organized around popular high-rise apartment complexes. In Wangjing, a vast array of Korean restaurants, hair salons, real estate agencies, and supermarkets were seamlessly integrated in residential neighborhoods. Stores selling imported goods from South Korea moved into the ground floors of the apartment complexes where the Korean migrants lived. Each year new apartment complexes were built in the areas surrounding New City, and continuous flows of South Korean migrants readily moved into new units as they became available. According to a map published by Baeyoung Real Estate, a popular Korean real estate agency in the enclave, there were forty-four different apartment complexes in Wanging in 2010. Of these complexes, the Korean population was largely concentrated within the eleven apartment parks surrounding New City.

The first group of Korean Chinese minorities who settled in Wangjing were recruited to work for a large factory located in Shunyi, thirty minutes north of Wangjing, opened by Hyundai as well as sixty-eight subsidiary companies under the conglomerate in 2002. As the new apartment units in New City were considered expensive by local standards, Hyundai purchased large sections of property in the neighboring area known as Nanhu [South Lake] to accommodate many of their Korean Chinese workers. Conditions were not comfortable, to say the least, as more than fifteen workers were crammed into small two-bedroom apartments.

A few days after I arrived in Beijing in 2009, Dr. Jung, a South Korean professor, gave me a tour of the enclave. As we walked around, he explained, "You can tell a lot about who a person is by asking where they live [in Wangjing]." According to Dr. Jung, most Korean Chinese migrants lived in Nanhu, a five-minute cab ride from New City. Insiders referred to Nanhu as the "Korean Chinese side" of the enclave. Interspersed within the apartment complexes in Nanhu were restaurants serving lamb skewers, chicken feet, and Yanbian cold noodles—delicacies of the ethnic villages in the rural northeast where the Korean Chinese had lived in isolation for many generations.

As we walked toward the New City apartments, Dr. Jung pointed out that the apartment complex by the large Walmart, known as the Huading complex, was where elite South Korean expats lived with their families. Near the entrance of Huading that day, I caught sight of a group of well-dressed South Korean women, chatting together in their high heels and perfectly coiffed hairdos. As we approached, a bus pulled up to the curb and dropped off children clad in tidy maroon plaid uniforms. The children handed their matching backpacks to their mothers as they spoke excitedly in Korean about what they did at school that day.

Just twenty meters away, I saw another South Korean woman hard at work in a small convenience store located near the front gate of the apartment complex. She wore a simple button-down shirt and jeans, and her hair was pulled back from her face. I noticed the white working gloves that covered her hands, as she busily tore open a pile of boxes near the street. I stood by for a while, waiting for the right moment to strike up a conversation, but she didn't notice me. The woman continued speaking to a Han Chinese man, presumably one of her vendors, in broken Mandarin, as she walked back and forth from the street to inside the store, carrying boxes of cereal and instant ramen noodles.

Typical monthly rent in Huading was around 20,000 RMB (or about 3,000 USD), more than six times the rent of New City's Third District. Expats were drawn to the comforts of Koreatown, because they expected to move back to Seoul within a few years and did not find it worthwhile to culturally or linguistically adjust to the foreign environment of Beijing. They were content to spend their inflated incomes on Korean language services and goods that bridged the gap between their small microcosm and the outside world. I would later learn that though the South Korean entrepreneurs sought to curry favor with the expats as lucrative customers, behind closed doors, the entrepreneurs resented the expats for their privileged lifestyles.

"Many of the South Korean entrepreneurs start off living in the Third District shortly after arriving in Beijing," Dr. Jung explained. "They come with their retirement money, rent out a separate office space for their business, and hire a troop of bilingual Korean Chinese minorities as hired help—a domestic worker to clean their house, a driver to take them around the enclave, and a secretary to help take care of their paperwork. A year or two later, the same person has moved to a smaller place in the Fourth District [*siqu*] and is running his business from his home, instead. A year after that, they lose their staff."

Dr. Jung led me to the dank basements of New City, where rooms were rented out for 50 RMB (almost 8 USD) a month. We passed a convenience store and signs for massage parlors, many of which served as brothels at night. The basements were close to the sewers, and the dimly lit cement hallways smelled of urine and spoiled food. Dr. Jung explained that while most South Korean entrepreneurs ultimately returned to Seoul after losing their savings, a few remained in the enclave and lived in the basements of New City among the Han Chinese migrant workers they had once hired as cheap labor. Having lost everything and with nowhere else to go, these South Korean grassroots migrants eked out a living, working odd jobs and buying just enough rice to eat for the week.

Chinese People Who Can Speak Korean

Although more than half a million Korean Chinese minorities lived and worked in South Korea when I was in Wangjing, for the most part, South Koreans arrived in Beijing with surprisingly limited understanding of who the Korean Chinese were. Dong-ho Lee, a thirty-year-old South Korean man who worked in a small South Korean enclave firm, described Korean Chinese minorities simply as "Chinese people who know how to speak Korean really well" [*hangukmal eul jal haneun joonguk saram*]. He went on to explain:

> I was really curious about what kind of people the Korean Chinese were [prior to coming to Beijing]. Why do they know how to speak Korean? How are these people able to carry on a conversation with me even though they are Chinese? How come they are in China? I was curious about things like that but honestly, because I didn't really have many opportunities to come across them [in Korea], I was more or less indifferent to them.

At first, I was taken aback by Dong-ho's comments during our interview because he had been so warm and kind to me as a newcomer in Beijing. When I had just moved to the enclave, Dong-ho had been the first to reach out to me and make me feel welcome. But by referring to the Korean Chinese as "Chinese people who can speak Korean," Dong-ho, perhaps unconsciously, re-enacted the widespread South Korean practice of demarcating the Korean Chinese as Chinese, rather than as coethnic, thereby disassociating himself from the ethnic minorities.

Cultural sociologist Eviatar Zerubavel's (1991) work on social classifications sheds light on why there was such a strong tendency toward differentiation and disassociation, despite the many similarities between the South Koreans and Korean Chinese in Beijing. "The most distinctive characteristic of the rigid mind," Zerubavel writes, "is its unyielding, obsessive commitment to the mutual exclusivity of mental entities" (34). He goes on to argue that ambiguous entities that do not fit neatly in mental categories of classification cause "a deep anxiety, even panic," because they pose "a serious threat to rigid classificatory structures, since, by their very existence, they call attention to the inadequacies of such structures" (35). Zerubavel points to the example of witches, who are widely feared because they "straddle the perceived boundary between civilization and wilderness," and the "transitional (and, therefore, ambiguous) yet unborn and just deceased, both of whom clearly defy the mental divide separating the living from the nonliving" (35). Furthermore, the anxiety and fear provoked by "ambiguous peoples," who threaten to "contaminate" social order, help account for the use of taboos and stigmas that often "mark" these individuals as deviant. Along these lines, if South Koreans who do not disrupt these taken-for-granted classificatory schemes are revered as "pure" because they reinforce pre-existing views of the world, then, culturally hybrid Korean Chinese, who are at once both Korean and Chinese, are "dangerous" as their very existence threatens to disrupt this order.

Empirically speaking, the enclave was inhabited by a rich spectrum of both South Koreans and Korean Chinese who occupied varying degrees of cultural hybridity. For instance, there were South Koreans who arrived in Beijing at a young age and spoke both Korean and Mandarin nearly fluently. Some matriculated into the Chinese education system as early as junior high school and went back to Seoul to attend college. Others attended university in Beijing and frequently traveled back and forth between Beijing and Seoul to visit friends and family. At the same time, while there were Korean Chinese minorities who spoke fluent Korean because they had grown up in the Yanbian Korean Autonomous Prefecture or because they had spent significant time living in Seoul, there were others who could not speak a word of Korean because they lived among mainstream Han Chinese prior to moving to Wangjing.

Notably, Korean Chinese minorities themselves recognized that the tendency among South Koreans to define someone as either Korean or Chinese, but never both, was unreflective of their social reality. Yet at the same time, they also seemed to understand that they lacked the cultural and moral resources to meaningfully challenge this social norm. I noticed this ambivalence during a particularly memorable interaction I had with Young-me, many years after I left the field.

The summer of 2017 in Seoul, Young-me texted me out of the blue, asking if I was interested in going out for a drink. I sensed that something was on her mind and invited her over to my apartment. When she arrived, we walked to a convenience store nearby to pick up some snacks and cans of cheap beer. Lying down on my living room floor, our heads propped up by some throw pillows from my sofa, we sipped our drinks and munched on potato chips. The conversation quickly turned to boys and marriage. On the brink of thirty, Young-me was anxious to get married. When she complained about the lack of eligible bachelors in her social circle, I asked her: "Aren't there any nice boys where you work?"

Young-me shifted her body to face the ceiling. I stared up and focused on the cream-colored ceiling, too. The low hum of the refrigerator filled the room as I waited for her to reply to what had only been intended as a casual question. With some hesitation, Young-me told me that it was hard for her to trust and become vulnerable to South Koreans; she didn't think that she could ever marry a South Korean man. Her sister, Mee-ryung, bitterly regretted her decision to marry her South Korean husband, and had unleashed her pent-up frustration in daily tirades to Young-me. After several years of fighting Mee-ryung filed for a divorce, only to re-marry her ex a year later out of pity for her young son, who would otherwise grow up without a father.

"My sister's lived in Korea for a really long time," Young-me told me. "She even naturalized—she's a South Korean national now. Honestly, I don't know if she's ever thought of herself as 'Chinese.' She grew up in a Korean village and went to a *minjok hakkyo* [a Korean ethnic school] her whole life, so she didn't ever have any [Han] Chinese friends. She can't even speak Chinese very well. And yet, she tells me that when she and her husband fight, he tells her that she can't possibly understand him because she is Chinese [*jungguk saram*]."

Young-me and I drank until midnight that day. But days and weeks after she left, her words continued to circle the back of my mind. Particularly during moments of silence throughout my day, I found myself replaying the comments that Young-me had made about her sister. It was clear from our interactions that day that Young-me was aware that no matter what steps she took to try to erase the differences separating her from other South Koreans—whether by marrying a South Korean man, or by changing the way she spoke, or even by giving up her Chinese nationality to take on a South Korean one—Korean Chinese minorities like herself would perpetually be marked as outsiders—as Chinese— even to those they considered family.

Migration scholars have long demonstrated how ethnic minorities face formidable barriers in feeling a sense of belonging and acceptance in the host society. In this sense, Young-me's skepticism toward successfully assimilating into South Korean society is unsurprising. There are two aspects of Young-me's situation that are quite remarkable, however. First, Young-me, though born and raised overseas, is an ethnic Korean who lived for most of her life in China within a secluded Korean enclave. It is thus noteworthy that she would feel apprehensive about her ability to fully integrate into South Korean society regardless of her ethnic, cultural, and socioeconomic background. If Young-me decides to raise her child in South Korea, will her stigma as a Korean Chinese minority continue to shape the life chances of her ethnically Korean second-generation children who have never before lived for a prolonged period of time outside the country of their ancestry?

Second, as we saw in the previous chapter, the ethnic enclave has historically provided a place of refuge for marginalized minorities. But this has largely ceased to be the case for Korean urban enclaves in the PRC. As a transnational enclave, Wangjing is tied to the social, economic, and political vicissitudes of Seoul. In the previous chapter, I demonstrated at length how media depictions of the Korean Chinese in South Korea continued to shape perceptions of the Korean Chinese in Beijing, and that because of these changing dynamics, Korean Chinese minorities have increasingly found themselves without a safe haven even in China. Their childhood villages have all but disappeared since the channels to transnational capital and labor opened between South Korea and China. Now the Korean communities that do exist are socially, economically, and politically dominated by first-generation South Korean migrants. Even the romantic image of their *joguk* [ancestral homeland] held so dearly by their ancestors when travel back to the Korean peninsula had been impossible during the Cold War, has become tarnished by the co-ethnic discrimination induced by increased contact and exposure. I explored the loss of this physical and psychological space of belonging for the Korean Chinese at length in chapter 2. Zerubavel likens this need for connection to one's place of "origin" as fundamental to the human existence. He states:

> Like having no navel, the embodiment of our genealogical embedded-ness, lacking a sense of ancestry is tantamount to being "cast out upon [a] sea of kinless oblivion." That explains why striking a person's name from his or her family's genealogical records used to be one of the most dreaded punishments in China. It also explains the identity crisis often prompted by the realization that one was actually adopted and the quest of many adoptees to find their "real" parents. Being cut off from their ancestral past, they often experience genealogical "bewilderment" and deprivation leading to the deep sense of existential vacuum. (2012: 7)

This struggle over identity and place of belonging between the South Koreans and Korean Chinese was a conflict that played out daily in the grounds of Wangjing. It was an emotional and psychological struggle that the South Koreans invested much of their energy into, and often "won," as recent arrivals. Economically precarious South Korean grassroots migrants made an intentional effort to distinguish them-selves from the Korean Chinese as members of a separate, more desir-able category of Korean because they had much at stake. If class and ethno-cultural background were easily interchangeable, then by losing their socioeconomic standing, South Korean migrants had a tacit fear that they would also lose access to a moral stature available to only "real" Koreans. I often noticed an unspoken anxiety among South Koreans living in China, who worried about becoming indistinguishable from the Korean Chinese if they lost their businesses and subsequently fell into poverty. There was a fear that by becoming impoverished ethnic Koreans living in China, they would by proxy become associated with all of the demeaning stereotypes (as inherently immoral, greedy, and traitorous) attributed to the Korean Chinese within the South Korean community. Subsequently, I found that even though the apartments in the Nanhu complex were much more affordable than the units in New City, I rarely came across a person speaking with a South Korean accent in Nanhu. More often, rather than move five minutes away to the Nanhu district, downwardly mobile South Koreans opted to either return to Seoul to live with extended family, or move to more isolated areas in remote China where they could lead lives of virtual anonymity.

For the South Koreans in Beijing, any association with China was undesirable: China was perceived as a Third World country whose people were culturally unsophisticated, poor, and rude. Interestingly, however, when I asked why they decided to migrate to Beijing, many praised China's booming economy. In the words of Hee-won Choi, a young South Korean woman in her early thirties, for instance, although Ms. Choi explained that she came to work in Beijing because she recognized its potential as a future economic powerhouse, she still retained an image of China as an undeveloped country:

> All of the major South Korean firms are offering better wages and benefits to people who can speak Chinese because they are really eager to tap into the Chinese consumer markets . . . Before I came, I saw China as an undeveloped country . . . like a country that is still uncivilized, you know? To be honest, I had a really negative image of China before I came.

When I asked Ms. Choi to elaborate on her impression of the PRC, she noted the slew of unflattering images of China she came across on the internet and in the mainstream media:

> For instance, you know how we use a lot of products . . . and foods from China, right? So if something was made in China, we expect it to break really fast. Or if we buy food imported from China . . . from the media, we are exposed to a lot of weird stuff . . . to give you an example, like chicken feet . . . they were showing these Chinese women eating chicken feet . . . but how can I explain it? They were ripping off the skin of the chicken and the way they were filmed, they looked really uncivilized. It was kind of disgusting. There were a lot of pictures of women on the internet. Or, there was this news story about a sandwich that was imported from China, and from the outside, it looked like there were eggs and ham like any other ordinary sandwich, but once you opened up the sandwich, there was nothing inside. There were only trimmings of egg and ham . . . So most of the pictures and news stories on China I came across on the internet and the TV were along these lines. It's really common for South Koreans to associate their impressions of the Chinese with something that is uncivilized, low quality, undeveloped, inferior, and boisterous.

To the South Korean migrants in Beijing, comparing the economic status of their country of origin to that of China was a way of bolstering their pride and identity as South Korean nationals. And by the same token, by categorizing the Korean Chinese as primarily Chinese, they implicitly saw Korean Chinese minorities as uncivilized, boisterous, and inferior by association, and thus unlike themselves.

Here, the socio-psychological concept of "schemata" is useful. Cognitive theorists argue that because people are constantly inundated with overwhelming quantities of information in everyday life, to process everything as independent and unique would be highly inefficient and lead to cognitive overload. Accordingly, cultural sociologist Paul DiMaggio (1997) points out that this has led to the human tendency to make connections where they do not exist—to forcibly impose stereotypes on even people who do not fit these perceptions neatly—and to habitually ignore encounters that seem to contradict preconceived expectations.

Thus, even when South Koreans encountered Korean Chinese minorities who were highly educated and sophisticated, rather than revise their imprecise perceptions of Korean Chinese minorities, there was a stronger inclination towards rationalizing these individuals as exceptional. I observed these tendencies throughout my time conducting field research. When I walked into a tea store I frequented to have tea with the Korean Chinese store manager, for instance, South Korean customers would emphatically express how the manager was so "gentle, soft-spoken, polite, and cultured," and so unlike the other Korean Chinese minorities they knew. Similarly, when I visited South Korean store clerks to hand out surveys with Young-me, some would remark how "neat and fashionable" she looked when they learned Young-me was Korean Chinese. Even among South Korean friends who were well-connected to the Korean Chinese community, I encountered similar tendencies on a regular basis. I noticed how a well-meaning South Korean minister, when introducing me to a young Korean Chinese couple he had a close relationship with, repeatedly mentioned throughout our conversation how the couple was "highly educated and intellectual" and thus, "trustworthy."

The Limits of Good Intentions

While psychologists have found that individuals can "override programmed modes of thought to think critically and reflexively" when sufficiently motivated, these instances are rare as deliberate thinking is highly inefficient (DiMaggio 1997: 271). Cursory interactions with Korean Chinese in everyday life were often too superficial to compel South Koreans to change their views. According to the theory of schemata, in order for South Koreans to feel motivated enough to question the assumptions they held towards the Korean Chinese, they needed a significant number of experiences that were irrefutably contradictory to their commonsensical perceptions. In other words, South Koreans would have to have enough close relationships with Korean Chinese minorities to start to see that their friends were not exceptional, but rather that their preconceived image of the Korean Chinese in general was in need of modification. The spatial divisions within the enclave, separating South Koreans from the Korean Chinese, however, made it difficult for these types of coethnic friendships to form.

By and large, my survey results confirmed suspicions that the South Koreans and Korean Chinese had a hard time fostering intimate relationships in their everyday lives. Only 20 percent of South Koreans I surveyed reported that it was easy to establish close friendships with Korean Chinese minorities. Nearly half (49.6 percent) of South Koreans did not have any close Korean Chinese, and only about one in five knew of at least one Korean Chinese person whom they could call during a time of need. In addition, only a small minority of South Koreans responded that they had Korean Chinese friends. These trends were similar among the Korean Chinese I surveyed. Eighty-seven percent of Korean Chinese surveyed responded that they felt uncomfortable when interacting with South Koreans, and nearly 70 percent did not have any South Korean friends. The vast majority of any meaningful interaction between the two groups took place within the emotionally charged context of the workplace, which only exacerbated existing resentment.

My survey findings demonstrated that while the South Koreans and Korean Chinese both recognized that they shared a common ancestral and cultural heritage, both groups reported considerable ambivalence over whether they belonged to the same in-group. For instance, although more than half (54.9 percent) of South Korean respondents acknowledged that they had more in common with the Korean Chinese than they did with the Han Chinese, only a small minority of South Koreans reported that they felt that they were members of a common ethnonation [*uri nara saram*].When I presented the same statement to the Korean Chinese, a striking 78.4 percent also responded that they had more in common—culturally and linguistically—with the South

Koreans, but very few responded that they felt more close and intimate to the South Koreans compared to the Han Chinese.

For many Korean Chinese minorities in the enclave, because they were aware that South Koreans tended to look down on them, there was a tendency to become tense and anxious when interacting with South Koreans. For Mee-sun Kim, a Korean Chinese woman I became acquainted with during my time in the field, the discriminatory treatment that she had endured while working in Seoul triggered feelings of anxiety when interacting with me, even in spite of our relatively intimate friendship. I noticed that she and her Korean Chinese friends had a difficult time disassociating me from my South Korean accent and mannerisms. They constantly questioned whether I was trying to get to know them because I genuinely liked and cared for them, instead of out of pity or an ethical duty as a sociologist.

On one particular occasion, I accompanied Mee-sun and another Korean Chinese woman to a hole-in-the-wall bar known for their delicious chicken wings and cheap beer. The restaurant was located only five minutes away from my apartment in the enclave. Mee-sun had been going through a hard time at home and that night she called me on my cell phone, saying that she did not want to drink alone. When we walked into the bar, she and her friend suddenly became aware of how decrepit the interior of the restaurant might look to a South Korean such as myself. She asked me several times if I felt comfortable. When I asked where the bathroom was, they expressed concern that I would be offended by its dirty, putrid conditions and asked if I wanted to go to a nicer restaurant.

After we had consumed five bottles of beer and were ready to leave, I attempted, unsuccessfully, to pay the bill. I wanted to pay for our drinks because I wanted to encourage a friend who was going through a difficult time. To my surprise, however, Mee-sun and her friend responded, "We're not poor. We can afford to eat out like this. You don't have to worry about it. Do you think we're poor?"

Money—and presumed disparities in class—was perpetually an issue in my attempts to forge friendships with the Korean Chinese minorities in the enclave. Spending large amounts of money in front of Korean Chinese friends was perceived as offensive and arrogant because they interpreted acts of generosity as demonstrations of wealth, as South Koreans often looked down on Korean Chinese minorities as people in need of material assistance. Along similar lines, showing discomfort toward the run-down conditions of local restaurants, stores, and bathrooms in Beijing was interpreted as viewing China—and by association the Korean Chinese—as inferior and unacceptably Third World.

This sensitivity to South Korean perceptions, however, made it difficult for the few South Koreans who genuinely wished to cultivate friendships with Korean Chinese minorities to overcome the barriers to do so. Facial expressions, choice in venues for meeting, comments about likes and dislikes, and consumption patterns were all potential landmines that would threaten to reify pre-existing stereotypes.

One negative comment or reaction made about China, for instance, could be interpreted as a negative comment about the Korean Chinese more generally. Or as Nam-hee Kang, a Korean Chinese college student remarked:

> I know it's not fair of me, but I react more sensitively to things that South Koreans say to me. I think it's because I have this bias that they look down on us Korean Chinese. Once, I was leading a group of South Korean tourists around major sites in Beijing, and one of the men in my group said something like, "Wow! I never knew that there were so many nice European cars in Beijing, too." I was really offended by what he said, because he seemed to imply that China was backwards and undeveloped. But then later on, he said that he had visited Beijing ten years ago, and back then, there were a lot of bicycles and not as many cars. I thought about it, and what he said made sense. I know that I was being a little sensitive with him because he was South Korean, but I can't help it. When a South Korean starts to make a comment about China, it kind of makes me put my guard up instinctively. That's just the way things are for us Korean Chinese.

Nam-hee admitted that her initial interpretations of the South Korean man's observation had been negative. Upon hearing his comment, she at first associated his impression of China with his presumably derogatory views toward Chinese people, and by default Korean Chinese minorities as well. But later on, after speaking to him at more length, she realized that he had made a simple comment on the decline in the number of bicycles in the streets of Beijing in the past decade.

Assumptions that the South Koreans looked down on the Korean Chinese as Chinese nationals and as distrustful outsiders, at times, made it difficult for well-meaning South Koreans to approach Korean Chinese minorities in the first place. Aware that Korean Chinese minorities were sensitive to comments that South Koreans made about China, many South Koreans feared that they would offend their counterparts. Dong-ho explained:

> When I see a Korean Chinese person, sometimes, I want to go over and start a conversation with him. But then, I think to myself, what if he thinks that I am suspicious or strange for wanting to talk to him for no apparent reason. What if he realizes that I am South Korean and feels intimidated by me . . . I want to go over and talk to him and become friends with him not because I want to help with something, but because he knows how to speak Korean. But I often feel silly for having these feelings. I feel like I would cause more problems if I did.

Dong-ho assumed that it was strange and out of the ordinary for a South Korean man to want to talk to a Korean Chinese minority without an ulterior motive. In Beijing, the bulk of relationships between South Koreans and Korean Chinese were born out of necessity. South Koreans sought the help of Korean Chinese migrants as translators and cultural intermediaries. Korean Chinese minorities, in turn, primarily interacted with South Koreans in the workplace and in shops. They often spoke to South Koreans, in spite of their distrust, because they were often hired to do so as drivers, workers, or shopkeepers. The roles that each group played established a set of predetermined expectations that structured interactions between South Koreans and Korean Chinese minorities in the enclave. It was thus considered so out of the ordinary for a South Korean man to approach a Korean Chinese minority outside of these rigid scripts—out of pure curiosity and without an agenda—that Dong-ho's behavior aroused suspicion rather than feelings of good will. These suspicions, in turn, precluded the type of small talk that could act as a social lubricant easing tensions and organically leading to friendship.

Questioning Perceptions of Reality

When I entered the field, I wondered how misperceptions between South Koreans and Korean Chinese minorities persisted in the enclave even in the face of such proximity in everyday life. On the one hand, I could understand how South Koreans in Seoul might persist in discriminating against the Korean Chinese; after all, in South Korea there were conceivably fewer opportunities to run into one another. But on the other hand, I thought that this rationale would no longer hold in the enclave where work and residential lives converged. Through the course of my fieldwork, however, I learned that people could live and work in proximity without feeling sufficiently motivated to form friendships. Thus, rather than assume that enclaves, by their very nature, facilitate the cultivation of a collective consciousness, I argue that it is more important to analyze whether the particular spatial configurations within the enclave help people get to know one another on a more personal level, cutting across class and cultural differences.

Along these lines, in analyzing why South Korean and Korean Chinese migrants experienced such a hard time becoming friends even in spite of their coexistence within the Korean bubble, I point to two reasons in this chapter. First, it is noteworthy that the vast majority of interactions between South Korean and Korean Chinese minorities in the enclave occur within the workplace where clear asymmetries of power exacerbate pre-existing tensions. In the workplace, both groups found ample evidence supporting their negative views that Korean Chinese workers were untrustworthy and that South Korean migrants were condescending and exclusive. Because spaces of leisure and residential life generally did not overlap, they in fact had few opportunities to spontaneously interact in more neutral environments.

Second, even in the rare instances when South Korean migrants like Dong-ho approached Korean Chinese minorities in their vicinity simply to get to know them, it was difficult for Korean Chinese minorities to not view these otherwise well-intentioned gestures with suspicion. People did not approach each interaction with a blank slate, but pre-existing patterns structured expectations for behavior, limiting who they opened themselves up to and trusted. Though there certainly were many cases where South Koreans and Korean Chinese minorities had been able to foster friendships, I argue that the barriers and suspicions—the potential land mines for misunderstanding—that both parties had to overcome to do so were extraordinarily high.

CHAPTER 4
....

The Feminization of Korean
Chinese Workers in the *Chaebol*

From my first visit to DN Group, a *chaebol* subsidiary in Beijing, I could sense tension pervading the office floors. I wanted to conduct interviews at various South Korean firms in the financial district to analyze patterns of upward mobility among highly educated Korean Chinese minorities. So, I asked Charles, a friend of a friend who worked in Human Relations (HR) at DN Group, to forward a carefully crafted email introducing myself and my research project to his Korean Chinese colleagues. To establish rapport, I stressed how my research was motivated by my own experiences with alienation as a second-generation Korean American growing up in a white American suburb. I also assured potential interviewees that I would guarantee confidentiality and refrain from probing into topics they felt were too sensitive.

The day I arrived to conduct interviews, Charles, upon greeting me at the lobby, sat me down with a nervous look on his face. He explained in a hushed voice that my email had "hit a sensitive nerve" among his Korean Chinese colleagues for reasons that he did not completely understand himself. Not only did no one express interest in my project, but some also explicitly stated their lack of desire to meet me. I was taken aback by the response. I had used similar letters to solicit interviews for other research projects before and had never encountered such a negative reaction.

Charles was a gregarious man from Oregon who, after having lived in Beijing for nearly a decade, spoke fluent Mandarin. But as a white American who worked for a South Korean conglomerate in China, he was unequivocally an outsider at the firm. Moreover, though Charles had worked as a HR manager recruiting and training several hundreds of Korean Chinese workers each year, I became skeptical about the depth of his relationships with his Korean Chinese colleagues when he vaguely (and rather imprecisely) referred to the ethnic minorities as the "Koreans who left the Korean peninsula hundreds of years ago."

Did the Korean Chinese workers react with such disinterest because Charles was not within their trusted inner circle, I wondered. While an introduction from an insider might have influenced my reception, in retrospect, I presume that the Korean Chinese minorities at DN Group were reluctant to meet me because it seemed, even from my brief email, as if I possessed the trappings of a privileged South Korean, the same category of Korean they associated with the haughty South Korean managers at their firm. Charles commented on my way out that day that the CEO of DN Group's China headquarters had over the years become increasingly concerned about the growing discontent among their Korean Chinese workers, and was desperate to quell the resentment simmering beneath the surface. I decided to return to DN Group to better understand the reasons behind their discontent; I wanted to analyze the interplay between power and ethnic politics within a multinational corporation, so central to the economic vitality of the enclave.

From my encounters that day, I realized that I would have to mainly rely on participant observation to collect data and invest time in delicately building relationships of trust with the workers. A few weeks after my visit, I returned to DN Group to work as an intern. I told Charles that I would be happy to work for free if I could use my observations as data, and promised to maintain the anonymity of the workers and the company. Charles helped me secure a position to work as part of a special task force that sought to improve cross-cultural communication among the employees. With my Han Chinese, Korean Chinese, and South Korean coworkers, I helped analyze survey data collected by HR on various problems among workers of different ethnic and cultural backgrounds. In addition to my work in the task force, I also attended early morning Chinese language classes with upper-level South Korean managers from different divisions within the company.

South Korean conglomerates served as an important site for be-longing and identity formation for middle class South Korean men during South Korea's "Miracle on the Han River." During the postwar years, the typical South Korean adolescent strived to gain admission to a prestigious university in Seoul, in order to be recruited upon gradu-ation to work for a *chaebol*. For employees who endured the grueling hours and authoritarian management styles of the postwar *chaebol*, the company took responsibility for the personal and financial welfare of their employees for life, supplementing their workers' salaries with edu-cation stipends when they had children, and granting them respectable pensions when it came time to retire. Employees were in turn expected to exhibit loyalty to the company and behave "in accordance with the company 'way'" (Jaeger 1983: 93).

In South Korea, the *chaebol* thus represented more than just a place of work. One's work life bled into one's private life. Personal sacrifices were made for the good of the company, and it was customary for work-ers to converse with their colleagues about problems they had with their wives, as well as potential business deals, late into the evening at a nearby bar, many hours after the workday technically ended. The company was perceived as a community, and cohesion within this community was prized above individual competence. Managers in Korean firms, thus, focused more on "character, aptitude and interpersonal skills than spe-cific job aptitude" in recruiting and evaluating their employees (Park Matthews 2005: 161). When asked about how potential hires were eval-uated, for instance, one *chaebol* manager explained:

> A rounded personality is still advantageous in a Korean employment setting. Bright people with creativity might be good for the success of the company but would not necessarily be well appreciated in the firm if difficult for the company and superiors to handle. They tend to break the unspoken rules and customs of company tradition or cul-ture. For this reason, they might be given challenging or important tasks to carry out, but would not necessarily receive the best evalua-tion by their seniors. (Park Matthews 2005: 161)

Whereas companies in the West have been known to selectively re-cruit and promote workers on talent and performance, in South Korean conglomerates, employees were typically recruited in large numbers directly from selective universities and were promoted according to se-niority rather than performance.

Although this so-called lifetime employment system was praised for rescuing the South Korean economy from the ashes of the Korean War during the 1980s, when the Asian financial crisis shook the economy in 1997 this organizational model was criticized as dysfunctional and incompatible with global (i.e., Western) standards (Haggard, Lim, and Kim 2003). Soaring debt-to-equity ratios among the major *chaebol* reached over 519 percent on the eve of the crisis and led to a series of corporate bankruptcies, the closing of 10 banks and 284 financial institutions, and per capita GNP plummeting from over 10,000 USD to 6,000 USD within a year after the fallout (Kim 2004: 222). And in late November of 1997, the International Monetary Fund (IMF) demanded structural reform of the *chaebol* in exchange for a bailout fund of 57 billion USD to help save South Korea's faltering economy.

In the years following the recession, South Korean conglomerates, facing declining consumer markets at home, entered Chinese markets at unprecedented rates. By 2002 Samsung owned several businesses in China, amounting to an aggregate value of 2.3 billion USD, including an investment company, twenty-four production-oriented legal-person enterprises, an R&D center, and a sales service company. These enterprises collectively employed a total of 38,000 workers and boasted a sales volume of 6 billion USD. According to the Beijing Daily News, Hyundai Motors in Beijing similarly demonstrated impressive rates of operational expansion. In 2003, the company accounted for 12 percent of Beijing's overall industrial output and planned on investing about 740 million USD in 2007. Life's Good, the South Korean conglomerate better known as LG, similarly contributed a sales volume of 7 billion USD in China and reports indicate that its subsidiaries employed nearly 11,000 local Chinese employees in 2003 (Zhan 2004).

The challenges of adapting to an increasingly diverse workforce within a global marketplace predictably caused significant workplace conflict at DN Group. On the surface, the company seemed to invest considerable resources in easing tensions among their workers because they saw the lack of mutual trust and cooperation as a major detriment to efficient operations. There were rumors that the firm was struggling to penetrate Chinese consumer markets. Sales were stagnant and the overall atmosphere of the company was pessimistic.

A few weeks into my internship the headquarters recruited Ms. Chang, a sturdy, middle-aged Han Chinese woman, as one of the departmental leaders on our floor in a feeble attempt to "glocalize."

From her first day, her reputation as a tough, no-nonsense manager rapidly spread across the different divisions. Only two weeks after she was hired, Ms. Chang laid off Joel, a white American who had worked in the cubicle next to mine. He had been known for taking frequent coffee breaks and for leaving precisely at six in the evening when the workday technically ended. Though Joel complained that he didn't feel particularly stimulated by the work at DN Group, he had mentioned to me on several prior occasions that he stayed because of the job security; he noticed that few people were ever fired. By swiftly laying off Joel so shortly after starting her position, Ms. Chang presumably sought to send a clear message to the other workers on her floor that under her regime, lackadaisical performance would no longer be tolerated. A few weeks later, Charles was also unceremoniously let go.

On the surface, it may seem as if Ms. Chang's draconian approach toward laziness demonstrated evidence of a changing workplace culture in the *chaebol* that prized competence over cohesion. There was a tacit awareness that Ms. Chang's power was limited, however, because she was Han Chinese. That she chose to fire Joel and Charles, the two Americans, while intimidating at first, ultimately belied her attempts to demonstrate power. Employees knew that Americans were on the fringes of the company—they were inconsequential. Had she fired two South Korean workers, by contrast, Ms. Chang's actions may have been more convincing, as South Koreans were generally untouchable, regardless of rank.

Instead, despite a few external attempts at organizational reform, management at DN Group continued to rely on old tactics—socialization to group norms and paternalism—in their attempts to overcome the new problems that they faced. In one of the few existing ethnographic works on the *chaebol*, Janelli and Yim (1993: 118) illuminate how during Korea's years of rapid economic development, the company aimed to ease resentment from the harsh disciplinary tactics imposed on subordinates by habitually referring to employees as "family members," and by drawing parallels between the "proper management of subordinates" and "the proper education of children." For instance, in an essay published by the company's monthly journal, one worker wrote:

> The managers have warm human affection, like a parent's devotion, toward the sawŏn [employees], cultivating the knowledge and

abilities of each individual and guiding their talents and ability to evaluate [their own] work. The sawŏn too, like sons and daughters toward parents, have faith in and respect for them, and fulfill their own responsibilities. (Janelli and Yim 1993: 119)

And just as in Janelli and Yim's ethnography, upper-level management from DN Group headquarters, even during a time of economic hardship, similarly seemed to relentlessly believe that they could dispel cross-cultural conflict by encouraging employees to share a common culture and identity as members of the DN Group family. Every other morning, workers gathered around one of the many flat-screen TVs that hung from the office ceilings to watch news shows produced by the Seoul headquarters, highlighting the firm's progress in Seoul and subsidiaries around the world. Occasionally, these broadcasts portrayed hypothetical scenarios of cultural conflicts between local Chinese and South Korean workers. The shows emphasized that workers could solve these conflicts by utilizing the methods of communication and cooperation laid out in the corporate manual.

Like the other employees at DN Group, I received a corporate manual when I was hired, and learned that new employees spent several weeks in intensive training sessions held throughout China and South Korea going over the key concepts that defined the corporate culture of DN Group. We were encouraged to explicitly refer to these key concepts in our daily interactions with coworkers and in business meetings with members of other teams. HR managers also trained new recruits to overcome cultural differences by incorporating the core values of the DN family in workplace interactions.

Moreover, the company invested resources in facilitating informal socializing among employees outside of the workplace. Twice a year each department went on a company retreat where employees played games, ate, drank, and spent time getting to know one another outside the office. To motivate intragroup bonding, the company also reimbursed food and entertainment expenses for informal outings that included workers of different cultural backgrounds. But despite the significant capital and effort invested in cultivating harmonious relations, tensions persisted. The Han Chinese and Korean Chinese employees, in particular, resented their South Korean superiors. They were aware that though their managers seemed amiable, local workers as ethnic and cultural minorities were effectively excluded from the inner DN Group circle. And as a result, despite the lip service South Korean management paid to the notion of the DN family, the vast majority continued to distrust the firm, its hierarchy, and its ethos.

A Bowl of Instant Noodles

During my time in the field, I was intrigued by the experiences of Jin-ho Shin, a Korean Chinese man in his early forties, who did not fit the stereotypical mold of a Korean Chinese worker who worked for a *chaebol*. He carried himself with pride and repeatedly expressed to me that unlike other Korean Chinese minorities I may have come across, he had managed to hold a certain fondness toward South Koreans. Although Korean Chinese minorities typically originated from the northern part of the peninsula, Mr. Shin explained that his grandparents were from Kangwon Province in the south. Thus, while his Korean Chinese friends often claimed northern Manchuria as their ancestral homeland, Mr. Lee explained that he continued to feel a deep emotional attachment to South Korea.

By the time of our interview, it had been more than a decade since Mr. Shin had quit his job at the *chaebol*. When I asked him how he came to his decision to leave his job so early in his career, he told me of a pivotal altercation he had with his South Korean *gwajang* [section manager], Mr. Choi, who had a reputation for bullying his Korean Chinese co-workers. Though his Korean Chinese colleague was of the same occupational rank and boasted a degree from the prestigious Qinghua University, Mr. Choi showed little restraint in treating him as his subordinate. Mr. Shin explained:

> He would order the Korean Chinese section manager to do this and that, and speak down to him. I would watch my colleague just patiently endure all this mistreatment, without a word of complaint or protest. I felt so bad for him, but at the same time, I was so angry that he wouldn't stand up for himself.

Assuming (rather accurately) that I would not understand why someone would flagrantly order around a coworker of equal rank, Mr. Shin paused, and then articulated for my benefit the unspoken rule in the *chaebol* that ethno-national background trumped rank. "If you are a South Korean expat, you have more authority and power in the company than a local [Korean] Chinese worker of a higher rank," he explained.

Mr. Choi's condescending attitude was by no means exceptional, but rather legitimated by a broader organizational culture that imparted preferential treatment on South Korean employees. Mr. Shin's Korean Chinese coworkers, for instance, silently watched their South Korean peers gleefully take home the latest electronic devices—newly designed mobile phones, refrigerators, and television sets—to test before they entered the market. While no one dared ask their superiors why they were excluded from these fringe benefits, Mr. Shin, who was known for his brash and assertive personality, refused to stew silently. He demanded equal treatment and was consequently the only Korean Chinese worker on the office floors who was occasionally given devices to test. This triggered hostility among some South Koreans, however. In his words:

> One day, my [South Korean] boss asked me why I had one of their new cell phones. He asked me to return it immediately. I got so angry that I threw down the phone in front of him and it smashed into pieces on the ground. Everyone was so shocked that I would dare stand up to him. He started cursing at me. I cursed back at him. I didn't back down. Eventually, he called the security guards. He asked one of the Korean Chinese secretaries to translate for him and started telling the guards I was being violent and disrespectful. I knew the [Korean Chinese] woman felt bad for me. She just relayed the general gist of what he was trying to say. She didn't translate everything because she felt sympathetic towards me. Eventually, the security guard got annoyed that he was brought in and told him that we should just figure it out by ourselves.

Though the conflict was eventually resolved after a drawn-out struggle that lasted several days, Mr. Shin decided to leave the firm a few months later. He explained that his decision to leave was not necessarily triggered by the event, but rather because he wanted to try something new. He was bored of the mundane routine of corporate life. During our conversation, as he reflected on his feelings toward South Koreans, he seemed torn by unresolved sentiments of disappointment:

> When I was young, I would just curse and get so angry at South Koreans who would treat me as if I were inferior. I don't do that anymore though. Now, even when I feel angry, I keep it inside. I don't let on that I feel offended or irritated. I try to treat them politely, even when I am burning up inside . . . Actually, I know that I said before that I had all these positive feelings towards South Koreans . . . but there are a lot

of times when I feel so used by them. I feel used when South Koreans treat me with such kindness and respect when they want something, but once I complete the favor for them and am no longer of use, they just go back to the way they used to be. They return to acting cold and indifferent towards me. There were so many times when something like that would happen, and I would feel so hurt.

One Korean Chinese minority I interviewed likened their existence to a bowl of instant ramen noodles. "Once used, we are carelessly thrown away," she said. This realization was particularly painful for Mr. Shin. Prior to his entry into the firm, he had hoped that if he was able to prove his competence, his South Korean superiors might one day accept and embrace him as a fellow Korean. In the end, however, it was hard for Mr. Shin to reconcile his desire to find recognition in the firm with the social reality that status and power revolved around whether or not he was a particular type of Korean.

"We Are Like Family"

The workforce at DN Group was roughly divided into four major ranks: the executive directors [*sangmu*], the department leaders [*bujang*], the section leaders [*gwajang*] and the staff. The staff were further broken down into different levels of power according to their length of employment at the company. Of the 585 employees who worked at DN Group, 26.3 percent were South Korean expats [*jujaewon*] brought in from the Seoul headquarters, 32 percent were South Korean "locals" [*hyeonjiin*] recruited in China, 21.9 percent were Han Chinese, 16.9 percent were Korean Chinese, and 1.9 percent were American.

The South Korean expats, who were at the top of the status hierarchy, dominated positions of power as executive directors (17 percent) and department leaders (22 percent). These expats lived in Beijing on a temporary basis, and a new group was sent to Beijing each year to replace the expats who left. According to internal statistics from HR, the 25th percentile of expats had lived in Beijing for 1.8 years, the 50th percentile 4.17 years, and the 75th percentile 6.7 years. In addition, their length of stay in Beijing largely corresponded with their rank such that executive directors often had lived in Beijing for a longer period of time than section leaders.

DN Group's corporate offices occupied many floors in a high-rise building, with one or two departments located on each floor. In the middle of each floor was a bank of elevator doors, with the bathrooms and café located nearby. The lounge area had been recently remodeled and was fully equipped with sleek tables and chairs, a water cooler, and an expensive espresso machine.

Each side of the floor was divided into clusters of cubicles arranged according to the department's teams. The desks and offices on the office floor were organized to mirror the hierarchy of power in the company. A large desk sat separate from the cubicles in the corner of each cluster; these were occupied by the section leaders. The department leaders and executive directors had enclosed offices that were located in the corners of the floor. Section managers were more integrated into the space where their team worked, allowing them to closely monitor their staff's daily activities.

The spatial layout of the offices corresponded to rank, making the relationship between background and rank physically apparent in everyday interactions. For instance, the expats, who had the most authority in the company, occupied the corner offices, removed from the hustle and bustle of the firm's day-to-day operations. They were paid significantly more than the other employees, earning twice their salaries in South Korea, in addition to luxurious stipends for housing, domestic help, personal drivers, and private school tuition. As the elite managers at a prestigious *chaebol*, the expats carried themselves with pride.

According to Mr. Kim, an executive director I interviewed, the expats at DN Group were part of an exclusive social circle that extended beyond the bounds of the firm. On the weekends, they met to relax and play golf together. Their wives and children were familiar with one another, and many of them even shared fond memories of working long hours together as entry-level workers in Seoul during their youth. Mr. Kim, who was in his late fifties, was recruited straight from Seoul National University nearly thirty years earlier.

"We are like family," Mr. Kim said of his relationship with other expats. They were casual and informal with each other, freely calling each other on the phone when one was in need. In his words, the expats were "friends who also happened to work together."

Mr. Kim explained that the Seoul headquarters perceived South Korean locals, who made up the largest proportion of workers in the China headquarters, as the "core workforce," or the "heart" of the Beijing subsidiary. South Korean locals were directly below the expats in the firm's hierarchy. Many started off at the bottom of the chain of command as staff and gradually worked their way up the corporate ladder. They followed the trajectory of seniority-based promotion reminiscent of the lifetime employment system. Like the expats, their rank largely corresponded to age and experience in the firm. Most of the older South Korean locals worked as department leaders, and many of their younger counterparts worked alongside Korean Chinese and Han Chinese staff in entry-level positions.

The company invested in South Korean locals like Mr. Baek. Mr. Baek had immigrated to China with his parents in the 1990s, when he was only fifteen years old. He had lived in Beijing for nearly half his life and spoke fluent Chinese, yet he made it very clear to me that he considered himself fully South Korean and did not at all identify with the experiences of the Korean Chinese minorities working at DN Group. Having graduated from a prestigious university in Beijing, he preferred to fraternize with the Han Chinese workers over the Korean Chinese. From the perspective of the expats, Mr. Baek as a South Korean who had spent enough time in China to understand local customs and norms represented the ideal mix of both cultures. At the same time, Mr. Baek had spent enough of his formative years in Seoul to have retained the "right" kind of South Korean "smell" [naemsae] in his demeanor; he knew how to easily procure trust and rapport with South Korean management in the Seoul headquarters. Moreover, like Mr. Baek, many South Korean locals planned to work at DN Group for life. Thus, expats like Mr. Kim felt a strong sense of responsibility to mentor young talent like Mr. Baek because he felt he could trust these local South Koreans to devote their entire lives to the company.

Though valued by the firm's executives, South Korean locals also experienced their own glass ceiling at DN Group, however. It was extremely rare for locals to become executive directors, for instance. They also received lower wages than the expats even when they shared the same rank and occupational status. They also did not receive the generous stipends the expats were given. As a result, even as the expats spoke glowingly of South Korean locals as representing the future of the company, the locals secretly resented the fact that they faced external limits to power and status in the firm.

The Han Chinese generally occupied positions beneath the South Korean expats and locals. Most were recruited from prestigious universities in China and hired for their technical expertise or their professional connections to Chinese government bureaucrats. While a number of Han Chinese workers occupied lower-tier entry positions within the company, some also occupied midtier managerial positions as section leaders, as in the case of Ms. Chang. By recruiting highly skilled Han Chinese workers to occupy these managerial positions, the firm hoped to better cater to the Chinese consumer market.

Filling the majority of the clerical positions at the lowest rungs of the corporate hierarchy were the Korean Chinese. Although some exceptional Korean Chinese workers were able to move up the corporate ladder to become section leaders, there were fewer Korean Chinese than Han Chinese workers who held these positions. Most of the Korean Chinese employees at DN Group were young, recent graduates recruited from the most selective universities in Beijing. As one Korean Chinese worker explained:

> There are a lot of Korean Chinese minorities like me, who have grown up in one of the three northeastern provinces in China, who have just graduated from college. We all attended universities in major cities like Beijing, Shanghai, Shenzhen and so on. When we graduate from college, we don't go back to our hometowns. If you go back to our hometowns in the northeast, the Korean ethnic villages have nearly disappeared. Only the elderly ethnic Koreans are left. No one is there anymore. All of the young people have stayed in the cities and have found jobs here, and most of the jobs that we find are at South Korean companies like this one.

Each section in the company had one or two Korean Chinese workers who took care of the clerical work and acted as translators for their South Korean and/or Han Chinese superiors. Many of the South Korean managers I interviewed mentioned Sun-mee Oh, a charming and soft-spoken young woman, who exemplified the ideal set of qualities they hoped to find amongst their Korean Chinese workforce. Ms. Oh grew up in Harbin, a major city in Heilongjiang Province of northeast China. She was recruited by DN Group after finishing her senior year at Peking University and had worked at the company for nearly five years. The older South Korean men at DN Group often praised her for her hard work and excellent linguistic skills. When I interviewed her, she commented that some of her South Korean colleagues would note that she was so poised that they often forgot that she was Korean Chinese. Though Ms. Oh enjoyed working at DN Group, she planned to quit after she and her husband started a family.

"A Woman Must Play the Part of a Woman"

Though DN Group recruited Korean Chinese workers from the same set of highly selective universities as their Han Chinese counterparts, Korean minorities were hired solely and expressly to work as cultural intermediaries for the firm. Just as women in postwar Japanese firms were expected to "play the part of a woman" no matter their value as workers (Rohlen 1979: 103), Korean Chinese workers were not differentiated according to their particular fields of expertise, but rather uniformly expected to "play the part" of a Korean Chinese minority.

As cultural intermediaries, Korean Chinese workers were expected to shadow their South Korean superiors throughout the workday, helping them communicate with local Chinese both inside and outside the office. While they spent a considerable proportion of their time engaging in "formal" transactions (i.e., translating business meetings and documents within the confines of the office), curiously, more than any other demographic group, Korean Chinese employees also spent much of their time engaging in "informal" transactions. Essentially, they were expected to act as the expat's living, walking survival guide in Beijing. As one local South Korean manager put it, "When South Koreans first come [to China] . . . they can't speak Chinese and so they rely on them [the Korean Chinese] to adjust." The manager went on to explain that the Korean Chinese were trained to help the expats survive comfortably in Beijing—from teaching the expats basic words they would need to use in their everyday lives, to learning how to ride a taxi or the subway in and around Beijing, figuring out which restaurants offered sanitary and healthy food, and understanding public safety laws in the city.

Though there were also a number of local South Korean staff at DN Group who were also bilingual, the expats preferred working with Korean Chinese minorities as cultural go-betweens. Compared to the local South Koreans, the ethnic minorities spoke colloquial Mandarin more fluently, and had a deeper knowledge of the subtle social norms in Chinese society that even local South Koreans were oblivious to. The expats also preferred working with the Korean Chinese over bilingual Han Chinese staff, because they felt a sense of intimacy and rapport with the Korean Chinese, as coethnic Koreans. Many expats in the past had complained of the emotional distance they felt towards the Han Chinese. According to one expat:

My Korean Chinese workers are a bit different [from the Han Chinese who can speak Korean fluently] . . . To give you an example, there is a Korean Chinese worker on my team who speaks with a strong regional accent from Gyeongsang Province [in South Korea], so right away, expats [from the same region] feel an immediate sense of intimacy with the Korean Chinese translator. . . . The Korean Chinese are our coethnic brothers [*dongpo*].

In a sense, the Korean Chinese were prized for not only supplying their cultural expertise, but also for providing a sense of familiarity and intimacy to expats who were suddenly faced with the formidable task of living in a foreign country. As cultural brokers who reminded the expats of both the home they left behind and the new world they now lived in, Korean Chinese minorities were hired to quell anxiety, ease misunderstandings, and provide reassurance. To use Arlie Hochschild's term, they were in many ways engaged in "emotional labor." Like the Delta flight attendants in Hochschild's study, Korean Chinese workers at DN Group were similarly required to coordinate "mind and feeling" to provide "the sense of being cared for in a convivial and safe place" (Hochschild 1983: 7).

In retrospect, I found Hochschild's theories on the role of emotions in the workplace helpful in understanding why my preliminary visits to DN Group had been perceived as so intrusive. For the Korean Chinese minorities, the emotional nature of their work was inextricable from their tenuous and ambivalent coethnic relationship with their South Korean managers. Although the Korean Chinese presumably felt betrayed and resentful of the expats, they catered to the emotional needs of their superiors because they understood that that was what they were hired to do. But by severing the emotional work they were expected to parlay from their actual feelings, Korean Chinese workers at DN Group felt even more alienated. In a coincidentally culturally appropriate example, Hochschild writes:

A graduate student of mine from Korea once gave me two masks with wildly happy eyes and broad smiles. These masks, she explained, were used by Korean peasants when confronting their landlord on specified occasions; holding the smiling masks over their faces, they were free to hurl insult and bitter complaints at him. The masks paid the emotional respects due the landlord and left the peasants free to say and feel what they liked. (Hochschild 1983: 80)

Emotional labor that runs counter to workers' actual feelings comes at a cost. By detaching themselves from their feelings to go through the motions of caring for their supervisors, the Korean Chinese grew more disenchanted with the self-serving agenda of the expats.

The framework of emotional labor is also helpful in understanding how the roles of the Korean Chinese in the *chaebol* were marginalized through the feminization of their labor. According to Hochschild, emotional labor is not only by and large relegated to women, but also the unconscious act of perceiving emotional labor as intrinsic to the work of women helps justify their exploitation. While exchanges between people of equal status are typically reciprocal, the exchange of emotional favors between workers of different status becomes more asymmetrical. That is, within uneven exchanges, managers typically feel entitled to the "emotional rewards ... the encouraging smiles, the attentive listening, the appreciative laughter, the comments of affirmation, admiration or concern" bestowed upon them by servants and women (Hochschild 1983: 85).

In the past, these gendered dynamics were used by postwar *chaebol* firms to devalue the contributions of women in the workplace. Janelli and Yim's (1993) ethnography, for instance, demonstrates how the *chaebol* legitimated tendencies to restrict women from opportunities to climb the corporate ladder by portraying unmarried female workers as the "darlings" and "daughters" of the company family. Whereas sons carried on the family legacy, the youngest daughters were "temporary members of their natal families," and accordingly, they were entrusted with "the least responsibility in terms of household chores" not only in the home, but also in the company (119). Workers thus quickly learned that the paternalistic benevolence of labor-management relations applied exclusively to young men. Women were expected to fulfill "the role of reducing friction in their departments," becoming the "basic bridges between personnel [literally, the basic stepping stones of business]" (119). Along similar lines, I found that while the South Koreans widely acknowledged the fact that the Korean Chinese played an important role in the firm, many failed to attribute the firm's ability to penetrate Chinese markets to the help of Korean Chinese cultural intermediaries. Instead, South Korean management by and large looked down on Korean Chinese workers and viewed their skills as interpersonal, easily replaceable, and not professional.

The ethnic minorities were thus explicitly undervalued and segregated in ways that were structurally similar to the ways women have been historically marginalized in the workplace. According to sociological studies of gender in the workplace, for instance, scholars have found that while male employees are often characterized as "aggressive, forceful, independent, and decisive," women are perceived as "kind, helpful, sympathetic and concerned about others" (Morrison, White, and Van Velsor 1987). In the case of South Korea, the segregation of male and female roles was further strengthened by paternalistic ideologies that framed the ideal role of women as subordinate to the dominant position of men (Kim 1986). While Park's postwar regime encouraged middle class men to work as "industrial warriors" in rebuilding the national economy, middle class women were sequestered to the domestic sphere. And gender stereotypes helped perpetuate the concentration of women in clerical positions, low-paying service sector jobs, and caretaking or educational occupations (Kang and Rowley 2005). In contrast to men, who dominated positions at the center of decision-making structures, the maintenance of internal and external networks, and the distribution of resources, women were by and large concentrated in departments that did not require professional expertise and primarily played supportive roles in day-to-day operations (Kang and Rowley 2005).

At DN Group, similar perceptions of the Korean Chinese as effeminate, incompetent ethnic minorities helped legitimize their sequestering into dead-end career tracks. "They [the Korean Chinese workers] weren't trained professionally as translators. They didn't graduate with degrees in translation. If they wanted to get compensated for their skills, they need to come with professional degrees in that area of expertise," Ms. Song, a South Korean section leader, argued. She thought that it was preposterous to think that skills obtained from one's upbringing could be recognized as professional or technical skills. Unlike Han Chinese or South Koreans, Korean Chinese were hired for their "soft skills"—their knowledge of how to adjust to everyday life in China, which the expats distinguished from "hard skills" such as technical expertise or business know-how.

Moreover, because many Korean Chinese youth arrived at DN Group without much previous exposure to South Korea and South Koreans, they typically spoke to their South Korean managers in strong rustic accents during their first few months working at the firm. Difficulty deciphering these regional accents, and the informal veneer of "unstandardized" Korean further justified the devaluation of their linguistic skills. Ms. Song went on to explain:

> I'm not trying to look down on the Korean Chinese, but those Korean Chinese! I feel that they cannot speak Korean proficiently! It's not that they can't speak Korean; they can carry a conversation with us, but [pause] I don't feel like they really understand what we are saying. And that's why they can't translate accurately. They're good at everyday conversation, but for things like formal discussion or a presentation . . . things that are a bit more complicated. . . . They don't use sophisticated language. They only know how to talk casually. They just figure out the basic message and just say it. They talk like they're little children. You can't speak as if you're still in elementary school at a business meeting.

Mr. Kim, a South Korean section leader in human resources, described this dynamic with surprising candor during a conversation one day by the water cooler. When I asked him how DN Group viewed Korean Chinese, he unabashedly asserted that "they are not seen as bringing anything else [other than their language abilities] to the table." He explained matter-of-factly that this was the reason even Korean Chinese workers who had been with the firm for over ten years were rarely promoted. Out of obligation the company gave Korean Chinese workers nominal promotions to section leader when employees stayed in the company for over seven years, but this raise in status was not accompanied by a raise in income.

"After such a long time, the company feels like they owe these [Korean Chinese] workers something. So they change their titles, but that's it," Mr. Lee said. He noted that there were no Korean Chinese workers who occupied a position higher than section leader at DN Group. Moreover, Mr. Lee divulged that South Korean superiors tended to underhandedly bully the Korean Chinese workers who chose to stay at the firm for over ten years despite the lack of career opportunities, because they preferred the stability of DN Group over the uncertainty of finding a new job. Just as career-driven women were taunted for abandoning their families upon marriage or childbirth, Korean Chinese workers who overstayed their welcome at DN Group were similarly the brunt of caustic jokes. In response to complaints about the lack of opportunities for promotion, South Korean managers donned a cavalier attitude, as if to say: "If you don't like it here, then leave. Where else are you going to go?"

High starting salaries ensured a perpetual backlog of young Korean Chinese minorities eager to take the place of those who quit. DN Group was known for attracting the best and brightest Korean Chinese youth each year. While most private Chinese firms offered a monthly salary of 2,000 to 3,000 RMB (300 to 440 USD) for recent graduates, DN Group offered twice that amount, from 5,000 RMB to 6,000 RMB (735 to 882 USD). And by securing a consistent supply of entry-level Korean Chinese workers, the firm implicitly encouraged a high turnover rate, leading to a concentration of Korean Chinese workers who were disproportionately young and often female.

Korean Chinese men were aware of the lacking opportunities for advancement at the *chaebol*. Those who were ambitious often chose the long-term strategy of taking a pay cut to work for a Chinese company more eager to invest in their careers. South Korean management, on their part, favored Korean Chinese women over men because they viewed the job of providing South Korean expats with linguistic and emotional support as they adjusted to their new lives in Beijing as more appropriate for women. This was not only because women were assumed to be intrinsically more nurturing and skilled at human relations, but also because women tended to terminate their positions after marriage or childbirth, helping maintain the appearance of a delicate status hierarchy shaped by age, gender, and cultural background. They preferred Korean Chinese women precisely because they were expected to quit while they were young. Korean Chinese men who wanted to stay in the firm for a long time were treated as eyesores in the company. They disrupted the façade that the firm universally rewarded workers who were loyal through years of devoted service.

Hee-won Kim, a young Korean Chinese woman, helped clarify why her peers were drawn to working at DN Group, despite the discrimination they faced:

> This is a great place for a woman like me to work. DN Group is a well-known company with global recognition. I am well paid for what I do here. The type of work that I do is not very difficult nor do they expect very much from me. . . . I figure, I will work here a few more years and then quit once I have a child. But if I were a man who had ambitions for myself, I wouldn't stay here. I would go to a Chinese company where I would be challenged and have opportunities to grow. . . . I don't really respect the [Korean Chinese] men who choose to work here. They don't seem particularly motivated to me.

The Significance of Working Overtime

At DN Group, perceptions of when the workday ended varied across the cultural backgrounds of the workers. For the local Chinese staff, the day ended when the clock struck six and they heard the pretty voice on the loudspeakers thanking them for another day of hard work. As one Korean Chinese worker articulated for me, "In China, your work is your work, and your private life is your private life." It was hard for the South Koreans to understand this notion of drawing hard boundaries between work and private life, however. For them, the workday never ended. The voice on the loud speaker represented a mere formality; they considered their colleagues their closest friends, and leisure time outside the office was often spent rehashing work-related issues over drinks. The Han Chinese, by contrast, complained that they did not understand the merit of socializing with their coworkers at the end of the workday. They were resentful of pressures to spend their personal time with their coworkers and loathed invitations to attend company events on the weekend.

These differences in attitudes became strikingly visible at the end of each workday, as the office floors started to empty out. The Han Chinese workers, true to form, deserted their desks promptly at 6 p.m., while their South Korean colleagues continued typing away on their computers. Even from the perspective of a foreigner such as myself, it seemed odd that the larger desks in the corner offices remained conspicuously lit as the many smaller desks scattered throughout the center of the floors were dark and bare. When I asked a South Korean expat what he thought of this situation, he responded that they allowed their Han Chinese workers to leave as they saw fit because they did not expect the Han Chinese to ever become "full" members of the company. "The Han Chinese would never completely understand the Korean ethos of the company as a family," he explained. The expat hesitated a bit before proceeding to comment that they did, however, hold a different set of expectations for the Korean Chinese because they were fellow Koreans who should "know better."

"South Koreans don't try to establish that kind of blurry relationship with the Han Chinese," a Korean Chinese worker explained to me. Surprisingly, for some Korean Chinese, the special bonds that they were able to cultivate with their South Korean managers made their jobs at DN Group worthwhile and meaningful:

I feel a sense of emotional closeness and warmth towards the South Koreans I work with . . . For instance, I feel a deep sense of satisfaction when I can go get a cold beer with my South Korean managers after a long day at work. I feel like we can just open our hearts to each other and honestly tell each other what's on our minds. It's really satisfying to be able to do that with the people you work with. It reminds me of what it feels like when I am at home talking to my parents. It's kind of strange . . . It's hard to put into words. It's this feeling of intimacy.

The vast majority of Korean Chinese minorities I worked with, however, were upset that they were held to a different set of standards as ethnic Koreans. Some even went as far as concealing their Korean Chinese backgrounds upon entering the firm, hoping to pass as Han Chinese, as in the case of Mei Lin. Shortly after she started her position at DN Group, however, Ms. Lin's coworkers soon found out that she had grown up in a small Korean village in Heilongjiang. "Once they find out that you are Korean Chinese, and that you can communicate with them easily, they expect to have that kind of [personal] relationship with you," she told me, in seeming dismay.

As a form of silent protest, many ignored the implicit pressures they felt from their South Korean managers to stay late and went home, alongside their Han Chinese coworkers, at the end of the workday. By turning off their desk lamps and shutting off their computers promptly at six, they were in a way demanding equal treatment: Why should they stay late if they were not rewarded like their South Korean colleagues with opportunities to climb the corporate ladder? Why were they expected to act as Koreans when it came to sacrificing their needs for the company, but conveniently not treated as coethnics when it came time to reap the fruits of their labor? Because of the lack of prospects for career advancement in the firm, most Korean Chinese viewed their time in the *chaebol* as temporary and did not feel motivated to sacrifice their personal comforts for an unavailing endeavor.

South Korean managers, however, interpreted the reluctance of the Korean Chinese to work overtime as a sign of laziness and a lack of devotion to the company. When I asked Mr. Lee, a South Korean section manager, what kinds of problems he encountered in managing his team, he replied:

Motivation. Since they [the Korean Chinese workers on my team] lack motivation, some people on my team work really hard, and others not so much. There are things like that, but you see, it's not just that the person who works really hard is just working hard to get things done, but that other people on his team can see that he is working hard and also feel motivated by his efforts to work hard together with him. . . . There's not a lot of that [hard work] on my team, though. . . . I am speaking from my personal experience, but for instance, there are Korean Chinese workers, Han Chinese workers, and South Korean workers on my team. [He draws on a napkin with his pen.] Then these people [pointing to the Korean Chinese workers who are drawn between the South Koreans and Han Chinese on a diagram on his napkin] need to help people over here [pointing to the Han Chinese] to come up to this level. But for instance, what we have is, I tell these people [pointing to the Korean Chinese] in the middle, "Since you guys can communicate better with me, please come up with me to this level." But then they might answer, "No, we're Chinese so we are only going to come up to this level." Or they might even work less so that they just satisfy the minimum requirements.

I suspected that Mr. Lee felt uncomfortable explicitly articulating his discontent, given that we were sitting in the lounge, in the middle of a high-traffic area between the water cooler and the bathroom. In my attempts to clarify what Mr. Lee was attempting to communicate, I asked if by "motivation" and "working hard," he was referring to working overtime. We engaged in the following dialogue:

MR. LEE: Overtime? Yes, we have a lot of that here.

ME: So are you saying that the Korean Chinese and Han Chinese workers are reluctant to work overtime?

MR. LEE: They don't seek it. No, absolutely not. They rather dislike it.

ME: And you're saying that that becomes problematic?

MR. LEE: I'm trying to say that that's why workers must be sufficiently motivated. They need to be motivated to help motivate the others on our team. It's not simply that I will order people on my team, "You need to work overtime today!" But rather, I try to show the others on my team, as a leader, that I am working very hard and explain to them why it is so important for us to finish this project by a certain deadline and why it's necessary for us to work overtime in order to meet that deadline. But even though I explain, they really dislike working overtime. They feel that I am infringing on their personal time and space.

Though workers were under no contractual obligations to stay in the office after six, working overtime signaled to their South Korean managers that they saw their jobs not merely as a means to an end, but rather as an integral part of their sense of personal wellbeing. Indeed, ever since the early years of the postwar era when the *chaebol* first emerged, overtime has symbolized devotion. In Park Chung Hee's efforts to rebuild the nation after the devastation of the Korean War, he exhorted citizens to discard their selfish interests for the good of the nation (Oliver 1993). Both blue-collar and white-collar workers alike were urged to embrace the Korean spirit of "diligence, self-help and teamwork" to fulfill their duties with a sense of responsibility and sincerity, doing "factory work like their own personal work" (Choi 1989: 182–183). For Park, an environment that fostered "a family-like atmosphere" and "complete harmony between employees and employers" was indelible to ensuring productivity (183).

Given the special currency that overtime has historically held in the *chaebol*, I could in some ways understand why Mr. Lee felt disappointed by his Korean Chinese subordinates. As fellow Koreans, he had expected the ethnic minorities to understand the importance of going beyond the call of duty for the collective good. From Mr. Lee's perspective, had the Korean Chinese adequately fulfilled their roles as true cultural intermediaries, they would have offered the company more than just their bilingual expertise. They would have understood that they had a personal duty and obligation—as people who understood the inner worlds of both South Korean and Han Chinese societies—to set an example for the Han Chinese on how to properly behave in a South Korean workplace. Mr. Lee believed that the Korean Chinese employed their own set of double standards, invoking their Korean ethnic identities when it was convenient for them to curry favors from their South Korean superiors, while emphasizing their Chinese cultural backgrounds when they were called to sacrifice their personal comforts for the company.

Turning Limitations into Opportunities

Given the series of disadvantages they faced, I had a difficult time comprehending why the Korean Chinese would continue to seek employment in the *chaebol*. In my interviews with the Korean Chinese entrepreneurs, I later learned that for the Korean Chinese, the *chaebol* represented an important stepping-stone for reaching their ultimate goal of starting their own entrepreneurial businesses. Korean Chinese workers recognized that the *chaebol* provided them not only with enough savings to fund their fledgling businesses, but also with the cultural know-how to cater to the subtle tastes and needs of the South Korean expats, their prospective clients.

Particularly for the older generation of Korean Chinese who were hired not long after Sino –South Korean normalization of ties, working at the *chaebol* provided a rare opportunity to fly to South Korea for the first time:

> I've been to South Korea several times for my work. The first time I went, I was sent for about a month for training when I first joined the company. We went to the Seoul headquarters and worked. We learned a lot of new things. They showed us how headquarters operated, but perhaps more important than the training that we received, I think that we were sent to the headquarters to get to know our South Korean colleagues who worked there.

At the headquarters, Mr. Shin, a Korean Chinese minority, worked alongside his South Korean colleagues for about a month. During his time in South Korea he was given a tour of the various factories they ran in the outskirts of Seoul, as well as many of the major tourist sites. A bright-eyed Korean Chinese youth, Mr. Shin had only ventured outside of his hometown in Harbin when he came to Beijing to attend college. "I had never been to Seoul before," he told me, his eyes sparkling with nostalgia. "I had heard stories about what it would be like, so when we landed in the airport, I was so excited. I was so excited that in Korea, everyone spoke Korean and everyone was Korean." Through these business trips, Mr. Shin was able to establish personal networks in South Korea that deepened his understanding of contemporary Korean society:

> When I go to the Seoul headquarters for business now, the South Korean workers are so kind to me. They are so kind because I came all the way from China . . . I made friends at different retail stores, at the factories, and at the headquarters. We help each other on personal matters, too. Even though I don't work at the *chaebol* anymore, when my former colleagues from the Seoul offices come to Beijing to sightsee, they call me up and I take them around for about two to three days. And when I go to Seoul, they meet up with me and we have dinner together.

By working in the *chaebol*, Korean Chinese workers learned to adopt the social and cultural norms of contemporary South Korean society in a way that would have been difficult for them to acquire without leaving Beijing. Ms. Kim, a Korean Chinese worker who had worked at DN Group for over five years, told me that her speech patterns naturally changed over time:

> After I started working at a major South Korean firm, I began to speak South Korean-style speech more regularly, and so naturally, over time, I just came to adopt this style of speaking as my own. Now, when I go back to my hometown in the countryside, I speak to them using what I thought would be a Korean Chinese accent, but my [Korean Chinese] friends sometimes respond to me strangely. They'll comment how I speak like a South Korean now . . . I don't know why, it just happened that way. I find myself changing. Also, because I am in contact with South Koreans often and I work with them on different projects, I find myself changing even more. Even in the way I think about things or approach issues. The South Korean managers at our company often tell me, "You really act and talk like a South Korean."

Others, like Ms. Cho, a shrewd Korean Chinese entrepreneur in her early forties, who was the sole breadwinner in her family, told me that she expended considerable effort in intentionally changing the way she spoke Korean. Ms. Cho worked for a major South Korean newspaper owned by a large conglomerate when she first came to Beijing. Her job consisted of translating Chinese news articles into Korean, and then uploading them onto the company website. For the first few assignments, however, her boss pointed out numerous mistakes that she had made in translating the articles. "My boss kept on correcting the articles I would send him and I would get so frustrated," she said. Her frustration motivated her to relearn the Korean that she had grown up speaking. On her way home from work, Ms. Cho took home old newspapers they had lying around in the office to read on her commute to familiarize herself with the South Korean style vernacular:

> I would read the newspaper and would memorize each sentence one by one. And before long [she paused] . . . the thing is, South Korean style Korean is not so different from the Korean I am used to. The differences are very subtle. You just have to remember a few rules.

Eventually, Ms. Cho was able to leverage the networks she made with South Korean businessmen at her old job to start a successful translation agency in the enclave. Most of her long-time clients worked as upper-level managers of major South Korean *chaebol* firms. When her Korean Chinese friends, who also operated translation agencies, asked her how she was able to attract such high-profile clients, she explained that the secret to her success lay in her ability to communicate with her South Korean clientele in a way that put them at ease:

> Some Korean Chinese people think, "That South Korean man is arrogant. He came to China, he should learn how to speak Chinese. Why should we change for him?" But I don't think that way. I think it's important to be considerate of what other people might want and need. I know there is a limit to how perfectly I can mimic South Korean style speech, but I feel like if I can speak Korean in a way that makes them feel more comfortable, then why shouldn't I try to make them feel more at ease when they interact with me?

Though she may have personally disliked the South Koreans, Ms. Cho recognized that they were critical to her business and livelihood, and she used the cultural capital that she acquired at the *chaebol* to strategically cultivate the skills she needed as an entrepreneur.

Gendered Perceptions of Competence

The *chaebol* hired only the best and the brightest. And the Korean Chinese minorities who were hired to work for DN headquarters were carefully culled through a rigorous screening process, often involving an entrance exam and several rounds of interviews. Certainly, not everyone was willing to jump through the many hoops required to gain entrance into a South Korean conglomerate. The brand name of the *chaebol* attracted a certain kind of person who derived a sense of self-worth from the prestige the *chaebol* represented—people like Sunmee Oh, the soft-soken Korean Chinese woman I introduced earlier in this chapter. Ms. Oh was the type of person who had spent her whole life working to the top. Upon graduating from Peking University, she fielded multiple offers when it came time to find a job.

But for people like Ms. Oh, precisely because she has identified so strongly with her ability to achieve her whole life, the disillusionment she felt when she looked around her and noticed that all her superiors were South Korean men was all the more overwhelming. Ms. Oh understood that no matter how hard she worked, or how evident her value to the firm was, she had no hope of ever rising to the top as a

Korean Chinese woman. What was perhaps even more frustrating to Ms. Oh was the fact that no one but members of her in-group—other Korean Chinese minorities, and perhaps to a lesser extent other Han Chinese workers—recognized that the rules to climbing to the top were predetermined. To the South Koreans who made these rules, there was an appearance of fairness and meritocracy as workers were evaluated according to a set of standardized criteria each year.

My aims for this chapter were twofold. First, I wanted to bring to light how the organizational culture of the *chaebol* helped legitimate a rigid hierarchy that privileged workers according to their age, gender, and ethno-cultural background rather than their individual skills. Readers will notice that someone as capable as Ms. Oh remained a clerical worker not because she lacked competence, but because she was, in spite of her impressive educational background, explicitly hired and trained to fulfill her role as a Korean Chinese minority—a cultural and emotional go-between smoothing out conflicts and any awkwardness between locals and South Korean expats in the firm.

Second, this chapter aimed to question the very ways in which job skills were conceptualized and measured. That is, I argued that the notions of competence and merit in and of themselves were highly subjective and worked to justify systems of inequality in the firm. While "hard" skills were legitimated as objective measures of merit through certificates, exams, or postgraduate degrees, skills that were not acquired through these more institutionalized routes were devalued. Given that the "soft" skills of the Korean Chinese were arguably more critical and irreplaceable than the technical expertise of the South Korean expats, why did multinational firms like DN Group not reward the skills of cultural brokers, particularly given their ambitions in globalizing operations in the aftermath of the fiscal crisis? In the chapters that follow, I show how these same skills empower Korean Chinese minorities to form tight-bonds of solidarity within their in-group and eventually build thriving businesses as transnational entrepreneurs.

CHAPTER 5

Are We in This Together?

Cultivating Solidarity in the Church

Although the residential neighborhoods and multinational firms in Koreatown were sharply divided along class lines, I wondered whether the enclave church provided Korean migrants with a more neutral environment where people could overcome their differences and form bonds of trust and solidarity. To learn more about the organizational role of the church, I traveled around Wangjing visiting various Korean churches in the area and interviewed the senior pastors and deacons there. At six of the eight churches I visited, I was granted permission to administer surveys following worship service to gauge the ethnic, cultural, and socioeconomic backgrounds of the congregations. I selected one South Korean megachurch, which I refer to as "Antioch," and one Korean Chinese underground church, which I call "First Presbyterian," as sites for in-depth participant observation. In this chapter, I compare the ways the Korean migrants at Antioch and First Presbyterian struggled to build a sense of community within the enclave.

Every Tuesday evening, I attended a Bible study hosted by Deacon Park, a third-generation Korean Chinese retired military official in his mid-forties, who lived in an apartment complex in the Nanhu District. The buildings in Nanhu were noticeably more run-down than those in the so-called South Korean side of the enclave. For instance, next to the front door of Deacon Park's building, a hole with stray wires hanging out marked where an intercom system used to be. The front doors were left unlocked and swung open to a dimly lit hallway of dusty cement. The first time I visited Deacon Park's apartment, I remember how confused I was to walk up three flights of stairs and face two nondescript doors, each without a sign or number. From the sounds coming from inside, I guessed that Deacon Park most likely lived in the unit on the left. Sure enough, when I knocked I was greeted by an elderly Korean Chinese woman who turned out to be Deacon Park's mother.

The apartment was small and old, but felt cozy and tidy. The living room was modestly furnished, aside from a large Samsung plasma screen television that hung on the wall. A pink plastic mat decorated with colorful cartoon characters and a small, worn coffee table lay in the middle of the floor. Against the wall, adjacent to the coffee table, there was a refrigerator and a piano, lovingly adorned by a motley assortment of tattered stuffed animals, a big plastic doll with blonde hair, and a collection of framed family photos.

Before long, we heard a knock on the door and two women entered. They seemed comfortable in Deacon Park's home and headed straight to the kitchen to grab the silverware, raving all the while how delicious the food looked. Eating at Deacon Park's home every Tuesday was the highlight of their week, they told me, as I helped them prepare for dinner. By the time we all sat down to eat, eight people—including Deacon Park and his wife, five women (including me), and a young man in his early thirties—squeezed around the coffee table.

Deacon Park placed a big pot of beef and potato stew in the middle of the cramped table and we dipped our spoons into the pot, heaping the stew into our rice bowls. Everyone gushed how delicious the food was and how talented Deacon Park was not only as a businessman, but also as a cook. The *kimchee* and other homemade pickled vegetables, still in their plastic containers, were scattered around the big pot, and the woman who sat next to me encouraged me to taste the different dishes. When I reached for the sautéed eggplant dish, she warned me that it was heavily garnished with Chinese herbs.

"South Koreans [*hanguk saram*] don't like these flavors," she said, compelling me to prove to them that contrary to their expectations, I was not a *hanguk saram* but rather a diasporic Korean, just like they were. I shoved a generous serving of the eggplant dish into my mouth. But as the eggplants hit my taste buds, I immediately realized that the flavors were indeed, as the woman had predicted, pungent and unfamiliar. I tried to conceal my shock as I nonchalantly reached for my glass of water. Throughout the meal, I noticed all eyes were on me. Everyone watched my facial expressions and my chopsticks as I picked up this and that, and I felt enormous pressure to show them that I accepted their food, and by extension, them.

Deacon Park played the role of thoughtful host as he ordered his wife to pour another serving onto my rice bowl, scolding her as she ladled stew into my bowl for missing the tastier ingredients.

"Don't forget to include the mushrooms. The mushrooms are good. And the potatoes, too. More potatoes," he chided his wife. In spite of my discomfort, for the first time in a long while, I felt an intimacy and warmth I hadn't felt since I last visited my family in New Jersey.

While Bible studies like the one I attended at Deacon Park's home may appear as nothing more than a humble meeting of friends, upon closer analysis I discovered that such meetings revealed how Korean Chinese minorities cultivated and mobilized bonds of solidarity to improve their quality of life in the enclave. For the Korean Chinese, the friendships that formed at church served as the lifeblood of their community. The sorrow and frustration they felt as minorities marginalized from both Han Chinese and South Korean societies fueled their desire to help one another emotionally and economically. They bonded over their feelings of alienation, and this sense of common fate motivated them to share whatever they had for the greater good.

In contrast to the warm, inviting environment of First Presbyterian, my experiences at Antioch, the South Korean megachurch I attended, were stilted and formal. I still remember the first time I noticed Mrs. Kim at a prayer meeting I had been attending for several months. She stood out because she was dressed unusually for a South Korean woman her age. The evening I met her she had on distressed jeans cuffed at the ankles, an oversized black jacket, and black sneakers and her silver, shoulder-length hair was kept in place by a headband. From the lines on her face and hands, I guessed that she was well into her sixties.

When I approached Mrs. Kim after our prayer meeting had ended, rather than introduce herself to me, she laughed awkwardly and diverted her eyes from mine. It was only after we started walking together outside toward the bus station that she started talking to me. Mrs. Kim revealed that she had been attending our church for several months, but had avoided attending main group functions. She liked going to prayer meetings because so few people came each week and she could come and go as she pleased. "I don't like telling people that I've been in China for so long because I don't have much to show for it," she explained as she looked down, kicking a stone across the street. As we stood waiting for our bus to come, Mrs. Kim told me how she and her husband had moved to China fourteen years ago to start a furniture business. They had had to downsize their company several times since then and were currently struggling to make a living.

After formally introducing myself to Mrs. Kim that Wednesday evening, I never saw her at church again. When I asked about her a few weeks later, one of the more veteran Bible study members explained that people like Mrs. Kim were common in Wangjing. People often disappeared as quietly and quickly as they appeared, without as much as a greeting or a farewell.

The contrastive images of Mrs. Kim, who always sat by herself at the back of the room, and Deacon Park's Bible study group huddled around his small coffee table illustrate a counterintuitive finding. Though the South Korean church was a powerful transnational organization with branches all over the world, the precarious grassroots entrepreneurs who attended the church, like Mrs. Kim, isolated themselves and were unable to benefit from the vast wealth that the church had access to. At the same time, while the Korean Chinese underground church was by far more humble in a materialistic sense, the church provided their members with considerable emotional and economic resources. I wanted to understand what types of conditions accounted for First Presbyterian's warm communal environment, and the lack thereof at Antioch. The pages that follow aim to address this question.

Divisions in the Korean Christian Community in Beijing

Over the past few decades South Korea has rapidly become a globally recognized Christian epicenter, with 29,820 Protestant churches and 55,989 pastors in 1989 (A. E. Kim 2000). By 2017, there were more megachurches (congregations of more than 2,000 members) in Seoul—including Yoido Full Gospel Church, the largest church in the world with nearly 800,000 members—than any other city, and South Korea had become one of the greatest dispatchers of missionaries in the world, second only to the United States.

When barriers to travel opened up between South Korea and China in 1992, South Korean missionaries disguised as businessmen and entrepreneurs flooded China, targeting Korean Chinese communities in particular. Some used funds from churches in Seoul to set up small businesses that were largely inactive to conceal their religious activities, whereas others found "covers" as employees of South Korean firms that were in fact funded by prominent missionary organizations.

During the early years, many South Korean missionaries attempted to establish institutional partnerships with Christian organizations in the PRC, but these efforts were for the most part ineffective due to strict laws against proselytization in Communist China. To circumvent state intervention, most South Korean missionaries eventually joined local underground grassroots movements in the PRC, planting churches, orphanages, and schools in Korean Chinese communities located in the Korean Autonomous Prefecture in Yanbian, Jilin Province. Despite the Chinese government's efforts to restrict the spread of Christianity, the religion spread rapidly throughout Korean Chinese minority communities in the early 1990s to such an extent that Pastor Kim, a Korean Chinese pastor of an underground church in Beijing, remarked:

> Christianity is not the religion of our ancestral heritage, but . . . today large numbers of Korean Chinese are Christian to the extent that other ethnic groups [in China] often exclaim, "You Korean Chinese have traditionally believed in Christ! It's part of your cultural heritage, isn't it?"

There are two types of churches in the Korean enclave in Beijing: state-sanctioned churches and underground churches. State-sanctioned churches are technically protected under the Chinese constitution, which guarantees the right to practice religion. Churches that are registered with the government, however, must abide by a long list of regulations, including laws that forbid members from meeting outside church grounds and proselytizing to Chinese citizens. Along these lines, Chinese citizens are prohibited from attending churches that are designated for foreigners, and Korean Chinese minorities were subsequently not permitted to attend state-sanctioned South Korean churches.

It was also widely known that the state regularly dispatched agents who attended weekly services to report back suspicious activities. One South Korean elder who attended a state-sanctioned church described:

> When there is a major church event, the deacons contact the government officials to let them know what type of event they are going to hold, the date and time of the event, and how many people they expect to show up. Then, on that day, government officials will come to the church grounds to observe whether or not we are holding the activities in line with the regulations.

He went on to explain that the Chinese state viewed churches as political organizations and invested considerable time and energy in regularly monitoring their activities. They were also aware that at times the government even sent undercover agents to make sure they were sticking to the rules, lending to an air of perpetual anxiety and tension among the deacons and elders. Many Korean religious leaders lamented that this degree of surveillance hindered the vitality of their ministry.

Frustrated by government surveillance and the numerous restrictions placed on church activities, a number of religious leaders in Wangjing set up underground churches. Underground churches were unregistered and took place in varying settings that ranged from the cramped spaces of someone's living room to the expansive spaces of large office buildings that were somewhat hidden from public view. Though state authorities were well aware that these churches existed, they by and large turned a blind eye to their activities and instead informally kept tabs on the religious leaders who founded these organizations. Large underground churches like First Presbyterian, for instance, experienced periodic threats that their services would be shut down for various (often arbitrary) reasons, but these moments of crisis were often mitigated through careful negotiations between church leaders and government officials.

Mobilizing Feelings of Alienation to Cultivate Solidarity

First Presbyterian was established in 2007, growing from only 20 Korean Chinese members to nearly 500 by the time I conducted fieldwork in 2010. The church offered two worship services: a morning service in Mandarin for nearly 300 Han Chinese members, and an early afternoon service in Korean for approximately 200 Korean Chinese minorities. The Han Chinese attendees were mostly young, well-educated urbanites, whereas the Korean Chinese membership included a wider range of socioeconomic backgrounds, from wealthy factory owners to elderly domestic workers.

In the six months I conducted in-depth observation at the church, I encountered only one South Korean family attending First Presbyterian. The lack of mixing between South Koreans and Korean Chinese members was readily apparent not only at First Presbyterian, but also at the vast majority of churches I visited in the enclave. I was told that the clear divide between South Korean and Korean Chinese churches was due to state mandates that prohibited Chinese citizens and foreigners from attending the same religious organization. And indeed, I found this to be true in the two state-sanctioned churches I surveyed (one of which was South Korean, and the other Korean Chinese). I became increasingly dubious, however, when I found similar trends in the remaining six underground churches I visited as well. Underground churches were by definition not restricted by Communist law, and yet even in these "illegal" churches, I was hard-pressed to find evidence of regular South Korean members in any of the Korean Chinese churches, or Korean Chinese members in any of the South Korean churches I visited, thus pointing to trends of self-selection shaping membership instead.

Like at most underground churches, there were no signs or physical markers indicating where worship services at First Presbyterian were held. There was merely a tacit understanding among people in the know as to where the church was located and what time services took place. I was introduced to First Presbyterian by a well-known South Korean missionary who was somewhat exceptional in Wangjing for having extensive social networks in both South Korean and Korean Chinese communities. The missionary led me, one Sunday afternoon, to a rundown office building tucked behind an alleyway. The first floor of the building was left dark, presumably intentionally. We waited outside until a deacon from the church arrived and walked us through the dark lobby to the elevator. I saw the first signs of life only after the elevator doors opened to a cheerful group of greeters waiting by the entrance of the third floor (see Figure 5.1). The church occupied the entire floor of the building, and the sanctuary was located in a large, modestly furnished room that was filled to capacity with rusty fold-up chairs.

As noted earlier, historically Korean Chinese underground churches in China, especially those in remote villages in northeastern China, received significant financial support from churches in South Korea (H. Kim 2010). In fact, many of my relatives who lived in the Seoul metropolitan area attended churches with similar outreach programs. My uncle happened to lead one of the missions programs at a prominent megachurch. Upon interviewing him about his involvement, I learned that my uncle frequently visited China to help build new churches. He explained that they cultivated relationships with Korean Chinese minorities while they were in Seoul working as low-wage laborers. When the

FIGURE **5.1** Inside the sanctuary of a Korean Chinese underground church.
Photo courtesy of the author.

Korean Chinese workers returned to China, the church provided them with funds to build churches in their hometowns. In his words:

> When new [Korean Chinese] people come to our church, we teach them about the Bible. . . . While these people are in South Korea, they join our community as fellow brothers and sisters in Christ and after a period of time, they go back to China. And so naturally, they start churches in the places where they live. These churches are built organically, and the leaders at the churches are people who had been members of our community in Seoul.

In total, my uncle's church supported twenty different Korean Chinese underground churches scattered throughout China, primarily in Jilin, Liaoning, and Heilongjiang Provinces. Each month, they sent their designated Korean Chinese leaders about 3,000 USD, in addition to an initial lump sum to fund the construction of new church buildings in their villages.

More recently, however, Korean Chinese churches, particularly those in large cities like Beijing, have begun to assert their financial and institutional independence from South Korean megachurches. This was particularly pronounced at First Presbyterian. Pastor Park, the senior pastor at First Presbyterian, was a highly educated Korean Chinese minority with degrees from a prestigious university in Beijing and a theological seminary in Seoul. Pastor Park explained that by remaining financially and institutionally autonomous, he was able to run his church as he saw fit and protect his congregation from the unsolicited advice of South Korean pastors who did not adequately understand their needs.

Several scholars have noted how financial support from megachurches in South Korea has in the past led to significant conflicts between South Korean and Korean Chinese religious leaders (H. Kim 2010). The same stereotypes that were responsible for creating tensions between the South Koreans and the Korean Chinese in the space of residential life (as depicted in chapters 2 and 3) continued to deter Korean Chinese clergy from working closely with South Korean pastors and from accepting their economic assistance whether from Seoul or Beijing. Many South Korean pastors, for instance, complained of feeling manipulated by Korean Chinese minorities who allegedly abused their religious cause to extract extravagant sums of money (H. Kim 2010).

Thus, although First Presbyterian regularly sponsored visits from guest speakers and mission groups from South Korea, they rarely utilized the church's transnational networks for material assistance. There was an implicit taboo against accepting money and an unspoken desire, among the leaders of First Presbyterian, to prove that they had no interest in financial entanglements. The emotional baggage attached to money outweighed the benefits. Moreover, many of the leaders of First Presbyterian spoke proudly of their humble facilities, wearing their ascetism as a badge of honor.

While the leaders of First Presbyterian fulfilled their moral obligation as Korean Chinese Christians to connect South Korean mission groups to local Chinese, their feelings of resentment colored their behavior. During the six months I spent at First Presbyterian, the church hosted one speaker and two mission groups from Seoul. On the surface, they did everything they were supposed to do: the Korean Chinese young adults met with the South Korean mission groups to sing, pray, and speak about the challenges they faced as an underground church in Beijing. The deacons also organized various outreach programs for their South Korean guests. Yet it was hard to overlook their perfunctory attitude. When I asked Deacon Park, my Bible study leader, about how he felt about the South Korean missions groups after dinner at his house one day, he replied:

> I feel so annoyed when I see South Koreans make photocopies of little Christian brochures on how to achieve salvation in our [church] office. I think to myself, "Who do they think they are? What use is a little pamphlet going to do when they don't even understand who they are talking to, who they are interacting with?"

Like Deacon Park, many of the Korean Chinese members of First Presbyterian felt a general sense of mistrust that the South Koreans came only to evangelize from a position of undeserved privilege. They assumed that any attempt to engage in meaningful discussion would not be met with an open-minded attitude, so many of the Korean Chinese minorities at the church did not feel compelled to go beyond their call of duty in getting to know their guests.

Pastor Park was aware that many of his Korean Chinese members struggled with feelings of marginalization as minorities who were neither Korean or Chinese. When counseling the members of his congregation, he made a concerted effort to articulate how their in-betweenness—their source of pain and alienation—could empower them to share the gospel with the Han Chinese in ways South Korean missionaries could not. He was quite intentional in using his sermons to inculcate a sense of pride within his Korean Chinese congregation, and his efforts did not go unnoticed.

Hee-sook Chang, a highly educated woman in her thirties who worked at a South Korean tech company in the enclave, revealed that she started to feel a sense of self-worth and pride in her identity as a Korean Chinese minority only after meeting Pastor Park and listening to his sermons. As a child, she wondered why she had been born a Korean ethnic minority in China. When Pastor Park stressed that God had sent their ancestors to Manchuria, many decades ago, for a special purpose, she finally was able to feel a sense of peace and comfort.

"What is so special about us is that [unlike South Korean missionaries] we do not look down on the Han Chinese," Ms. Chang explained to me over dinner one day. "It is natural for us pray for the Han Chinese and embrace this country [China] without any judgment . . . because we were born here [in the Chinese countryside] . . . If I had been a stronger person, perhaps, God would have arranged for me to be born in North Korea [to fulfill his purpose there]!" she said with a chuckle.

In the world of evangelicalism, China and its expansive population represented an enviable, untapped market for proselytization—a market that the South Korean missionaries were failing to effectively take ahold of. Despite their extensive knowledge of the Bible and spiritual maturity, South Korean missionaries were impaired by their pride and comfortable upbringing, Ms. Chang explained. For the Korean Chinese, however, establishing rapport with locals came effortlessly.

Investing in Relationships

My foray into the South Korean community was by no means as difficult as my attempts to gain access to the Korean Chinese community. From my first week at Antioch, I was immediately welcomed by the leaders and encouraged to join various activities. Antioch was officially registered with the government, but nearly impossible to find. The church was located behind a large warehouse on an undeveloped dirt path that branched off a major street. From the street, all I saw was the warehouse. Curiously, all of the taxi drivers in Wangjing knew where Antioch was located. When I told them to take me to the big South Korean church by the factories, they asked me if I wanted to go to the one behind the warehouse, or the one by the big seafood market (where a different Korean Chinese underground church was located).

At the entrance of the building, two men in black suits stood behind a table with a big sign taped to the front reading "Passport Check" in Korean letters. The leaders at Antioch learned from the mistakes of their predecessors that it was important to maintain harmonious ties with the Chinese government, so they enforced strict regulations on church participation in line with state guidelines. Due to their successful efforts in maintaining peace with the government, Antioch grew to serve over two thousand members, nearly all of them South Korean expats or South Korean entrepreneurs.

The first day I didn't have my passport with me, so I pulled out my New Jersey state identification card instead. One of the men standing behind the table asked me in perfect English where in New Jersey I was from, casually mentioning that he had received his doctorate in engineering at Rutgers University. Our conversation was cut short by hordes of women and their children who had just gotten off one of the many shuttle buses that had arrived. The charter buses were free of charge and fully operated by the church. They made rounds to all of the major apartment complexes in the enclave and members rode them to attend Sunday worship services and various church events during the week. When I checked a map of the bus routes, I discovered that none of the buses stopped by the Nanhu district, where many of the Korean Chinese lived.

South Korean churches in Beijing generally received more direct institutional support from partner churches in Seoul than Korean Chinese churches. Antioch, for instance, was a local branch of a well-known church in South Korea that trained missionaries to spread the gospel around the world since the 1980s. The church facilities, though hidden from plain view to ordinary Han Chinese passersby, were impressive, filling an expansive plot of land with several different buildings for the various ministries and programs they offered. There was a separate worship hall for the children's group, the women's group, and the English-speaking group, in addition to the main chapel. Each of these sanctuaries could fit several hundred people. The main chapel occupied several floors and was equipped with the latest technology, a large pipe organ, and a separate viewing room with a nursery.

The Seoul headquarters of the megachurch, had, over the years, grown to become a powerful transnational organization with twenty-five branches around the world. At the time of my study Antioch's global congregation numbered over 75,000 individuals, and the megachurch supported more than 1,000 missionaries in different countries scattered across the globe. The headquarters also operated their own publishing house that supplied its overseas branches with highly polished spiritual texts and curricula for various programs. Monthly newsletters from the headquarters kept overseas congregations apprised of major church news and events. Similar to the *chaebol*, the core pastors and leaders at Antioch in Wangjing were trained and dispatched from Seoul.

Some South Koreans in Beijing who did not attend Antioch suggested that the church had grown quickly in size and prominence because it received so much financial and institutional support from the Seoul headquarters. Pastor Choi, who led a South Korean underground church in the enclave, commented how Antioch represented a "brand." "It's connected to a very famous church in South Korea. Subconsciously, it taps into an image of a church that is modern and sophisticated. If you go to Antioch, you feel this atmosphere of a First World country. I think that the people who go to Antioch are attracted to this type of image and ambience," he explained. Indeed, even the praise band leader of the English worship service was a well-known K-Pop star.

At Antioch, I volunteered as a temporary keyboardist for the Japanese Ministry. I was filling in for a woman who had to go back to Japan to care for her ailing parents over the summer. The Japanese ministry sought to evangelize to Japanese foreign residents in Beijing, but few were interested in Christianity to begin with, and even fewer were interested in attending services held in a massive South Korean church. I chose to become involved in the ministry because the South Koreans who attended the service were mainly deacons and elders who were prominent members of Antioch. Though the group was small, they represented a subset of members who were well-connected and extremely committed—the Japanese Ministry represented only one in a long list of activities that the members were involved in. Many regularly attended daybreak prayer meetings during the week, Friday night Bible study, and Saturday staff meetings.

The congregations at both First Presbyterian and Antioch were highly volatile and constantly fluctuating—an inherent trait of transnational populations. Farewell parties and welcome banquets were a part of everyday life at Korean churches in the enclave. At Antioch I attended parties for South Korean youth who were preparing to return to Seoul after earning their college degrees in Beijing. I similarly helped send off South Korean expats whose short-term assignments in Beijing had ended, and watched South Korean entrepreneurs quietly disappear from Beijing after hearing rumors that their businesses had gone bankrupt.

When I asked Ms. Choi, a South Korean woman at Antioch, how long most members of the Women's Ministry (WM) stayed in China, she answered:

> About an average of three years, probably. Three years for the most part. . . . For those who stay longer, maybe five years. . . . Of the people who have lived here for over ten years, some are expats . . . some are entrepreneurs, but to give you a percentage . . . it's very small. Even if you include everyone, I know maybe ten [out of 200] people . . . Maybe not even that many.

Though Ms. Choi had served Antioch for merely four years, she was easily one of the most veteran members of the ministry.

First Presbyterian's congregation was also highly mobile, but the patterns of mobility were distinct from Antioch's. At First Presbyterian, most of the people who moved back and forth between Seoul and Beijing were young adults who sought better training, education, or work experience in South Korea. In addition, most Korean Chinese minorities who left Beijing planned to return and ultimately settle permanently in China. This perception of China as their final destination strongly influenced their attitude towards investing in relationships.

Deacon Lee, a member of First Presbyterian, migrated to Beijing from Harbin in 1990 to attend a highly selective university. He was nineteen years old when he first arrived and had lived in Beijing for over twenty years. His father passed away in 1991, and his mother went to Seoul in 1994 to work as a domestic worker for a wealthy South Korean family. She was able to obtain a visa through one of her relatives in South Korea. Deacon Lee explained that because his mother naturalized in South Korea, he could easily obtain a South Korean passport as well. But when I asked him why he didn't seize the opportunity to live in Seoul with his mother, he was indignant:

DEACON LEE: Who's gone to South Korea [out of the people we know at church]?

ME: Aren't there a lot? There are a lot of Korean Chinese people who . . .

DEACON LEE: Those people are from the countryside. They're country bumpkins. Out of college-educated Korean Chinese, who do you know who has gone to South Korea?

ME: There's no one?

DEACON LEE: Very few people who have graduated from college go to South Korea [to live].

ME: Aren't there people who start businesses in South Korea? I heard that some Korean Chinese go to—

DEACON LEE: Well, there are probably some who do, but not a lot. People who are capable stay in China. Why would they go to South Korea to work [in the low-wage labor market]? Maybe there are a few who go to South Korea to open some kind of entrepreneurial firm, but most of the people who go are usually middle-aged men and women from the countryside who have nothing better to do . . . Ah, I guess there are a few young Korean Chinese who go to South Korea to study abroad. People who graduate from universities in China don't go to Seoul. Why would they want to go to Korea to work in such harsh conditions? For what? To make a few thousand dollars? I wouldn't go even if they offered to give me a few thousand dollars.

Deacon Lee was already a successful entrepreneur in Beijing. He owned several real estate properties in Beijing and drove a European sports car to church. He was understandably offended by my presumption that Seoul was a better place to live than Beijing. Like him, other college-educated Korean Chinese minorities at First Presbyterian were transnational migrants in the sense that they visited Seoul several times a year to import goods and visit family, but unlike the South Koreans, they saw Beijing as their home.

By contrast, most South Koreans viewed Beijing as only a temporary destination. One pastor of a South Korean underground church remarked during our interview that in the six months he had served the church, about 10 percent of his congregation had left to return to Seoul. He sensed a cloud of uncertainty hanging over the heads of his parishioners, shaping their behaviors and decisions:

> No one comes to China thinking that this is the place they want to settle for the rest of their lives. . . . People come here thinking that they're only visiting temporarily, so there's no sense of emotional stability. They are always a bit anxious, wondering how they will go back to South Korea, how the move will affect their children's education, their retirement plans, and so on.

This element of uncertainty affected how South Koreans interacted with other members of their congregation. Because departure always seemed imminent, many felt unmotivated to invest deeply in relationships with others at church. "Why invest in someone who might at any point leave? Why invest myself in the community here, when *I* might leave at any point?" was the common attitude.

The expectation that members of the community could at any time pack their bags and return to Seoul made it difficult to establish trust. Many admitted they were careful when interacting with other South Koreans in need of economic help. Mr. Suh, a South Korean man in his early thirties, told me about a man he met:

> The South Korean man I met didn't ask me for money directly, but I could sense something was a bit off. . . . We met a couple times for

drinks and he started explaining how he was starting this business and needed to borrow some money. As we shared beers, he asked me to help him. . . . Or there are people who explain that they are in some kind of crisis situation and urgently need to borrow 1,000 or 2,000 RMB [150 or 300 USD].

Mr. Suh explained that after the man asked him for money, he turned down subsequent requests to meet because he felt suspicious of his intentions. He pointed to the numerous public service announcements in major Korean magazines in Wangjing warning people of South Korean con men who had run off after borrowing money from several friends.

The highly fluctuating nature of the population also made it difficult for small South Korean underground churches, which were dominated by entrepreneurs, to sustain their activities over a prolonged period of time. South Korean underground churches were notorious for disappearing not only because they were constantly running away from government officials, but also because they had a hard time maintaining a core leadership. According to a South Korean pastor of an underground church:

It seems as if once someone is ready to become a leader or an active member at church, they have to leave. People who undergo training have to stay around to serve more actively and take on more responsibilities, but they end up leaving just as they've finished training. So when new members join our church, we train them from the very beginning all over again. But these people end up leaving too, after a few years. People are constantly dropping out of the congregation. It's a vicious cycle of training people and watching them leave once they are ready to serve.

This problem of maintaining core leadership contributed to the pervasive atmosphere of uncertainty and instability in small South Korean underground churches, exacerbating entrepreneurs' reluctance to trust and rely on others during times of hardship. The only churches that had staying power were megachurches like Antioch because they relied on external support from South Korea to sustain their activities.

The Church as a Safe Haven

From an organizational perspective, whether state-sanctioned or underground, the enclave church generally possessed traits ideal for facilitating bonding among its members (see Figure 5.2). These organizational traits, which have over the years become distinctive of Korean churches more broadly, can trace their roots back to the early 1900s,

FIGURE **5.2** A Korean Chinese volleyball tournament held at the gym of a South Korean church.
Photo courtesy of the author.

when Christianity entered the Korean peninsula. Korean-style evangelicalism originated during a time when the Korean peninsula was on the verge of Japanese invasion. According to the Presbyterian missionary William N. Blair, Korean intellectuals and independence fighters exiled in Korean enclaves in Manchuria at the time desperately looked to Christianity as a means to hold onto national sovereignty:

> All eyes were turned upon the Christian Church. Many Koreans saw in the Church the only hope of their country. There is no denying the intense loyalty of the Korean Church. Christianity gives men backbones. There were not lacking many hot-heads in the church itself who thought the church ought to enter the fight. The country wanted a leader and the Christian Church was the strongest, most influential single organization in Korea. (Lee 2010: 19)

Emotional and organizational reliance on Christianity intensified following the Russo–Japanese War (1904–1905), culminating in the Great Revival of 1907, a watershed moment in the history of Korean Christianity.

Timothy Lee (2010) highlights in particular two characteristics about Korean-style evangelicalism that are relevant to the present study. He notes that during the Great Revival of 1907, Koreans felt compelled to prove that they were authentically "born-again" by demonstrating how devoted they were to the church through their investment in time, and their emotional fervor.

To this day, time spent at church is used as a benchmark for measuring the strength of someone's faith. Korean Christians are often noted for their extraordinary commitment to church activities. In the case of Beijing, the high frequency of meetings at church helped create a regular, structured environment where people were able to strengthen their relationships with one another. This was true for both South Korean and Korean Chinese churches in Beijing. For instance, Ms. Park, a leader in the Women's Ministry (WM) at Antioch, commented how "relationships fostered at choir were reinforced at coffee meetings after worship service on Sundays and Bible study meetings midweek." Furthermore, Ms. Park frequently encountered people she knew from various activities at church in going about her everyday routine in the enclave. She said that at least within the confines of Koreatown she didn't feel like a foreigner, but rather like she was part of a small, tightly knit community.

Devout churchgoers like Ms. Park easily spent over seven hours at church on Sundays alone. Every Sunday, Ms. Park arrived at church at around 8:00 in the morning to pray and prepare for worship service. When service ended at around noon, she ate lunch with her friends at the church cafeteria and attended choir practice at 3:00 p.m. After choir practice, she sometimes went to get a quick bite to eat with her friends at a nearby Korean restaurant, returning home late in the evening. When I asked if she went to church on other days of the week, Ms. Park cocked her head to the side, apparently confused that I would expect otherwise. She proceeded to give me a rundown of a typical week:

> On Saturdays, I am involved in Family Prayer meetings and breakfast fellowship at church in the morning, and then, in the afternoon, I have choir practice . . . On Mondays, the church is open for individual prayer. On Tuesdays, we have intercessory prayer meetings. On Wednesdays, there is the women's group, on Thursdays, we have our outreach program, and on Fridays, there is a small group Bible study.

Though many Korean migrants were not as actively involved in church as Ms. Park, according to my survey nearly 40 percent of the

South Korean respondents who attended church spent more than six hours in church-related activities each week. By contrast, only about 10 percent of the South Korean respondents who attended church spent the same amount of time in other organizations.

Similar trends characterized Korean Chinese churches in the enclave. At First Presbyterian, members regularly gathered for volleyball practice on Sunday evenings, Friday night prayer meetings, and midweek Bible studies, among other activities. In addition, they frequently contacted one another during the week to meet for an impromptu dinner or for drinks. Nearly everyone lived and worked within a five-mile radius, so it was easy to synchronize their schedules with one another without much prior planning. Indeed, even my process of gaining entrance into the Korean Chinese community at First Presbyterian helped reveal how the organizational culture of the Korean church facilitated trust and intimacy.

When I first started to attend First Presbyterian, perhaps because my introduction came by way of a South Korean missionary, I was immediately marked as a South Korean. I sat alone at the back of the pews for many weeks before my presence was acknowledged. Pastor Park would often nod hello and ask me how I was doing, but for the most part, week after week, I struggled to make small talk with the people around me.

In an effort to cultivate friendships, I tried to join the church choir after hearing Pastor Park announce after worship service one Sunday that they were in dire need of new members. When I eagerly chased down the choir director shortly thereafter, however, I was told that I would need to undergo an intensive interview process to join. I wrote my phone number down in the director's notebook and waited for her to contact me. But three weeks passed without a phone call. For the first three months I spent at First Presbyterian I experienced numerous similar episodes of rejection.

One morning, I found myself lying awake in bed at the break of dawn, unable to fall asleep. On a whim, I decided to take a cab to attend the daybreak prayer meeting [*saebyeoggido*] held every morning at First Presbyterian. Daybreak prayer meetings, and a ritual known as unified vocal prayer [*tongseonggido*], which typically erupts at the end of the prayer meetings, originated during the Great Revival of 1907. Today, these two rituals have become emblematic of Korean-style evangelicalism. In accounts written by Graham Lee, a missionary who led worship

service at Pyongyang Presbyterian Church during the height of the revival, the raw emotional vulnerability that the early Korean Christians
demonstrated as they prayed through the night is striking:

> After a short sermon . . . man after man would rise, confess his sin,
> break down and weep, and then throw himself on the floor and beat
> the floor with his fists in a perfect agony of conviction . . . Sometimes
> after a confession, the whole audience would break out into audible
> prayer, and the effect of that audience of hundreds of men praying
> together in audible prayer was something indescribable. Again, after
> another confession, they would break out into uncontrollable weep-
> ing and we would all weep together. We couldn't help it. And so the
> meeting went on until [2:00] a.m., with confession and weeping and
> praying. (Lee 2010: 77)

Among overseas Koreans, it was customary to seek out daybreak
prayer meetings during desperate times because the church often
formed the organizational hub of the Korean community. Perhaps because I was so well-acquainted with this practice as a diasporic Korean
myself, I found myself seeking out this morning ritual to soothe my
anxieties. I arrived at First Presbyterian half an hour early that day. With
nothing to do, I sat idly on the front steps of the building waiting for
the others to arrive. At 5:30 in the morning the dark building was ac-
cented only by the flashing rainbow neon light sign of the KTV room
next door. Two skinny girls who wore identical red body-skimming
dresses—presumably, hostesses who had finished their last shift—
smoked cigarettes about fifty feet away from where I sat.

The assistant pastor was the first to arrive. He seemed surprised
to see me sitting on the cement stairs and ushered me inside, asking
if everything was okay. Fourteen people—including Pastors Park and
Kim, two middle-aged couples, one elderly woman in her seventies, one
woman in her late thirties with her autistic son who was about seven,
one single mother in her thirties, one single woman in her forties, a man
in his forties, and two single women in their late twenties—attended the
prayer meeting that day. Of the people who came that day, four were
from my Bible study. They all seemed taken aback to find me there.

After Pastor Park finished his sermon, he turned off the lights and
turned on a recording of some hymns. At first I just sat quietly, listening
to the hymns and the others around me enumerating their concerns
in a loud, impassioned voice. There was something about my physical

and mental state of exhaustion, combined with the melancholic music playing in the background, that seemed to trigger something within me. I suddenly found myself unable to hold back my tears and my body started shaking, overcome with grief. After a while, Deacon Park's wife came to sit next to me and silently placed her hand over mine.

As people finished praying, one by one they exited the room. I heard the door open and close. I was among the last to stand up and leave. When I walked out the door, I heard laughter and chatter in the room next door. I peered in to find everyone sitting around a long table, eating rice porridge and Korean Chinese–style pickled vegetables. The somber mood of the room I had just left was a sharp contrast to the happy, lively ambience of everyone eating breakfast family-style. One of the men from my Bible study pulled out a chair, motioning for me to join them. I was still too shaken to immediately transition into the jovial revelry that enveloped that small room. But as I sat listening to them laugh and talk, I felt, for the first time, their sympathy.

I continued to attend daybreak meetings every morning, for the next three months after that day. Many of the stories and conversations that were shared around the breakfast table after the prayer meetings gave me valuable insight into the nature of the everyday struggles of the Korean Chinese minorities in the enclave. In addition, the core leaders of the congregation—the deacons and the elders—who saw me at the break of dawn every day started to protect and vouch for my presence in my interactions with the other Korean Chinese minorities at church.

I often look back at that moment during my time in the field, and find myself pondering what it was about that specific experience that might have caused people who had been ordinarily so distrusting to open their hearts to me. Most likely, ordinary Korean Chinese minorities who sought to attend First Presbyterian were welcomed more readily into the community than I was. Still, I suspect that in cultivating ties with the more established members of the church as newcomers, the same dynamics applied: emotional vulnerability and commitment in time demonstrated someone's sincerity and trustworthiness.

Certainly, Antioch, the South Korean megachurch that I attended in the enclave, also held daybreak prayer meetings every day. On Saturdays I spent the entire day at Antioch, getting up similarly at the break of dawn to start my day with prayer, followed by a group breakfast, Bible study, small group fellowship, and other extracurricular activities. At times I volunteered at the church cafeteria to help prepare the meal served after daybreak prayer meetings. The structure of the prayer meetings, and even the nature of the group breakfast that followed afterward, was nearly identical to that of First Presbyterian. After the pastor delivered a short sermon, he turned off the lights as the praise band played melancholic music in the background, prompting the congregation to break out in unified vocal prayer. During breakfast, we were encouraged to sit with the people who were in our Bible study groups.

Why was it that the same organizational dynamics emblematic of Korean-style Christianity at Antioch failed to inspire the same bonds of trust that formed in First Presbyterian? Certainly, the members of Antioch were not lacking in their commitment to the church. I would often hear impassioned cries even among many of the ordinarily stoic male deacons and elders during unified vocal prayer sessions. During group breakfast at Antioch one Saturday, I overheard one of the church elders praise Deacon Kim, a department chief at Samsung headquarters in Beijing, who woke up at five to attend daybreak prayer meeting before heading to work every day. According to the elder, Deacon Kim had a (virtuous) habit of kneeling on the floor of the sanctuary when he prayed, and would weep in full prostration as he bared his soul to God. When I asked what he prayed about, Deacon Kim spoke about his spiritual growth.

I do not doubt that Deacon Kim's intentions were sincere. In the months I spent getting to know him, he seemed genuinely devoted to the church and to his faith. But there was a distinctively performative element in the emotional fervency that he and many of the other South Korean attendees demonstrated at Antioch. I noticed that while it was acceptable to demonstrate emotional vulnerability within the context of spirituality, it was rare for someone to open up about their failing business or broken marriage during fellowship hour. Frequent meetings and emotional fervency in and of themselves were insufficient in facilitating communal bonding. To be effective, these organizational traits had to be combined with the right type of infrastructural arrangements that helped people focus on what they had in common rather than their differences.

Anomie at Antioch

Deacon Kim was exceptional among South Korean expats in that he had lived in Beijing for nearly ten years. Like most expats, he lived in one of the more exclusive apartment complexes in the enclave with his wife and children. At Antioch, I observed that the entrepreneurs and expats didn't seem particularly close with one another even though they worked closely together in various ministries like the Japanese ministry. When I asked Deacon Kim one day why expats and entrepreneurs didn't hang out together more often outside of church, he seemed baffled by my question.

"What do you mean? We might go to the same church, but we have nothing in common," he responded. I pointed out that he and Mr. Choi, an entrepreneur who was part of the same small group we joined, both volunteered in the praise team and enjoyed playing music. He paused and seemed to carefully consider his words before explaining that though they served together at church in various capacities, it was hard to get to know people like Mr. Choi. The entrepreneurs never really shared what was going on in their lives during small group meetings. There was a sense of shame in revealing your weaknesses at Antioch, perhaps because the expats lived in such comfort and luxury.

There was a tacit understanding that though the expats and entrepreneurs attended the same church, they lived in two different worlds. Deacon Kim seemed sympathetic toward the plight of the entrepreneurs but could not understand how to interact with them in a way that did not make them confront the real gaps in living standards that separated them. He said:

> It's hard to go out to eat or hang out with them. We just have such different lifestyles. I feel bad going to an expensive restaurant because I know that they probably can't afford it. At church, we're nice to each other because we share a common faith, but honestly, our relationship is not very intimate. Outside of church, I only socialize with other men who work for other major South Korean companies. We go play golf on the weekends and drink at nice bars. We just live in two different worlds.

Mr. Choi was in his sixties and had moved to Beijing more than fifteen years ago to start a small business. When his business became bankrupt, he dabbled in this and that before opening a small Korean restaurant in the center of the enclave. Everyone in my small group seemed to know that Mr. Choi had gone through many painful experiences during his time in China, but no one dared to ask him specific details about his struggles for fear of embarrassing him.

These divisions in class were even more conspicuous in the Women's Ministry, which was by far one of the most prominent organizations at Antioch. The WM was designed to provide South Korean women who arrived in Beijing with the social networks and resources they needed to confront the challenges they faced as mothers and wives in a foreign country. The women were organized into small groups based on the age of their children. When I asked Ms. Park, the leader of the WM, what they talked about during meetings, she explained that most of their topics of interest were about their children's education:

> Many of our children go to international schools, which are completely run in English. For children who have only attended school in South Korea, suddenly they find themselves having to learn English in addition to Chinese. . . . We talk about how to deal with the stress that our children encounter here. Because that is what our children struggle with the most, the mothers in our ministry come together and listen to each other's experiences and try to help each other.

Though programs like the WM were intended to help South Korean women in general, the focus often fell on the interests of the expat wives, and glossed over the significant differences separating the experiences of the South Korean entrepreneurs from those of the expats. As described in greater detail elsewhere, the expats occupied a distinct social strata within the enclave and the workplace, and the problems that they discussed during small group meetings were unique to the circumstances of the privileged. These programs subsequently engendered feelings of alienation among South Korean entrepreneurs and their wives, who felt ashamed of their precarious economic circumstances.

To provide a concrete example, South Korean expats sent their children to prestigious international schools known as so-called A-level international schools that offered classes taught by Western faculty and advanced curricula that were geared towards admission into selective universities in the United States. For tuition alone, the schools charged from 180,000 RMB (26,500 USD) to 200,000 RMB (30,000 USD) for each child per year. Because the expats received generous stipends from the *chaebol* to cover their children's education expenses, they could easily afford to send their children to these schools. South Korean entrepreneurs, however, sent their children to Korean private schools that charged a tuition of about 20,000 RMB (3,000 USD) per year. Those who were struggling even more financially sent their children to Chinese public schools within the enclave that charged Korean students 5,000 RMB (735 USD) per year.

During WM small group meetings at Antioch, the South Korean mothers who sent their children to A-list schools were obsessed with sharing information on which afterschool SAT or TOEFL program in Wangjing could best prepare their children for admission into an Ivy League college. Paying fees upwards of 2,000 RMB (300 USD) each month per subject matter for additional tutoring and after-school cram schools, the expats spent an exorbitant amount of money on their children's education that was unfathomable for the South Korean entrepreneurs, who according to my survey earned a median monthly income that ranged from about 10,000 RMB (1,500 USD) to 20,000 RMB (3,000 USD). Instead of feeling a sense of solidarity or support, the wives of South Korean entrepreneurs who were privy to these conversations became more acutely aware of their relative deprivation. They were afraid of feeling judged by the South Korean expat wives and kept their problems to themselves.

Furthermore, while the wives of South Korean entrepreneurs were busy working around the clock, helping their husbands run their businesses, South Korean expat wives lived like queens without a care in the world. Pastor Choi explained:

> Whereas in Korea, the wives were busy running errands, cleaning the house, and taking care of the children, in Wangjing, they can afford to hire a housekeeper to clean the house and take care of the errands, as well as a driver who can take them places. They have no responsibilities, other than to meet with their friends at expensive restaurants for lunch and get their hair done every day. They have time to go to Bible studies and other church functions during the week. All the while, I only see the wives of South Korean entrepreneurs on Sunday for worship.

Overcoming Differences at First Presbyterian

Unlike the members of Antioch, the Korean Chinese minorities at First Presbyterian were able to form strong bonds of trust and solidarity not necessarily because they were more homogenous. In fact, many of the ethnic minorities at First Presbyterian were separated by strong regional differences, which at times created tension. The Korean Chinese from Yanbian, for instance, spoke a distinct dialect of Korean from their counterparts from Liaoning, and were broadly rumored to be untrustworthy and duplicitous even among other Korean Chinese minorities.

In addition, depending on whether they grew up in a more rural or urban area within the Northeast, the Korean Chinese also varied in their perceptions of self and their fluency in Korean and/or Chinese. While some identified more strongly as Chinese, others—and, in particular those who attended Korean ethnic schools—perceived themselves as first and foremost Korean. There were also class differences within the community. While some Korean Chinese minorities graduated from elite universities in Beijing, others had only completed elementary school and worked and found jobs as low-wage workers.

Why then were the Korean Chinese members of First Presbyterian church able to overcome their various socioeconomic and regional differences? First, as I alluded to earlier, intergroup conflict—feelings of marginalization from both South Korean and Han Chinese societies—served to solidify a strong sense of collective consciousness as ethnic minorities who fit neither here nor there. Korean Chinese minorities perceived their regional differences as insignificant when compared to the feelings of alienation and discrimination that they collectively experienced.

Second, because most Korean Chinese minorities migrated from farming villages, their socioeconomic differences were on the whole not as vast as the gaps separating South Korean entrepreneurs from the expats at Antioch. In fact, the socioeconomic differences that did exist were dependent not on their family backgrounds (whether they came from a wealthy or working class household), but rather on their life-stage (how old they were or what generational cohort they were a part of).

But perhaps more importantly, fellowship programs at First Presbyterian were organized in a way to bring together people who shared key demographic characteristics. Depending on the time of year, the church sponsored between six and ten Bible study groups, and each group had ten or more members. Formally, Bible study groups met at the homes of the group's leader to share their struggles and pray together for a few hours each week. Informally, members of each group met numerous times throughout the week to socialize and help one another during times of hardship.

Because the Bible study groups were primarily organized by age—which in turn, often overlapped with their socioeconomic backgrounds—members were able to commiserate with each other over similar life experiences, hardships, and frustrations. Most of the Korean Chinese youth who attended First Presbyterian, for instance, had migrated to Beijing to attend university, and many later found jobs working for one of the major *chaebol* firms in the financial district. The oldest age group consisted mostly of elderly Korean Chinese minorities who had recently returned to Beijing after having worked as domestic workers (for women) or construction workers (for men) in South Korea in the 1990s. Most had retired and returned to China to live with their adult children in Beijing. In between these two age groups, the vast majority of middle-aged Korean Chinese were employed as managers of South Korean firms or ran their own entrepreneurial businesses in the enclave. Socioeconomic differences at First Presbyterian—and within the Korean Chinese community at large—were thus perceived as life-stage differences, rather than differences of class or social status.

In addition, the disparities in wealth that did exist among the members of First Presbyterian paled in magnitude when compared to those at Antioch. For instance, income differences among middle-aged entrepreneurs at First Presbyterian were much smaller than those between South Korean expats and entrepreneurs at Antioch. According to my survey findings, Korean Chinese minorities who were between the ages of 30 and 60 were evenly distributed in terms of their income brackets, and only 21.6 percent of the population earned more than 10,000 RMB (1,500 USD) a month. This range in incomes was much more exaggerated among South Koreans of the same age group who participated in my survey, of whom 79.4 percent earned more than 10,000 RMB (1,500 USD) a month, and within this population, 23.4 percent made more than four times this amount, earning a monthly salary upwards of 40,000 RMB (6,000 USD). At the lower end of the spectrum, 13.6 percent of South Koreans earned less than 6,000 RMB (900 USD) a month.

Because gaps in income within the Korean Chinese population were not as jarring, rather than sentiments of envy or alienation, the Korean Chinese minorities were more prone to see themselves as part of a larger collective. There was a sense of communal welfare that did not exist at Antioch—the members of First Presbyterian saw their individual well-being as tied to the general well-being of the community. And the Korean Chinese minorities I met were eager to contribute whatever skills and knowledge they had to help a member of their community advance socioeconomically.

Soo-yun Lim, for instance, was an active member of my Bible study group who regularly received assistance from other members of our group in running her online shop. Ms. Lim was one of few Korean

Chinese minorities at First Presbyterian who had assimilated so fully into Chinese society that aside from her Korean name, she was virtually indistinguishable from a Han Chinese person. Ms. Lim understood conversational Korean, but could not speak it and had only recently started learning how to read and write her ancestral tongue. Though Ms. Lim was born in a small Korean village in Heilongjiang, she moved to a Han Chinese village when she was six years old. There were no ethnic Korean schools in the area, so she attended a local Chinese school. The only other Korean minorities she knew were her relatives, who remained in the Korean village her parents left behind. Growing up, she saw herself as no different from her Chinese peers:

> We didn't understand what our identities [as Korean Chinese] entailed [as we were growing up]. I was too young to understand back then. It's possible that at times, I might have understood [that I was different from my Han Chinese peers], but we didn't have a strong impression [about the significance of our ancestral heritage]. Because there were no people I could compare myself to—comparative cases that I could draw from—we had no reference point. Everyone [around us] was Han Chinese. There's a saying that goes like this. If you put a goose inside a group of chickens, then he'll think he's also a chicken. That's the way it is in life, don't you agree?

Ms. Lim's father, who had worked as a doctor in a Chinese state collective, had always felt limited by his lack of Mandarin fluency. Because he had faced barriers in career advancement as a Korean Chinese minority under the Mao regime, he encouraged his children to assimilate to avoid discrimination.

In 2002 Ms. Lim migrated to Beijing from Heilongjiang Province to work as a journalist, but quit her job after a few years. She later started her own online business selling miscellaneous religious goods such as hymnals, Bibles, crosses, and church gowns imported from major manufacturers in South Korea to the growing number of churches and other religious organizations in China. Though she felt at ease interacting with her Chinese clients, her inability to communicate with Korean vendors was a major obstacle.

During Bible study meetings at Deacon Park's house, Ms. Lim frequently complained about the language barriers she faced over dinner, and each week several members from our group volunteered to stay late to help her. On one particular occasion, after Bible study ended

I tried to help Ms. Lim order some wooden crosses from a South Korean website but found that the vendor did not accept foreign credit cards. After we clumsily fiddled with the website for an hour, Ji-soo Yang, a Korean Chinese entrepreneur who had a lot of experience importing goods from Korea herself, quickly came to our aid and called the customer service line in Seoul. Ms. Yang had lived in Yanbian for most of her life and was fluent in Korean. True to form, she had no trouble communicating with the customer service representative. After spending a few minutes on the phone, she learned that the only way Ms. Lim could purchase the wooden crosses was by setting up a bank account in Seoul that would electronically wire money directly to the website. Ms. Yang then called her sister who was working as a waitress at a restaurant in Seoul. Her sister immediately went online and purchased the items for Ms. Lim, and Ms. Yang then wired money to her sister's account on Ms. Lim's behalf. Later, I heard that Ms. Yang's sister had also helped set up a bank account under Ms. Lim's name so that she could purchase more items from the website without any future hassle.

The following day I met the two women at daybreak prayer meeting, and Ms. Yang again stayed late to teach Ms. Lim how to make purchases from the website, patiently guiding Ms. Lim through each of the steps over and over again. Without the aid of her friends from Bible study, it would have been almost impossible for Ms. Lim to run her business efficiently. But by relying on others in the Korean Chinese community, she was able to overcome her individual shortcomings to build a successful niche business. Her experience was not unique. On countless occasions, I watched people at First Presbyterian use their differences as a strength by sharing the knowledge and experiences they had as a collective to fill the gaps they faced as individuals—Korean Chinese minorities who had strong Chinese networks willingly connected other members to their Han Chinese friends; those who had thriving restaurant businesses shared information on vendors; those who spoke other foreign languages translated advertisements so that their friends could expand their clientele base.

Creating an Environment for Vulnerability

Finding access to a community can make all the difference in shaping the life chances of migrant entrepreneurs. This chapter demonstrates how for transnational migrants, the ability of transnational organizations to effectively cultivate a sense of community and solidarity among its members was more important than their actual material wealth. I show how while Antioch, as a powerful South Korean megachurch, had access to rich transnational resources, the South Korean entrepreneurs who attended the church were largely unable to benefit from them. By contrast, First Presbyterian, though relatively poor, provided struggling Korean Chinese migrants with emotional support and collective know-how during times of hardship.

In the beginning of this chapter, I introduced the story of Ms. Kim, the wife of a South Korean entrepreneur, who went through the motions of going to Bible studies and Sunday worship services at Antioch, all the while isolating herself from deep involvement. Because Ms. Kim didn't open up about her experiences or emotionally invest in the people she met at church, she could not benefit from the resources that were available within her community. Thus, in spite of the sharp business instincts she may have had as an individual, her entrepreneurial skills were limited in guaranteeing success especially in uncertain institutional environments. Because other South Korean entrepreneurs similarly isolated themselves, it was highly likely that they were making the same set of mistakes as their peers and predecessors unbeknownst to themselves.

So why didn't Ms. Kim integrate herself more at Antioch? This chapter highlights two factors in shaping migrants' social integration in civic organizations. First, the tendency to isolate, I argue, is significantly shaped by migrants' attitudes towards their place of residence. Korean Chinese minorities were for the most part transnational migrants who, in spite of their frequent trips to Seoul, were firmly rooted in Beijing. By comparison, South Korean migrants by and large saw their lives in Beijing as temporary, and were perpetually mentally prepared to return to Seoul. As this chapter demonstrated, the actual amount of time migrants ended up staying in Beijing was not as important as whether or not they perceived Beijing as a place they wanted to settle down in. These attitudes powerfully shaped how Korean migrants in the enclave approached relationships, and in turn, the type of emotional practical support they had access to.

Second, the particular organizational environments that migrants find themselves in can also influence how effective they are in cultivating solidarity. While Antioch has access to a vast wealth of resources, these resources had little impact on enhancing Ms. Kim's quality of life. Bible study groups at Antioch took place on the church grounds because of the legal restrictions on foreign religious activities in the PRC, and conversations were dominated by *chaebol* executives and their wives, who treated spirituality as a proxy for morality and status. At First Presbyterian by contrast, many of my Korean Chinese friends shared tears of frustration and anxiety over a hot meal every weekday in the cozy confines of their homes. Had South Korean entrepreneurs like Ms. Kim participated in a Bible study with other entrepreneurs who were just as economically precarious as they were, perhaps they would have been more amenable to making themselves more vulnerable during fellowship hour. Instead, Ms. Kim was ashamed of her desperate circumstances and further distanced herself from the only community she had access to in Beijing.

CHAPTER 6

Building Small Businesses
in the Transnational Enclave

It was a bitterly cold morning in Beijing when a well-known Korean boutique closed its doors. The steel shutters that covered the entrance caught everyone by surprise. Employees who had arrived early that morning to start their daily shifts were shocked to read the letter that was taped onto the storefront: "Customers with pending purchase orders may visit our store on January 10th for a full refund. Please contact Miss Jin [*Jin xiaojie*] at 800-555-1212."

The number provided was useless, however, as Miss Jin was nowhere to be found. In the weeks following Miss Jin's disappearance, rumors spread that the boutique owner had sold her property some six months ago and had secretly run off to Seoul. This incidence of fleeing by night had become increasingly widespread among South Korean entrepreneurs in Beijing's Koreatown. While precise statistics were difficult to obtain, the Chinese Academy for Social Sciences estimated that about 20,000 or 30,000, or about one in three South Korean migrants, had left Beijing over the course of 2009 due to economic hardship (*Chosun Monthly* April 2009). Many packed their bags and returned to South Korea, while others fled to less developed areas in China where the cost of living was much lower.

Located only a five-minute cab ride away was a thriving shopping mall where the majority of the stores were owned by upwardly mobile Korean Chinese entrepreneurs (see Figure 6.1). I worked part-time in

FIGURE **6.1** The entrance of a popular Korean Chinese shopping complex in Wangjing. Photo courtesy of the author.

one of the shops owned by Joo-mi Chang, an attractive Korean Chinese single mother in her mid-thirties. Ms. Chang had spent her childhood in a Korean ethnic village in the outskirts of Harbin in Heilongjiang Province. After graduating from a two-year junior college in Harbin in 1998, she and her boyfriend followed the thousands of Korean Chinese minorities who left their hometowns to fill the growing demand for low-wage labor in Seoul. Over a period of six grueling years in Seoul's garment district, Ms. Chang worked as a waitress, delivering meals to people who worked in the clothing booths, and later as a sales clerk in the wholesale markets.

In Seoul, Ms. Chang earned lower wages and worked longer hours than her South Korean coworkers, but in spite of the many difficulties she faced, she was ultimately able to save enough money to open her own clothing boutique. In 2005 she moved to Beijing when her relationship with her boyfriend (and the father of her daughter) ended. Given the nature of our friendship, I felt uncomfortable asking Ms. Chang how much she made each month, but it was clear from her lifestyle that she was faring quite well: a live-in Korean Chinese nanny cooked her meals and took care of her daughter six days a week, and in addition to the two-bedroom apartment she lived in, she owned a second home in the southeastern part of Beijing, as well as two commercial properties. Just to pay off the monthly rent of her apartment, the mortgages on her three properties, and the monthly wages for her nanny, Ms. Chang needed to make well over 30,000 RMB (4,400 USD) each month—an income that was higher than that of an average South Korean entrepreneur in the enclave. But perhaps more impressive than her wealth was the fact that Ms. Chang had been able to sustain her business for over seven years in the highly volatile and competitive clothing markets of Beijing.

Why did South Korean entrepreneurs in Beijing experience such widespread downward mobility? And why were the Korean Chinese, by contrast, able to achieve upward mobility in the enclave? Not only did the South Korean migrants have privileged access to a lucrative niche market, but they also arrived with prestigious college and graduate degrees, extensive job skills, and sufficient seed money to start their own businesses.

What I encountered in the field flew in the face of past theories on immigrant entrepreneurship. Since the 1980s, migration scholars had praised the Korean immigrant experience in the United States for representing the epitome of the American Dream. Despite the initial poverty and formidable linguistic barriers they faced overseas, Korean immigrants in the United States were able to pull themselves up by their bootstraps as small business owners of humble nail salons, grocery stores, and dry cleaners. Specialists of immigrant entrepreneurship largely pointed to these first-generation Koreans as evidence of how immigrants facing discrimination and linguistic barriers in the mainstream job market could use entrepreneurship as a means to secure a middle class lifestyle (Light and Bonacich 1988).

In explaining the success of the Korean immigrant entrepreneurs in the United States, past research placed particular emphasis on schooling. Many argued that though the college degrees of the Korean immigrants did not carry much value in securing employment in American firms, they were still able to benefit from their foreign-earned human capital when setting up neighborhood businesses (Sanders and Nee 1992). They pointed to the fact that similar trajectories of entrepreneurial success were conspicuously absent among resource-poor ethnic groups, such as Latin American immigrants in America, who had lower levels of education (Portes and Rumbaut 2001). To date few Mexicans in the

United States have ventured into entrepreneurship, and most remain stuck in low-paying menial positions in the service sector, manufacturing, and construction.

These theories did not seem to apply to the experiences of the Koreans in Beijing, however. In spite of their reputation as the nation's "model minority," high levels of schooling only provided a partial explanation for why the Korean Chinese had been able to attain socioeconomic mobility as entrepreneurs. While the Korean Chinese were more educated compared to other Chinese citizens, they still fell behind the South Koreans both in terms of their overall levels of education as well as in the quality of schooling they received. Of 381 South Koreans I surveyed, for instance, 82.9 percent had degrees from a four-year college. In stark contrast, I learned from my interviews that the vast majority of Korean Chinese minorities went to schools where there was a lack of high-quality teachers, resources, and facilities because of the limited access to resources in the Chinese countryside under Mao.

When I consulted South Korean scholars about my findings, many of them argued that Ms. Chang's success could be traced to her knowledge of local Chinese culture and her fluency in Mandarin. They reasoned that the South Koreans, as foreigners in the PRC, faced intimidating obstacles in breaking into local markets. I found this explanation unsatisfying, however. While I recognized that the Korean Chinese minorities, as Chinese citizens, did not face the same institutional and cultural barriers that the South Koreans did, this perspective was contradicted by widespread trends of downward mobility among the hordes of Han Chinese rural migrants, who, like the Korean Chinese, were fluent in Chinese and understood local organizational customs.

In this chapter, I argue that success and failure for Korean entrepreneurs in Beijing lay in their ability to act as cultural brokers within the transnational enclave. Though previously I showed how the same role had pigeonholed the Korean Chinese into dead-end career tracks in the *chaebol*, interestingly, this chapter shows how what was once a weakness could be turned into a powerful resource depending on the institutional environment that migrants were in. Whereas cultural intermediaries were devalued for their "soft" skills as workers of multinational corporations, this structural position placed them in a locus of power within small firms as middleman minorities capable of culling resources from a diverse set of non-overlapping networks within a highly competitive market.

Communication Barriers with Local Workers

I was introduced to Mr. Kang, a South Korean entrepreneur, through a friend I knew at Antioch. Early during our interview, I found it telling that Mr. Kang mentioned several times how he found solace in a popular saying that in China, "It was not the strongest man who survived, but rather the man who survived, who was the strongest."

Many of the South Korean entrepreneurs I interviewed were men, who like Mr. Kang had arrived in Beijing with ambitions of finding wealth and success in China. The shame that these middle class men felt in losing their ability to financially provide for their families was palpable in the strained nature of our conversations. Along with his disappointing experiences with entrepreneurship, Mr. Kang felt that he had also failed as a father. Several times during our interview, he asked me to turn off my digital recorder as he relayed the vulnerable details of his experiences.

In describing his former self, Mr. Kang said that he used to be a workaholic who had derived immense pride in his capabilities as a businessman when he lived in Seoul. He worked for an advertising agency in his youth and migrated to Beijing in 2002, with the second wave of South Korean migrants who crossed the Sino–South Korean border after China entered the World Trade Organization (WTO) in 2001. In the beginning, the agency sent Mr. Kang on a business trip to gather information about opportunities to expand into the Chinese market. And two years later, they told him to pack his bags to help open a branch office in Beijing.

Only a few months into his stay in Beijing, however, the headquarters started experiencing financial difficulties and Mr. Kang was summoned to return to Seoul. He explained:

> That was in 2004, so there weren't any big problems [economic recession] in South Korea or China at the time, but the headquarters was struggling for some reason. They told me not to get too comfortable in Beijing, and asked me to come back. [pause] I was called back, but I didn't go.

Confused and a bit surprised by his boldness, I asked him what he did upon quitting his position. He responded:

> I stayed and just continued to do the work that I had been doing in advertising. I had already formed relationships with clients, and I continued to work with them, only on my own terms as an entrepreneur from that point forward.

Mr. Kang was unable to sustain his business for long, however. Shortly after he took over the company, he found himself unable to compete with local Chinese firms because of the vast wage differentials separating local Chinese and South Korean workers. Whereas local workers were paid an average of 2,000 RMB (300 USD) each month, South Korean workers received about ten times this wage, or about 20,000 RMB (3,000 USD). Because Mr. Kang hired a large number of South Korean employees at his firm, the high costs of labor made it nearly impossible to keep prices low and competitive with local advertising agencies.

Understandably, he still looked back at the situation with a great deal of frustration and bitterness. Mr. Kang felt that the local markets were rigged against foreigners like himself. He argued that the high wages given to South Korean workers were justified given their technical expertise and job experience. South Koreans designed advertisements that stood out from those of their local competitors in creativity and quality of execution. They were specialists in their field and had painstakingly honed their craft over many years of training and experience. Mr. Kang believed that South Korean designers like himself deserved to be properly compensated for producing a higher quality product, but they were helpless to local industry customs that did not grant advertising agencies legal rights to the finished product. Once the designs were finished and ready to go into production, their clients negotiated with several different agencies to publish the advertisements, and South Korean companies unsurprisingly lost bidding wars to local companies that charged much less.

When he realized that his years running the advertising agency were numbered, Mr. Kang quickly folded his business and set up a small chain of retail stores selling lifestyle products imported from South Korea instead. He borrowed money from his friends and relatives in Seoul to open one main store in Wangjing and nine other stores in nearby neighborhoods outside of the enclave. Given his past predicaments with maintaining healthy profit margins, Mr. Kang knew that he had to hire local workers to remain cost effective, but he continued to feel insecure about his Chinese language abilities. In his words:

> Communicating with my Chinese personnel was the hardest part of my job. Because of my limited Chinese, even though I wanted to treat them well and encourage them to work hard in my heart, it was so hard for me to express all of my feelings in Chinese.

Even prior to moving to Beijing, Mr. Kang had spent much time, money, and effort in learning Chinese, studying intensively with private tutors for several months. When he continued to struggle to speak to his staff in Chinese no matter how hard he studied, Mr. Kang felt he had no choice but to hire a Korean Chinese manager to help him communicate his vision of how he wanted certain tasks executed in monthly staff meetings.

As Mr. Kang's Chinese improved, however, he started to realize that his manager wielded considerable discretion in shaping the channels of communication that flowed between him and his Chinese employees. Though he felt uncomfortable speaking in Mandarin himself, over time he started to understand more of how his words were translated, and he grew concerned about the vast liberties his manager took in relaying his original message:

> Sometimes, after we gave the presentation, I would ask him [my Korean Chinese manager], "Why did you leave this or that part out of my speech?" He was a pretty smart guy, though. He knew how to discern what parts to translate and what parts to leave out. He would explain to me that certain parts of what I wanted to say would actually have a more negative effect on my staff, so he intentionally left that part out. So for instance, if I spoke about three different things, of the three, one of my points wasn't going to have a positive impact on my staff, so he would just leave that part out. He would only talk about the other two points. And when I asked him, "Why didn't you talk about this third part?" Afterward, he would explain to me why that part was not really appropriate. I trusted him because I believed that he understood more about their culture than I did.

Unlike many of the other South Korean entrepreneurs I interviewed, Mr. Kang did not once make a derogatory comment about his Korean Chinese manager, but was quite intentional in taking responsibility for his circumstances. He explained that he fully trusted his Korean Chinese manager—they had worked together for nearly seven years, ever since he started his advertising agency in 2004, and Mr. Kang trusted him like a brother. But by constantly deferring to his manager's judgment, he felt handicapped in his ability to decisively shape the course of action at his own firm. Four years after opening his lifestyle business, he found himself saddled with mounting debts and decided to closed his business venture once again, this time with a heavier heart.

I met Mr. Kang nearly two years after he had given up on his dream of growing a successful business in China. In those two years he had agonized over why his businesses had failed and endlessly ruminated over how the linguistic and cultural barriers he faced had blocked him from success. I found it noteworthy that Mr. Kang never learned to speak Chinese fluently even though he had lived in Beijing for nearly a decade, because of the abundance of Korean Chinese middleman services available to South Korean migrants in the enclave. While he was able to live comfortably in Beijing without ever having to adapt to the local environment by remaining in the enclave, the enclave also blocked him from gaining the tools he needed to succeed. Findings from my survey data confirmed my impression that the enclave insulated South Koreans from adapting to their host environment. The data showed no correlation between the number of years of residence in China and Mandarin proficiency among South Korean entrepreneurs. For the majority of South Koreans, low levels of Mandarin proficiency persisted regardless of how long they had lived in Beijing.

Under the Façade of Power

Like many other South Korean entrepreneurs in Beijing, Mr. Yook arrived in Seoul with his retirement fund in hand to open a small Korean restaurant in the enclave. And like his predecessors, Mr. Yook's restaurant had also closed shortly after opening because of growing misunderstandings and tensions that brewed between him and his staff. In our interview, he stressed that effective communication was at the heart of running a smooth restaurant kitchen:

> In a restaurant kitchen, people are divided into various groups. Some people are in charge of fried foods, some are in charge of sautéed foods, others are in charge of baked foods, and so on. So, if there is one chef who is in charge of the overall flow of the kitchen, you have to make sure you communicate effectively with him in order to produce good food. The manager needs to be an effective intermediary between the chef and the owner, but often, the relationship between the chef and owner turns sour.

When problems arose among the workers in his kitchen, Mr. Yook trusted his Korean Chinese manager to mediate because of his limited Chinese. This arrangement quickly went awry, however:

> Once, I told my manager to carry out a specific task. I found out later that what he actually did and what I asked him to do was totally

different . . . I found out that the manager told the chef things that were different from the original message that I had intended to relay to him . . . the manager just told the chef whatever he thought was best, as if it was his business to run. Later on, people working in the kitchen got so angry that they all quit their jobs.

Confused by the dramatic response from his workers, Mr. Yook hired a third-party translator to investigate why his staff had quit so suddenly. When he sat down with each of his workers, he realized that his manager had taken matters into his own hands, discerning for himself the best course of action. Frustrated by his apparent powerlessness, he implored:

How can you run a business when all your workers suddenly decide to quit? Do you know how difficult it is to hire and then train a new set of workers again? How cost effective would it be if something like this kept on happening every six months or so? You just can't run a business this way.

Mr. Yook's experiences help illustrate how in many ways power in the enclave was shaped not by money or social status, but by the breadth of one's cultural expertise. The power dynamics between a Korean Chinese manager and his South Korean boss, for instance, depended proportionally on how alienated or integrated the South Korean entrepreneur was with Chinese society. Recently arrived South Korean migrants who rarely left the cultural bubble of the enclave, like Mr. Yook, were more vulnerable to losing control of their businesses compared to migrants like Mr. Kang, who could at least understand Chinese even if he could not speak it fluently himself.

Both Mr. Yook and Mr. Kang struggled to come to terms with their newfound feelings of vulnerability in the PRC. Through their bouts of failure, the entrepreneurs were confronted with the stark reality that they were at the mercy of their Korean Chinese managers, despite asymmetrical power dynamics that initially placed them in positions of authority as owners of their businesses. Over time they realized that though they had the external appearances of power, control was actually in the hands of their Korean Chinese employees.

South Korean entrepreneurs were also quite vulnerable because of their unstable legal statuses. Because the Chinese state had not institutionalized a program granting long-term residence to foreigners, most South Korean owners of small or medium-sized businesses lived as short-term visitors, extending their tourist visas every year or so regardless of whether they had resided in China for just one year or over ten years. Subsequently, the South Koreans who experienced bankruptcy were highly susceptible to poverty. They had no rights to social welfare or public healthcare. They were barred from sending their children to Chinese public schools without paying a relatively high tuition. And many had become ineligible for welfare back home, as they had stopped paying taxes to the South Korean government.

Towards the end of our interview, Mr. Kang confessed that he felt afraid of starting another business in the enclave. He felt a general sense of powerlessness, not only in terms of controlling the fate of his business, but also in terms of securing a stable future for his family:

> Nowadays, I don't have access to the type of seed money nor do I feel the same type of ambition that I used to. I find myself dipping my toes in this and that, to test and see if I could make it [a new business] work if I decided to pick it up. After having experienced life in Chinese society for seven years, I realize just how difficult it is to run a business in this country . . . whether it be in terms of filing for taxes or figuring out how to follow various fiscal regulations, or hiring and managing personnel, the legal regulations are very strict.

Rumors of Korean Chinese Con Men

Along with difficulties in managing local workers, Mr. Kang noted that it was difficult to navigate China's legal system as a foreign entrepreneur. Chinese government policies were notoriously volatile despite the many improvements that had been made since market reforms. Property rights remained insecure and laws were constantly changing. As a result, businesses were often subject to unpublished regulations and the whim of the court. Moreover, entrepreneurs had to deal with the local, provincial, and central governments, which often had different and sometimes conflicting agendas. The inability to understand how this fickle and often arbitrary legal environment worked placed entrepreneurs at high risk.

In the case of South Korean entrepreneurs, because they often placed Korean Chinese managers in charge of administrative tasks, their managers had open access to confidential information about the companies they worked for, as well as direct lines of communication with influential bureaucrats. Among South Koreans in the enclave, rumors circulated that the downward mobility of the South Korean entrepreneurs was largely caused by Korean Chinese managers who took advantage of their employers' linguistic handicap to find minor loopholes or legal infractions that could be used as blackmail. Mr. Shim, a South Korean expat who had lived in Beijing for over ten years, told me that he had witnessed many naïve South Koreans fall victim to swindling Korean Chinese managers throughout his many years in China:

> There are people I know whose businesses have failed because of Korean Chinese minorities. When [my friend] just arrived from Korea, he obviously couldn't speak or understand Chinese . . . he needed someone who could communicate in Chinese, so he hired a Korean Chinese minority who could help him. But because my friend couldn't speak Chinese very well, it was easy for his Korean Chinese employee to relay misleading information to the Chinese bureaucrat [on his behalf]. And because the Korean Chinese worker also handled all of the accounting documents for his firm, it was easy for him to slip money for himself between the cracks . . . They [the Korean Chinese] are able to manipulate regulations to their advantage because they can speak Korean and Chinese fluently. Whether tax regulations, accounting regulations, business license requirements . . . they [the Korean Chinese] start prodding here and there [to see where their boss' weak spot is]. If it turns out that his boss was renting a space without a proper business permit, it is easy for the Korean Chinese manager to use that against his boss . . . So, even if the South Korean entrepreneur initially had been able to open up a store . . . once a report is filed [that he was illegally renting commercial property] it's all over. He [the entrepreneur] has to leave the space; he has to either leave or pay a fine of tens of thousands of Chinese yuan. When you are hit with unfortunate events like this and lose tens of thousands of yuan a few times, it's not long before you are left with nothing. How can you run a business under these circumstances?

Stories such as these pervaded everyday conversations among South Koreans in the enclave, reinforcing perceptions that Korean Chinese minorities were untrustworthy and blinded by money. I often heard similar rumors at the teahouse I frequented located in the heart of enclave, near the Wangjing New City apartments. Ms. Yong, a South Korean woman I met on one of my visits, replied that she had been brought to China by "fate." Prior to leaving Seoul, she had met a fortune teller who told her that she would experience hardship in China and return to South Korea in a couple of years.

After hemming and hawing over the particularities of her current living situation, Ms. Yong revealed that she had tried to open a small retail business with her husband in Wangjing. Within three years of moving to the enclave, their business failed and they had decided to pack their bags and move back to Seoul. Understandably, Ms. Yong hesitated in elaborating on the details of her experiences. At first, she cryptically commented that the Korean Chinese had "loftier goals" than the South Koreans, and that it was hard to compete with them. After some prying, Ms. Yong eventually explained that the Korean Chinese didn't show their true feelings to the South Koreans they worked with. "They might say one thing, but aim to accomplish something completely different—they will never fully disclose what their real intentions are," she said. "South Koreans, however, are more simple-minded [*dansun*] and sentimental [*jeongi manta*]."

Ms. Yong and her husband had worked closely with a Korean Chinese manager with whom they had felt an emotional bond and trust. She seemed to think that their manager, however, had concealed feelings of superiority over them. "While on the outside, he made it seem as if he liked us and felt emotionally close to us," she explained, "we found out later on that he had been waiting for the right time to lock us into a vulnerable position and take advantage of some minor legal infraction we had committed." She let out a heavy sigh and hung her head as she muttered under her breath how she regretted using her emotions to guide her interactions with her manager. She wished she had kept her distance from him instead.

South Koreans, who saw it as their duty to warn others from falling victim to unscrupulous Korean Chinese minorities in the enclave, made an intentional effort to share these cautionary tales with newcomers in the community. After a while, I started to ask why entrepreneurs would continue to hire Korean Chinese managers given their allegedly scheming ways. To these inquiries, I was told quite matter-of-factly that the South Koreans and Korean Chinese were inextricably linked by fate. The South Koreans could not survive in Beijing without the linguistic and cultural assistance that the Korean Chinese provided, and the Korean Chinese could not survive without the transnational capital and employment opportunities that the South Koreans brought to the enclave.

I had difficulty accepting the logic of this argument, however. If Korean Chinese workers were responsible for the downfall of most South

Korean businesses, why were South Korean entrepreneurs reluctant to hire young, bilingual South Koreans to work as managers in their stead? According to Mr. Kang, young South Koreans who recently graduated from college were not only too expensive to hire, but they were "too proud" to work under local Chinese workers. South Korean youth took for granted that by virtue of their ethnic and cultural backgrounds they would be hired into positions of authority, regardless of their age, prior job experience, or educational credentials. Moreover, Mr. Kang felt that South Korean youth added little value to the firm because they lacked the type of cultural insights necessary for troubleshooting problems the entrepreneurs encountered on a daily basis. Mr. Kang explained:

> The South Koreans I hired thought and approached things the same way I did, since you know, at the end of the day, we are all South Korean. And even though there are a lot of advantages to having these similarities, I found that the types of obstacles that my South Korean employees faced in trying to make things happen in the for-eign environment of China were the same types of obstacles that I faced as their boss and as an entrepreneur. We ended up facing the same types of obstacles, so I thought to myself, "I'm paying this guy so much to work for me . . . wouldn't it make more sense to just let him go and hire even just three or four more Korean Chinese employees in his place?"

Because Korean Chinese managers played such a vital role in en-clave firms, South Korean entrepreneurs who sought to grow businesses in Wangjing had little choice but to work alongside them. But because of the rampant feelings of distrust between the two groups, even well-meaning South Koreans such as Mr. Kang were cautious of their Korean Chinese managers. They learned from the mistakes of their peers by withholding internal documents from their managers and refrained from sharing details about the problems they faced.

The Korean Chinese, for their part, sensing these feelings of sus-picion and distrust, often responded in kind by also distancing them-selves from their employers. Thus, while it was difficult to ascertain the extent to which Korean Chinese con men were culpable for the losses of South Korean entrepreneurs, the rumors were significant in that they shaped mutual perceptions, and in turn behavior. Suspicion caused the South Koreans to expend significant energy in keeping their managers in check rather than collaborating with them. And it also caused Korean

Chinese workers to keep their South Korean employers at arm's-length, preventing them from fully investing in the companies they worked for.

Guanxi and Gatekeepers

Mr. Lee was one of the few South Koreans I met who had been able to amass wealth as an entrepreneur in Wangjing. His experiences highlight the sheer value cultural capital had in sustaining a thriving enclave business. The day we met for our interview, Mr. Lee was dressed in a white button-down and slacks. He carried himself with an air of formality and seriousness, and periodically glanced at his wristwatch, as if to signal that he was taking time out of his busy schedule to speak with me. When we sat down at his desk, he opened his black leather notebook and laid a silver pen down on top of a blank page (to presumably take notes).

At the time of our interview, Mr. Lee had sustained his firm for over eight years. His company had started out as a small-scale real estate agency catering to South Korean migrants in the enclave, but within a few years, the company business had expanded to include large-scale import-export services, as well as a travel agency. The day I visited his office to conduct the interview, I saw his company logo on the doors of four different office spaces that when combined, spanned across the entire floor of a large commercial building. When I mentioned how impressed I was at the size of his company, Mr. Lee casually mentioned that he owned several additional office spaces in other buildings as well.

Like Mr. Kang, Mr. Lee had relied on support from his personal networks in South Korea to secure seed money for his business:

> I used some savings that I had stored up over the years, and the rest, I asked my friends in Korea. Even though I am out here [in Beijing], I still keep in touch with my friends back home and I told them about a business I wanted to start and asked if they wanted to be investors. Most of my friends are working for large companies in Seoul and they have comfortable lifestyles. And then, as my business started growing in size and scale, I was able to gain the interest of other investors [in South Korea].

When I asked him if it had been difficult to acquire such a large sum of money, he responded:

> Fundamentally, I believe that everything starts with trust, the type of trust that you are able to build when you form relationships with

other people. At that point, I had already built a strong foundation of trust with my friends [in Seoul], so gaining access to funds was not a problem. I also wasn't asking for an exorbitant amount of money either . . . about 10,000 USD or under? I asked several friends for about 10,000 USD each and was able to gather several tens of thousands of dollars. I didn't need much money. At that time, the currency exchange rate with China was favorable enough that you didn't need so much to start a company.

While his peers struggled to navigate the local bureaucracy, Mr. Lee was successful in avoiding the same pitfalls. He gave me an example of how such a situation might unravel:

Let's say that you need to have five fire extinguishers according to stipulations of the Fire Department. But we only have four. That's breaking the law, right? But let's say that the inspector who comes to visit our office is someone I know. He might let it just slide. He'll probably say, "Hey, you're missing one. Ah well. No big deal." And then, he'll just leave . . . But let's say I don't have a relationship with that person. He'll say, "You don't pass the requirements. Pay this failed inspection fine."

On the surface, Mr. Lee's anecdote resonated with widespread perceptions—both among academics and in business circles—that *guanxi* [social connections] with local officials was critical to running a successful company in China. Barriers in understanding how to navigate the unpredictable—and often arbitrary—legal environment in the PRC placed entrepreneurs at high risk. Mr. Lee confirmed my impression that local bureaucrats held considerable power as gatekeepers of local businesses in China:

Let's say that you felt that you were unjustly fined and tried to file a lawsuit complaining about your case. You could be waiting forever to get a chance to fight the case in court . . . the same government division that reviews lawsuits also happens to be the same division that files inspection reports. And so what happens is that they keep on pushing your case further and further back. So even if you were supposed to appear in court to fight your case a month later, you might find out that your documents are pushed back another six months. That means that your store will be closed for another six months, and since you stopped running your business, you're losing money during this time and it's not like we have unlimited funds, right? So you end up waiting six months, then a year, and so on, and you're still waiting for your court date. You might not have done anything wrong according to the law, but after having lost so much time and money waiting for a court date, your business approaches bankruptcy.

In light of these trends, many China scholars have gone so far as to claim that *guanxi* is the primary determinant for entrepreneurial success in China (Gold, Guthrie, and Wank 2002; Krug and Mehta 2001). For instance, Hsing (2003), in her study of Taiwanese investors in mainland China, argues that cultural affinities and strong coalitions with local officials were part and parcel to their success. And along these lines, her ethnography details how the nuanced Chinese cultural customs of holding banquets and gift exchange helped Taiwanese entrepreneurs curry favor with bureaucrats.

Studies such as these depict *guanxi* as deeply rooted in the Chinese cultural way of life (Yang 1994). For some scholars such as Lucian Pye (1986), *guanxi* cannot be simply reduced to Western notions of social capital or social networks. Pye argues that the Chinese view "society as a web of human relationships and associations" and as a result, have a cultural tendency to rely on social ties as a means to an end (173–174). Hwang (1987) similarly highlights how *guanxi* encompasses a cluster of indigenous concepts such as *bao* [reciprocity], *renqing* [empathy], and *mianzi* [face or dignity], distinguishing *guanxi* from Western notions of social capital. *Guanxi* practice must be convincingly imbued with a culturally intricate set of rituals encompassing *ganqing* [loosely translated as emotion] in order to be fully effective (Gold, Guthrie, and Wank 2002).

While few would go so far as to make the essentialist argument that *guanxi* is exclusive to the Chinese, China experts have nonetheless overwhelmingly emphasized the importance of local gatekeepers in securing entrepreneurial success. How, then, was Mr. Lee able to overcome these obstacles? In some respects, I found that Mr. Lee was able to succeed as an entrepreneur because he was somewhat integrated into Han Chinese society. By experiencing life outside the enclave in his youth, he, unlike his South Korean peers, understood how to establish rapport with local Chinese. Mr. Lee described himself as a young man from a privileged family who was at a loss as to what to do with his life. Upon graduating college in Seoul, he dabbled in graduate school, but continued to wrestle with feelings of restlessness even after obtaining his master's degree. In 1999, he ventured to Beijing and enrolled in a six-month language program hoping to find a better sense of direction in life.

Mr. Lee's emotional state can be better understood within the broader context of economic recession in South Korea following the Asian financial crisis in 1997. He was part of a larger generation of South Korean youth who fled overseas in an effort to escape mass lay-offs and declining employment opportunities in their home country. While Mr. Lee had been able to secure a degree from an elite university in Seoul, many who migrated to Beijing in the late 1990s did so after failing to find a job or gain entrance into their university of choice.

As others drowned their sorrows in alcohol, Mr. Lee backpacked around China with his girlfriend for a few years after his language program ended. "I went to about every major city in China," he boasted. To my surprise, Mr. Lee became uncharacteristically more animated as he spoke about his experiences traversing the remote corners of the country. "I spent a lot of time in Tibet and Xinjiang. I started near the border between China and Kazakhstan and traveled all the way down towards the border between China and India. I didn't travel on a short-term basis, either. I stayed in each of the cities I visited for one or two months at a time."

Mr. Lee explained that he wanted to write a travel guide to intro-duce South Koreans to what life was like in different parts of China. All of the travel guides available in Korean back then had been trans-lated from Japanese. He wanted to write a book from the perspective of a South Korean, uncovering the lives of Chinese people from lesser known regions—areas of the countryside where Koreans had never dared to venture before. To write this travel guide, he and his girlfriend backpacked across the country, and took pictures as well as meticulous notes of the places they visited and the people they met.

Although they ultimately did not publish their book, the trip was a formative one. By the time he returned, he had fallen in love with the coun-try he had traversed, as well as the woman who had accompanied him on his journey. In the months immediately following their trip, he decided to remain in Beijing, eager to deepen his understanding of the Chinese, and lived with an elderly Chinese couple in a homestay arrangement:

> I didn't see the point in hanging out with other South Korean col-lege students in Beijing. I guess you could say that I was with Han Chinese people around the clock, twenty-four hours a day. I didn't do anything in particular, though . . .When my homestay father went out to play mahjong with his friends at the park, I would tag along with him. When my homestay mother went to the market to buy groceries, I would accompany her.

Unlike many of the other South Korean entrepreneurs I interviewed, Mr. Lee was never interested in merely learning Mandarin as a means to an end. Instead, Mr. Lee claimed that he was driven by a desire to connect with locals and form relationships with them. Granted, as a man in his late twenties at the time, Mr. Lee was not in the desperate situation of running a business in a foreign country to support a family. He lived off financial support from his wealthy parents in Seoul, and free from the immediate pressure of having to secure a job, he had the luxury of learning a language solely to satisfy a growing curiosity. When he was not spending time with his homestay parents, he was conversing with the private tutors he hired. He stressed how he had expressly asked his Chinese tutors to teach him how to speak like a local.

"There are people who can read all sorts of books and understand what's written in the newspapers, but if you ask him to carry a simple conversation with a local, he has no idea how. If you ask him to go out and listen to what a local is saying, he can't tell you what that person is saying," he told me as he discretely alluded to the problems that the South Korean entrepreneurs often complained about. Mr. Lee emphasized that he rarely used textbooks with his tutors, but he asked them to bring newspaper clippings every day to provide fodder for discussion instead.

Over the four years that Mr. Lee spent traveling around China and living with his Han Chinese homestay parents, he was able to acquire a comfort in engaging with locals that was rare for South Koreans in the enclave. He had not been aware at the time that the leisurely afternoons spent playing mahjong with his Chinese homestay father and strolling the markets with his Chinese homestay mother would come to his aid later in life. But I noticed how he exuded confidence when he interacted with his Korean Chinese workers. It was clear from the way he handled clients who dropped by his office during our interview, and the way he delegated tasks to his employees, that Mr. Lee was the central authority figure in the room.

Mr. Lee revealed that oftentimes, when they encountered some type of legal issue, he would send one of his Korean Chinese workers to go and negotiate with the local official. "It's not something that I can do all on my own," he said. Given the scale of his business, he had to rely on his workers to maintain harmonious ties with key bureaucrats on his behalf. But because he was able to communicate directly with the bureaucrats when necessary, Mr. Lee was not paralyzed with fears of possibly falling vulnerable to ill-willed Korean Chinese middlemen.

That Mr. Lee was able to successfully navigate the Chinese bureaucracy through his employees shed light on the scope of influence
that *guanxi* played in entrepreneurship. Was Mr. Lee able to sustain his
business for so long because of his ability to mobilize *guanxi* with local
bureaucrats? Or was it because he was able to effectively manage his
Korean Chinese workers—a feat that other South Korean entrepreneurs
struggled to achieve? If we presume that *guanxi* can be mobilized in-
directly, how critical was it for foreign investors to master this set of
culturally nuanced rituals in order to succeed as an entrepreneur in
Beijing?

While China scholars are wont to emphasize the singular importance of *guanxi* in sustaining businesses in the PRC, to tie Mr. Lee's success exclusively to his access to *guanxi* would overlook the many other
factors that have abetted the growth of his businesses. I was more con-
vinced by the notion that Mr. Lee's success as a transnational entrepreneur hinged on his ability to reap the benefits of both South Korean and
Chinese societies. He had access to both the financial and social capital
of his home country, South Korea, as well as the abundant supply of
cheap local labor in China. His linguistic and cultural expertise allowed
him to cultivate healthy relationships not only with powerful bureaucrats in China but also his local staff, his South Korean clientele, and his
South Korean investors.

By the same token, the downward mobility of the South Koreans
cannot be explained solely by their lack of *guanxi*. Rather, broader
cultural barriers South Korean entrepreneurs typically faced impeded
them from gaining access to a host of important resources. For instance,
by secluding themselves within the enclave, South Koreans also blocked
themselves from gaining access to important channels of information.
Many of the South Korean entrepreneurs I interviewed struggled to
keep up with surmounting fines from failed inspections not because
they failed to host the right types of banquets, but because they were unaware of what laws pertained to their businesses and what licenses they
were required to apply for. As Mr. Lee noted, although *guanxi* could be
used to smooth over friction with local bureaucrats, "you still need to
understand how to follow certain laws while reacting flexibly to others."

Ms. Chung, a Korean Chinese manager who worked at an advertising agency in the enclave, found that many of the competing South
Korean firms in her neighborhood disappeared within a few years of
opening due to fines incurred by failed inspections. Her firm did not

have that problem, as her Korean Chinese boss was meticulous about following local regulations:

> There are inspections [twice a year], but we don't run into major problems when we go under inspection because we follow all the laws and regulations carefully. We've been running this business for over thirteen years now . . . Among South Korean advertising agencies, however, all but a few don't publicize their addresses and contact information. They hide their information. Do you know why? They move around a lot. One day they are located here, and the next, it's somewhere else. It's because they are trying to run away from the government. They don't want to get inspected.

Later, I learned that Ms. Chung's employer had initially started off working for a South Korean entrepreneur in 1993. He took over his boss's company a few years later.

Cultural Brokerage and Transnational Entrepreneurship

While the peripheral positionality of the Korean Chinese minorities often exposed them to both economic and social disadvantages in the enclave, this structural position allowed them to reap immense rewards as transnational entrepreneurs. As ethnic minorities on the margins of two disparate worlds, Korean Chinese entrepreneurs were able to capitalize on their roles as cultural brokers, bridging "structural holes"—or gaps in social networks—separating different groups from contact (Burt 2009). Studies on social networks have long demonstrated how brokers are able to wield considerable power "in situations where the levels or groups they mediate between are separated or segmented by barriers of culture, language, distance or mistrust" (Gould 1989: 54). By mediating between two groups who were otherwise not connected, Korean Chinese intermediaries were able to benefit from 1) access to diverse, non-redundant sources of information and resources; 2) control over information and resources that flow between the disconnected parties; and 3) the ability to play one party off against the other to secure their position or accrue greater benefits from their role (Brass 2009). In analyzing social interactions in the enclave, the concept of cultural brokerage—brokering ties between two groups of people divided by cultural and linguistic barriers—can help illuminate why and how Korean Chinese entrepreneurs were in a uniquely advantageous position to mobilize transnational resources for upward mobility.

As I have alluded to earlier, the expats represented a privileged class within the enclave. Paid extravagant salaries commensurate to upper middle class standards of living in South Korea, the expats continuously injected transnational capital in the form of their foreign earned incomes into the enclave economy by spending lavishly on Korean cultural goods and services. Considering the rampant distrust between the South Koreans and Korean Chinese in Beijing, I thought that the South Korean entrepreneurs would enjoy a distinct advantage in luring expats. After all, South Korean entrepreneurs grew up in the same cultural environment as the expats and were presumably better equipped to appeal to the more sophisticated palates of their customers. I was surprised, however, to find that Korean Chinese-owned shops by and large fared better in attracting more expat clients than their South Korean counterparts.

This is not to deny the fact that the South Koreans benefited from their access to Korean cultural capital as recent arrivals. For instance, South Korean-run restaurants were particularly sought after by expats because they provided the right type of ambience, service, and cuisine. During dinner with two South Korean friends at a Korean restaurant in the enclave, for instance, my friends noticed right away that the owner was Korean Chinese. They pointed to the subtle, yet important differences in the flavor of the *kimchee* that arrived with our entrees:

FRIEND 1: If you taste the *kimchee*, you can tell right away. You
    can, right?
ME: Why? What kind of taste is it? How is it different?
FRIEND 1: How is it different? Hmmm . . . [South Korean
    kimchee] doesn't taste as sour or old. See if you look at
    this *kimchee*, there's a lot of dried red pepper flakes and it's
    bright red, but you can't really taste the ingredients [even
    though you can see that they are there].
FRIEND 2: South Korean *kimchee* tastes fresh even when it's old.
FRIEND 1: Yeah. There's a lot of flavor in the sauce and it's
    crunchy.
FRIEND 2: The way people here make *kimchee*, they use cheap
    ingredients so it tastes old and rotten even if they just made it.
FRIEND 1: I wonder if it's because they don't use expensive ingredients. I think that the way they [Korean Chinese] make
    it is just different.

It was common for South Korean consumers in the enclave to differentiate South Korean restaurants and bars from Korean Chinese ones. From the subtle flavors of the food to the nuanced differences in décor, South Korean establishments were perceived as more authentically Korean and higher quality than Korean Chinese ones.

But while certain service industries such as the restaurant business or clothing boutiques were more influenced by subtle differences between South Korean and Korean Chinese styles, South Korean consumers often preferred Korean Chinese-owned businesses for "middleman" services (Bonacich 1973) such as real estate agencies, language schools, clinics, law offices, travel agencies, and advertisement agencies. South Korean expats sought services that would help buffer the social costs of migration precisely because they planned on returning to their home countries within a few years. They were thus drawn to life in the enclave because it sheltered them from the inconveniences of having to adjust to a new foreign environment. As a result, even though Korean Chinese-owned establishments at times did not perfectly satisfy expats' nuanced cultural preferences, the Korean Chinese were perceived as more effective in providing niche services that bridged the gap South Koreans faced in Chinese society.

Ms. Choi, a South Korean expat who moved to Beijing to work for Korea Telecom (KT), explained that it was customary for expats like herself depend on Korean Chinese intermediaries who could help them settle into their new lives in the enclave:

> One of my coworkers introduced me to her brother-in-law's friend
> . . . He told me that he had used this particular [Korean Chinese real
> estate] broker when he arrived [in Wangjing]. Because I had no way of
> comparing prices at the time, I was just grateful that they were warm
> and provided me with good service.

As in the case of Ms. Choi, expats were often intimidated by the prospect of living in Beijing and sought to remain in the enclave where they had access to a variety of services that catered to their specific needs. Ms. Choi commented that she felt more comfortable hiring a Korean Chinese real estate agent over a South Korean, who presumably faced the same set of linguistic and cultural barriers in China as she did.

Moreover, South Korean expats were happy to pay a premium for Korean Chinese agents because they were known for going beyond the call of duty to help their South Korean customers feel at home.

Ms. Choi's real estate agent, for instance, not only helped her find a new living space in the right neighborhood with the right set of facilities, but he also understood that she felt scared about the prospect of living in a place so foreign. She noticed that her real estate agent did everything he could to assuage any feelings of uncertainty and anxiety she had:

> They helped me move all my belongings, they helped me contact the local police office [to apply for alien registration], if I think about it now, I feel like they helped me in ways that went beyond what they were required or obligated to do. For instance, even when I went to the supermarket, I had no idea how to find the things I was looking for. And since I'm unfamiliar [with the transportation system], I would take the wrong buses and even if I took a taxi, I didn't know how to describe where I wanted to go. So they would solve all of my problems for me. They would tell me that in order to buy this and that, I would need to go to such and such a market, and then, they would actually take a cab with me and personally take me to the market. Then, they would wait for me outside while I shopped and help me carry my shopping bags back to my new apartment. They told me that the standard rate for "black cars" [illegal cabs] was 10 RMB (1.50 USD) if I wanted to travel within Wangjing so I wouldn't get ripped off by the cab drivers, and so on. They would help me get acquainted with this type of common knowledge—information that everyone knows. And so, I was really grateful for how kind they were to me.

The emotional labor of these middleman services was an integral part of their businesses. Part of the reason why Korean Chinese venues were so popular was because they provided their expat patrons with the feeling that they were living in a home away from home.

In addition to real estate agencies, the Korean Chinese dominated the *minbak* market as well. Like many South Korean sojourners who were planning to relocate to Beijing, I stayed at a *minbak*—a Korean bed-and-breakfast—during my first few weeks in Wangjing (see Figure 6.2). When I first moved to Beijing to conduct fieldwork, my uncle, who was himself a South Korean entrepreneur, advised me to stay at one in order to familiarize myself with my surroundings and introduced me to several blogs that featured different *minbak* in Wangjing.

As a Korean American unfamiliar with the concept of *minbak*, I found the experience of staying in the home of a stranger unnerving. When I arrived at the place I was to stay at for the night, I had to check the address that I had printed out several times before I was able

FIGURE **6.2** A sign for *minbak* (short-term lodging) in Korean in the middle of the Wangjing New City apartments.
Photo courtesy of the author.

to muster up the courage to knock on the door of what appeared to be an ordinary residential unit inside the Wangjing New City apartment complex. I almost turned to leave upon ringing the doorbell, when a middle-aged Korean Chinese woman greeted me at the door. Behind her, I saw an older Korean man lounging on a sofa inside the living room, watching a South Korean game show on TV. The scene so closely resembled that of a private home that for a second I panicked, wondering if I should go inside or just stay at the Holiday Inn Express nearby. My host grabbed my suitcases and ushered me inside her home. She led to me to a modestly furnished bedroom that had two twin-sized beds on each side of the room. As she rolled my suitcase to the side of one of the beds, she handed me a clean towel and told me to wash up.

When I walked inside the bathroom to take a shower, I was surprised to find the shampoo, conditioner, bars of soap, extra towels, and bathroom slippers laid out in ways that reminded me of the homes of my extended family in Seoul. The products were all familiar South Korean brands that were most likely purchased at one of the Korean grocery stores in the enclave. Compared to the chaotic environment outside where everything seemed so unfamiliar, the *minbak* put me at ease.

After finishing my shower, I walked into the living room to see that my host had prepared a traditional Korean meal for me on the dinner table. She wrote out the names of the subway stops phonetically in Korean letters on a map of the Chinese metro system and showed me where the best tasting Korean restaurants and largest Korean grocery stores were located as I ate the warm meal prepared before me. After I finished my meal, she went with me to buy and set up a mobile phone, and introduced me to her friend, a Korean Chinese entrepreneur who ran a real estate agency on the bottom floor of the apartment complex.

South Korean businessmen like my uncle perceived *minbak* as an important means of gaining insider information on what life was like in Wangjing. Ms. Kwon, a South Korean woman who served as a pianist at the church I attended, told me of how she and her husband were introduced to First Presbyterian through a *minbak* owner. Prior to moving to Beijing, her husband stayed at a Korean Chinese-run *minbak* in Wangjing for six months to secure a place to live. She said:

> The company where he worked was located in Koreatown, so we knew that we wanted to live in the vicinity. During his stay at the *minbak*, he was able to . . . find out where we would send our children if we were to live here. We found out that our children would not be able to attend other Chinese public schools [outside of Wangjing] because of their South Korean nationality. Fortunately, the public schools in the enclave accept South Korean children if you pay a certain fee. So in the end, that's why we decided to live here in Wangjing because it was near my husband's work and the schools our children would attend.

The Korean Chinese also dominated Korean media outlets in the enclave. The most popular ethnic media consisted of monthly magazines that contained advertisements and an expansive telephone directory of local Korean businesses in the enclave. In Wangjing, three companies— Kyung Han Advertising, Han Wool Tari ["under one umbrella"], and KOREAN—commanded the widest circulation of readers. All three of these magazines were owned by Korean Chinese entrepreneurs, who catered to a predominantly South Korean readership. According to a Korean Chinese managing director at one of these firms:

> We have more South Korean clients [than Korean Chinese or Han Chinese]. Mainly because South Koreans come here from a foreign

country. In South Korea, they are used to being exposed to advertisements in magazines like these. They have this mentality that if you want to operate a business, you have to advertise first. That type of mind-set is already well-established. But when we first started our business, there were no media outlets or magazines that could produce these advertisements.

The Korean Chinese CEO was able to capitalize on this unfulfilled demand in the enclave because he was aware that South Koreans were accustomed to advertising through local magazines in Seoul. He was also cognizant of the needs of South Korean readers, who could benefit from a monthly magazine that connected them to middleman services and products. The manager said that the magazine showcased information that would be simple to read, but useful to South Korean migrants in Beijing:

> We publish articles that recommend good restaurants, where you can order takeout, which hotels are best to stay at during which season . . . Also, we give information on different schools in the area. A lot of [South Korean] people worry about which schools to send their children . . . Or, we show our readers how to take the subway, if, for instance, you want to go to the airport, if you should go to Terminal 1 or Terminal 2.

I came across new issues of these monthly magazines at a vast array of venues in the enclave, including South Korean churches, restaurants, real estate agencies, and business offices. Within the South Korean community the magazines represented an important resource, a kind of survival guide to living in Beijing. The telephone directories were regularly consulted in finding translation services, places to eat, and hotels to book.

A Cultural Ambassador

I return now to the story of Ms. Chang, the Korean Chinese single mother I introduced at the beginning of this chapter. Her experiences show how in spite of her limited material resources, her knowledge of the inner workings of both South Korean and Han Chinese societies served as a powerful asset when building her business in the enclave.

Perhaps in understanding the key to her success, it is important to first understand that Ms. Chang's small boutique sold not only trendy clothes imported from South Korea, but also the cultural experience of South Korea's fashionable image to people in the enclave. When I walked into Ms. Chang's stores, my eyes were immediately drawn to the magazine cutouts of South Korean celebrities who were wearing clothes similar to the ones hanging on the racks. In the background, Ms. Chang's iPhone played tracks from the latest South Korean soap operas, and even Ms. Chang herself looked like one of the South Korean celebrities that hung on the walls of her store. She was an attractive woman to begin with: slender, doe-eyed, with a pale complexion. But perhaps more noteworthy about her appearance was how distinctly South Korean she looked, from her hairstyle to her clothes to the style of her makeup.

Ms. Chang made a concerted effort to keep up with the latest South Korean fashion trends. She watched the South Korean news and the hottest South Korean television shows over the internet. When the shop was empty we often watched these shows together on her laptop, and she would point out to me which actresses were popular and would ask me what I thought about their outfits. From the many hours of South Korean TV she consumed, Ms. Chang knew which celebrity couples had recently gotten married, which colloquial expressions had become popular, and which K-Pop groups were trending. She knew the plotlines of all the major South Korean soap operas and could discuss the pros and cons of why so-and-so should not run off and marry so-and-so in striking detail. When South Korean customers came into her store, I watched Ms. Chang make references to celebrity gossip and discuss the latest plot developments in the hottest shows. On other days, Ms. Chang and I flipped through one of the many South Korean fashion magazines that lay around her store. I watched her flag outfits that some of the models wore and make note of what types of clothes to buy at Dongdaemun on her next business trip to Seoul, and how to dress the mannequins in the display window.

Every two weeks Ms. Chang flew to Seoul to pick out a new shipment of clothes from the garment district, where she had worked over a decade ago. I accompanied her on one of her business trips, and as we sat inside a Starbucks sipping our lattes, she expressed how comfortable and familiar the surroundings felt:

> I've been working with the same vendors [in Dongdaemun] for several years now. They know when to expect me and what kind of

clothes I like to sell at my store, so by the time I go visit them, they've already picked out a few things for me. They give me a better price than they do for other shop owners because I've been working with them for so many years now.

When Ms. Chang bantered in Korean with her vendors, she spoke "standardized" Korean. The vendors playfully called her "older sister," pulling out a chair and a can of ice coffee from one of the vending machines nearby. I found it hard to imagine how a Han Chinese person, even after many years of Korean-language training, could mimic the light-hearted chatter she engaged in.

"This shirt has been selling like hot-cakes. You know, it's just like the one that X wore in that movie that just came out. Have you seen it?" A vendor dug up a T-shirt with a printed flower design on the front. "I think she wore it with a skirt that looked like this one." The vendor rushed behind the curtains separating her stock from the next stall and pulled out a blue skirt with buttons down the front. Ms. Chang asked if the skirt came in different colors. A new shipment was scheduled to arrive in two weeks, but Ms. Chang was scheduled to be back in Beijing by then. The vendor offered to mail a package over to her store in China if she paid up front, so Ms. Chang bought several skirts, two shirts, some matching cardigans in different colors, and a few scarves. As she picked out the scarves, she looked over to me and remarked how she didn't think her South Korean clients would like the scarves, but that her Han Chinese clients would.

Every time she came back from a business trip, Ms. Chang sent out fifty or so text messages to her regular customers, letting them know a new shipment of clothing had arrived from Seoul. She kept a running log of how much each client spent and where they lived. Many of her regulars were Han Chinese women who had frequented her store for many years. Some were young Korean Chinese hostess bar workers who were dating older South Korean men who gave them generous spending allowances. Others consisted of middle class South Korean women who lived in Wangjing. To the Han Chinese women in particular, Ms. Chang represented a type of cultural ambassador who introduced them to the elusive world of South Korean fashion. They all seemed to want to look like her, and asked for advice on what was popular in Seoul, and how to pair certain accessories with different articles of clothing.

On slow days, Ms. Chang visited nearby shops on her floor to chat with the other shopkeepers. They all looked to her for advice. Her shop had been there the longest and was recognized as one of the more successful ones on the floor. When Ms. Chang passed by their stores on her way to the bathroom, which was located on the opposite end of the floor, they would all greet her and strike up a short conversation, asking how her daughter was doing, or complaining about how business had been slow. Sometimes, she would step into their stores for a few minutes to give them pointers on how to dress their mannequins or how to better streamline their clothing racks by style and color. She effortlessly transitioned from fluent Mandarin to impeccable Korean, depending on whom she spoke to.

Toward the end of my stay in Beijing, Ms. Chang had put up signs on her front door that she was looking to hire. The Han Chinese woman who had worked with her for the past two years was planning to go back to her hometown in the countryside because her mother had grown ill. Ms. Chang told me that she wanted to hire a fashionable Korean Chinese woman this time around. After having spent several months with her at her store, I could understand why.

From my experiences interacting with the sales staff in the nearby shops, I saw how the Korean Chinese approached different clients according to their cultural and ethnic background. When I walked inside their store they would look me up and down, and know from my appearance that I was not Korean Chinese or Han Chinese. Even if I initially spoke to them in Mandarin, they would respond to me in standardized Korean. Some would offer me a cup of instant coffee imported from Seoul, affectionately calling me "older sister," as they showed me their recently arrived stock of clothes from Dongdaemun. Their demeanor changed almost instantaneously when a Han Chinese woman walked into their store. They haggled more aggressively—without batting an eyelash they would explain how they had received the garment the customer wanted from Seoul just the night before, that no other store in the vicinity had anything like it, so if they didn't want to buy it then they could just go ahead and leave.

The Double-Edged Sword of Transnational Enclaves

For the South Koreans, the enclave economy acted as both a blessing and a curse. On the one hand, the Korean enclave provided them with privileged access to transnational resources and a lucrative niche market for Korean goods and services. On the other hand, the enclave also isolated the South Koreans from Chinese society, perpetuating their dependence on Korean Chinese intermediaries to conduct their businesses. In contrast to their Korean Chinese counterparts, for the South Koreans, the linguistic and cultural barriers they faced limited their ability to gain access to information on legal regulations, manage and control their workers, and form harmonious relationships with local officials.

Many of the South Korean entrepreneurs I interviewed did not mention the importance of specific Chinese cultural practices such as the exchange of gifts when speaking of their relationships with local bureaucrats. It is particularly noteworthy that the few South Korean entrepreneurs who were fluent in Chinese and had many Han Chinese friends were able to successfully manage institutional uncertainty by forming good relationships with local officials. I argue that what was more important to entrepreneurial success was not necessarily *guanxi*, but rather the ability to broadly establish rapport with culturally diverse groups of people—including not only Chinese locals but also foreign consumers like the South Korean expats.

By continuing to emphasize the impact of *guanxi*, there is a tendency in the field to implicitly project an image of local bureaucrats as having a near monopoly on resources and power in postreform China. While local bureaucrats do continue to hold considerable power, it is important to appreciate the alternative ways in which Korean Chinese rural migrants have used their cultural and linguistic skills as cultural brokers to mobilize resources in both the host society and their country of ancestry to carve out an alternative pathway to upward mobility.

In this chapter, I demonstrated how cultural brokers flourish not in large, well-established corporations but rather in entrepreneurial settings where the size and scale of the business is small enough for workers to handle a more broad and flexible range of roles. As managers of small South Korean businesses in the enclave, Korean Chinese workers often acted as their bosses' right-hand men. They were entrusted with translating highly sensitive business transactions with Han Chinese bureaucrats. They had privileged access to the writing and signing of important legal contracts. They controlled day-to-day operations by supervising Han Chinese workers who did not understand Korean and could only communicate with their employer through their Korean Chinese managers. Their South Korean supervisors consulted with them when making important business decisions that affected the future viability of the firm. Because these various transactions were all mediated through one or two Korean Chinese managers, these managers often held more decision-making power and control over the company than even their South Korean employers.

Moreover, as entrepreneurs, the Korean Chinese were able to utilize their position as cultural brokers to access a wider range of resources in both South Korean and Han Chinese societies for their collective benefit. As we saw in chapter 5 with the church, Korean Chinese minorities who had experience working in South Korea advised their friends on how to manage their South Korean clientele and how to mobilize critical resources in South Korea. Others who worked in the low-wage market provided important contacts to Han Chinese workers who would provide high-quality labor for a competitive price. College-educated and politically connected Korean Chinese elites shared their insights on how to establish rapport with Han Chinese bureaucrats. Through this sharing of know-how, the Korean Chinese entrepreneurs were able to dominate middleman industries that catered to wealthy South Korean expats who were willing to pay a premium for services that buffered cultural and linguistic barriers from the local society.

CHAPTER 7

The Lost Youth

While most South Korean students in Beijing lived near Wudaokou, a neighborhood known for its concentration of colleges and universities, many, like Jay, attended church in the enclave. Jay always seemed to be at church when I called him on the phone. When I asked him how many hours a week he spent at Antioch, he had a hard time coming up with a figure—he spent over ten hours there on Saturdays and Sundays alone, and in addition to his weekend duties, he also led a Bible study for college students, was involved in the church outreach program, and attended daybreak prayer meetings a few times a week. Jay explained that he felt that his faith gave his life a sense of purpose:

> I felt directionless when I first came to Beijing. All of my friends felt similarly depressed and lost. Many of them came to Beijing because they didn't get into the college they wanted. We know that we are just going to go back to Seoul after we graduate, so we would just go to clubs and karaoke salons in Wangjing and get wasted drunk several times a week . . . The adult entertainment industry here is really [hesitates] developed, and the culture among Korean students here [pauses] . . . it's the norm to get drunk several times a week. But after about three years of partying like crazy, I started feeling more empty and depressed. I kept on wondering if this was it and what the point was. A lot of my friends had gone back to Korea, so maybe I was feeling lonely. I don't know. Once you feel like you get close to someone, they leave and go back. It's hard to build deep relationships here.

I started to seek out a deeper meaning to my life by going to church. Going to church fulfills me in a way drinking doesn't.

Every time Jay went back to visit his family in Seoul, he heard his friends tell depressing stories of joblessness. Raised by middle class parents, Jay had grown used to a certain standard of living—he liked nice clothes, fancy cars, and modern living spaces. But this standard of living has increasingly become out of reach for him. In Beijing, Jay relied on his parents for financial support. Of the 170 South Korean college students who participated in my study, 60 percent received more than 10,000 RMB (1,500 USD) from their parents in South Korea each month to cover their living expenses. This figure was roughly the same as the average monthly salary of South Korean entrepreneurs and nearly double that of most Korean Chinese college-educated workers.

Middle Class Precariousness

When the South Korean won dropped in value relative to the Chinese yuan after the 2008 Beijing Olympics, many South Korean college students started to search for part-time jobs to support themselves. Students whose parents were struggling financially ended up going back to Seoul without finishing their degrees. Those who stayed behind felt that they had somehow missed the boat in South Korea, where so much of one's self-worth was defined by educational pedigree. Jay was afraid that a degree from Peking University would not get him far in the South Korean labor market. And in fact, he knew that even *chaebol* firms in Beijing gave lower salaries to South Koreans who had graduated from local universities, in spite of their fluency in Mandarin and considerable cultural know-how.

Afraid to face reality back home, Jay stayed in Beijing even though he had no intentions of living permanently in China. Like many of the South Korean grassroots migrants I wrote about earlier, because Jay was perpetually preparing to return to Seoul, he was reluctant to invest himself deeply in relationships in Beijing. It was hard to chastise Jay for his behavior, though. As he mentioned, people were always moving in and out of his life and he had learned to keep people at a distance, no matter how well they got along. By the time I met Jay in 2010, he had lived in this limbo state—too afraid to return and too afraid to stay—for more than ten years.

Older members of the congregation at Antioch believed that South Korean youth in Beijing lacked the emotional tenacity and drive to figure out what they wanted to do with their lives. The youth were perceived as wallowing in self-pity and drowning their sorrows in reckless partying. I often heard them yelling late at night on the streets picking fights with random strangers or harassing women passing by—behavior that irritated middle class Han Chinese residents in the enclave, who stereotyped South Korean youth as arrogant, good-for-nothing drunks.

Global fiscal crises and labor market deregulation have triggered serious levels of youth unemployment not only in South Korea, but also the OECD more broadly (Choudhry, Marelli, and Signorelli 2012). The sharp decline in the demand for labor following the Lehman Shock of 2008 has disproportionately affected recent college graduates all over the world. Many are initially hired as irregular workers and remain stuck in precarious jobs even many years after the economy has recovered amidst intensifying competition for a limited number of full-time positions.

In the case of South Korea, around 288,000 youth—or 8.6 percent of people in the fifteen-to-twenty-nine-year-old age bracket—were unemployed in 2017 according to Statistics Korea, making the rate of unemployment among youth more than double what it was for the general population (Kim 2017). Unemployment has become commonplace even among the college-educated. In 2003, more than one-third of South Korean youth who were jobless had college degrees (Bae and Song 2006). Those who turned to self-employment as a way to circumvent the system have also by and large failed to keep up with surging real estate prices and the decline in consumerism. According to the National Tax Service, among 228,460 businesses opened by South Koreans between the age of fifteen and thirty-four in 2011, only 23.5 percent sustained their businesses for more than five years (Kim 2017).

South Korean journalists refer to today's youth as the "*sampo* generation"—a neologism describing young adults who have given up on relationships, marriage, and children. For the vast majority of young South Koreans, finding a stable job has become an intangible dream. The select few who can afford to get married and have a family are those who are hand-picked to work for the *chaebol*.[1] On top of high incomes, South Korean conglomerates continue to offer their employees year-end bonuses, better working conditions, job security, and social status. But for 81 percent of the workforce employed by SMEs, average incomes have shrunk to 62.9 percent of those of large firms (Koo forthcoming). According to a Gallup Korea survey of 850 people between nineteen and thirty-one years old (excluding college students), in 2017 the average monthly income was only 1.58 million won ($1,338 USD) (Kim 2017).

Across the globe, a deepening class divide and grim prospects for stable employment have caused numerous highly skilled young adults from advanced industrialized countries to migrate in search of better opportunities. In the West, a new group of middle class youth leave their home countries planning to return after a year or so, only to end up staying for much longer. Francis Collins's (2014) work documents the precarious lives of young Americans who have migrated to South Korea to find jobs as English teachers. Though they often describe their motivations for leaving as rooted in a desire for self-exploration and adventure, many of the young graduates Collins interviews are also saddled with heavy student loans and scant means to pay them off. After working a series of part-time jobs in their countries of origin, they typically hear about a strong demand for native English teachers overseas through friendship networks (51). Collins and Shubin (2015) speak of an "in-betweenness" among these English teachers that was reminiscent of what I found in Beijing. According to one of their interviewees:

> [Those] people who are here temporarily, if you walk into their apartments, they're still living out of bags even if they've been here three, four years, they're still thinking along the lines of how affordable they can make their lives so they can ship it all back on the plane back home. (100)

Pei-Chia Lan's work shows how Westerners living in Taiwan have formed highly stratified communities similar to Beijing's Koreatown, with "higher-end professional migrants, such as diplomats and managers in multinational corporations" at the top of the social hierarchy (2011: 1683). Like the South Korean expats in Wangjing, these global elite lead relatively insular lives, distinguishing themselves from English teachers, who are stigmatized as "'drifting losers' with a lifestyle of excessive partying and drinking" (1688–1689).

Research on Japanese expat communities also demonstrates growing class divisions "between the descendants of old Japanese immigrants who left the country earlier, mostly to escape from poverty, and new corporate migrants" (Goodman et al. 2003: 10). As large Japanese companies expanded overseas in the 1980s, they created a new group of elite migrants whose lives of privilege set them apart from diasporic Japanese who had migrated out of necessity. Unlike other grassroots migrants, Japanese expats had access to a wide range of social and economic benefits including "housing provision, support for the establishment of social clubs and organizations, [and] the financing of the construction of Japanese Schools" (9). More recently, growing levels of Chinese foreign investment in Africa have led to similar patterns of social stratification within overseas Chinese communities (Lee 2017).

Neoliberal Reform and the Ethnic Enclave

This book helps demonstrate how the global expansion of companies and neoliberal reforms have created stratified flows of migration. I contribute to the existing literature by analyzing how notions of status, morality, and ethnic identity are constructed and negotiated within different configurations of space within migrant communities. As others have shown before me, multinational corporations have played a core institutional role in the enclave by stimulating the circulation of both formal and informal transnational capital. But perhaps more importantly, my book aims to show how conglomerates have also acted as key organizations, reproducing notions of worth and competence by manipulating a moral sensibility tied to ethnic membership.

Within these communities, increasingly a common ancestral heritage is not enough to procure a sense of shared fate and solidarity. Instead, we see how market deregulation has led to cleavages within the middle class, such that some highly skilled grassroots migrants who may appear privileged on the surface actually lead emotionally and financially precarious lives. While migration had once been utilized as a means to circumvent stunted mobility at home, in this new social order of global capitalism, oftentimes migration exacerbates precariousness as people are cut off from structures of social and institutional support that they had access to in their home countries.

Moreover, a pervasive sense of anxiety has led to intensifying conflicts within the middle class. Narratives of mobility and identity often commingle within a language of ethnic morality, reflecting "different visions of the state, different modes of capitalist (re)production, and . . . different forms of subjectivity" (Heiman et al. 2012: 14). Thus, the class solidarity that once propelled Korean factory workers into organizing labor strikes and social protests during South Korea's authoritarian regime in the 1980s has become fractured in recent years. Instead, South Korean entrepreneurs in Wangjing blamed their Korean Chinese managers for their downfall. They similarly criticized South Korean university students in the enclave for creating their own circumstances of misery. South Korean university students, for their part, adamantly claimed that they had nothing in common with Korean Chinese minorities even though many had spent nearly half their lives in China. How have cleavages within the middle class affected the future of politics and social movements within migrant communities? This is a question I hope future scholars will answer.

Endnote

1. Korean sociologists have argued that economic restructuring following the Asian financial crisis has triggered a growing gap in wealth and social stability between employees of large and smaller firms. As it has become more difficult for small- and medium-sized companies (SMEs) to survive in an overly saturated market, SMEs have relied heavily on *chaebol* firms for subcontracting jobs. While South Korean conglomerates have expanded their operations overseas, only a small number of SMEs have been able to survive economic downturn, leading to severely unbalanced levels of growth and power (Koo forthcoming).

REFERENCES

....

Alexander, P., and A. Chan. (2004). "Does China Have an Apartheid Pass System?" *Journal of Ethnic and Migration Studies* 30(4): 609–629.

Anderson, B. (1991). *Imagined Communities: Reflections on the Origin and Spread of Nationalism*. London: Verso.

Andreotti, A., P. Le Galès, and F. J. Moreno-Fuentes (2015). *Globalised Minds, Roots in the City: Urban Upper-Middle Classes in Europe*. Hoboken, NJ: Wiley.

Bae, J., and C. Rowley (2003). "Changes and Continuities in South Korean HRM." *Asia Pacific Business Review* 9(4): 76–105.

Bae, S. H., and J. H. Song (2006). "Youth Unemployment and the Role of Career and Technical Education: A Study of the Korean Labor Market." *Career and Technical Education Research* 31(1): 3–21.

Becker, H. S. (1986). *Writing for Social Scientists: How to Start and Finish Your Thesis, Book, or Article*. Chicago: University of Chicago Press.

Behar, R. (1996). *The Vulnerable Observer: Anthropology that Breaks Your Heart*. Boston: Beacon Press.

Bian, Y. (2002). "Chinese Social Stratification and Social Mobility." *Annual Review of Sociology* 28(1): 91–116.

Bonacich, E. (1973). "A Theory of Middleman Minorities." *American Sociological Review* 38(5): 583–594.

Bourdieu, P. (1993). *The Field of Cultural Production: Essays on Art and Literature*. New York: Columbia University Press.

Brass, D. J. (2009). "Connecting to Brokers: Strategies for Acquiring Social Capital." In *Social Capital: Reaching Out, Reaching In*, edited by V. O. Barktus and J. H. Davis, 260–274. Northampton, MA: Edward Elgar.

Burt, R. S. (2009). *Structural Holes: The Social Structure of Competition*. Cambridge: Harvard University Press.

Chan, K. W., and L. Zhang (1999). "The Hukou System and Rural-Urban Migration in China: Processes and Changes." *China Quarterly* 160: 818–855.

Choi, J. J. (1989). *Labor and the Authoritarian State: Labor Unions in South Korean Manufacturing Industries.* Seoul: Korea University Press.

Choudhry, M. T., E. Marelli, and M. Signorelli (2012). "Youth Unemployment Rate and Impact of Financial Crises." *International Journal of Manpower* 33(1): 76–95.

Coleman, J. S. (1988). "Social Capital in the Creation of Human Capital." *American Journal of Sociology* 94: 95–120.

Collins, F. L. (2014). "Teaching English in South Korea: Mobility Norms and Higher Education Outcomes in Youth Migration." *Children's Geographies* 12(1): 40–55.

Collins, F. L., and S. Shubin (2015). "Migrant Times Beyond the Life Course: The Temporalities of Foreign English Teachers in South Korea." *Geoforum* 62: 96–104.

Cumings, B. (1997). *Korea's Place in the Sun: A Modern History.* New York: Norton.

Davis, D. (ed.) (2000). *The Consumer Revolution in Urban China* (Vol. 22). Berkeley: University of California Press.

Davis, D. S. (1995). *Urban Spaces in Contemporary China: The Potential for Autonomy and Community in Post-Mao China.* Cambridge: Cambridge University Press.

Davis, D., and F. Wang. (2009). *Creating Wealth and Poverty in Postsocialist China.* Stanford, CA: Stanford University Press.

Desmond, M. (2016). *Evicted: Poverty and Profit in the American City.* New York: Broadway Books.

DiMaggio, P. (1997). "Culture and Cognition." *Annual Review of Sociology* 23: 263–287.

Dufoix, S. (2008). *Diasporas.* Berkeley: University of California Press.

Ellis, C. (2007). "Telling Secrets, Revealing Lives: Relational Ethics in Research with Intimate Others." *Qualitative Inquiry* 13(1): 3–29.

Fleischer, F. (2007). "To Choose a House Means to Choose a Lifestyle: The Consumption of Housing and Class Structuration in Urban China." *City & Society* 19(2): 287–311.

Freeman, C. (2011). *Making and Faking Kinship: Marriage and Labor Migration between China and South Korea.* Ithaca, NY: Cornell University Press.

Gelézeau, V. (2008). "Changing Socio-Economic Environments, Housing Culture and New Urban Segregation in Seoul." *European Journal of East Asian Studies* 7(2): 295–321.

Glazer, N. (1954). "Ethnic Groups in America: From National Culture to Ideology." In *Freedom and Control in Modern Society*, edited by M. Berger, T. Abel, and C. Page, 158–173. New York: Van Nostrand.

Goffman, E. (1951). "Symbols of Class Status." *British Journal of Sociology* 2(4): 294–304.

Gold, T., D. Guthrie, and D. Wank (eds.) (2002). *Social Connections in China: Institutions, Culture and the Changing Nature of Guanxi* (Vol. 21). Cambridge: Cambridge University Press.

Goodman, R., C. Peach, A. Takenaka, and P. White (eds.) (2003). *Global Japan: The Experience of Japan's New Immigrant and Overseas Communities*. New York: Routledge.

Gould, R. V. (1989). "Power and Social Structure in Community Elites." *Social Forces* 68(2), 531–552.

Haggard, S., W. Lim, and E. Kim (eds.) (2003). *Economic Crisis and Corporate Restructuring in Korea: Reforming the Chaebol*. New York: Cambridge University Press.

Han, D. (2010). "Policing and Racialization of Rural Migrant Workers in Chinese Cities." *Ethnic and Racial Studies* 33(4): 593–610.

Heiman, R., C. Freeman, M. Liechty, K. Fehérváry, C. Jones, and C. Katz (eds.) (2012). *The Global Middle Classes: Theorizing through Ethnography*. Santa Fe, NM: SAR Press.

Hochschild, A. (1983). *The Managed Heart*. Berkeley: University of California Press.

Hsing, Y. T. (2003). "Ethnic Identity and Business Solidarity: Chinese Capitalism Revisited." In *The Chinese Diaspora: Space, Place, Mobility and Identity*, edited by L. J. Ma and C. L. Cartier, 221–235. Boulder, CO: Rowman and Littlefield.

Hwang, K. K. (1987). "Face and Favor: The Chinese Power Game." *American Journal of Sociology* 92(4): 944–974.

Jaeger, A. M. (1983). "The Transfer of Organizational Culture Overseas: An Approach to Control in the Multinational Corporation." *Journal of International Business Studies* 14(2): 91–114.

Janelli, R. L., and D. Yim (1993). *Making Capitalism: The Social and Cultural Construction of a South Korean Conglomerate*. Stanford, CA: Stanford University Press.

Jin, S. (1990). "The Rights of Minority Nationalities in China: The Case of the Yanbian Korean Autonomous Prefecture." In *Koreans in China*, edited by D. S. Suh and E. Shultz, 31–43. Honolulu: University of Hawaii Press, 31–43.

Jo, J. Y. O. (2017). *Homing: An Affective Topography of Ethnic Korean Return Migration*. Honolulu: University of Hawaii Press.

Kang, H. R., and C. Rowley (2005). "Women in Management in South Korea: Advancement or Retrenchment?" *Asia Pacific Business Review* 11(2): 213–231.

Katigbak, E. O. (2015). "Moralizing Emotional Remittances: Transnational Familyhood and Translocal Moral Economy in the Philippines' 'Little Italy.'" *Global Networks* 15(4): 519–535.

Kim, A. E. (2000). "Korean Religious Culture and its Affinity to Christianity: The Rise of Protestant Christianity in South Korea." *Sociology of Religion* 61(2): 117–133.

Kim, A. E. (2004). "The Social Perils of the Korean Financial Crisis." *Journal of Contemporary Asia* 34(2): 221–237.

Kim, E. J. (2010). *Adopted Territory: Transnational Korean Adoptees and the Politics of Belonging.* Durham, NC: Duke University Press.

Kim, H. (2010). *International Ethnic Networks and Intra-ethnic Conflict: Koreans in China.* London: Palgrave MacMillan.

Kim, H. H. (2003). "Ethnic Enclave Economy in Urban China: The Korean Immigrants in Yanbian." *Ethnic and Racial Studies* 6(5): 802–828.

Kim, J. (2016). *Contested Embrace: Transborder Membership Politics in Twentieth-Century Korea.* Stanford, CA: Stanford University Press.

Kim, J. (2017). "A 'Lost Generation' in South Korea Bears the Brunt of Rising Inequality." *Nikkei Asian Review*, December 14. https://asia.nikkei.com/Economy/A-lost-generation-in-South-Korea-bears-the-brunt-of-rising-inequality.

Kim, S. (2000). *Korea and Globalization.* New York: Columbia University Press.

Kim, S. J. (2003). "The Economic Status and Role of Ethnic Koreans in China." In *The Korean Diaspora in the World Economy*, edited by C. Bergsten and I. Choi, 101–127. Washington, DC: Institute for International Economics.

Kim, S., and J. Finch. (2002). "Living with Rhetoric, Living against Rhetoric: Korean Families and the IMF Economic Crisis." *Korean Studies* 26(1): 120–139.

Kim, Y. C. (1986). "Women's Movement in Modem Korea." In *Challenges for Women*, edited by S. W. Chung, 75–102. Seoul: Ewha Women's University Press, 75–102.

Finch, J., and S. K. Kim (2012). "Kirŏgi Families in the US: Transnational Migration Education." *Journal of Ethnic and Migration and Studies* 38(3): 485–506.

Koo, H. (2001). *Korean Workers: The Culture and Politics of Class Formation.* Ithaca, NY: Cornell University Press.

Koo, H. (2016). "The Global Middle Class: How is it Made, What Does it Represent?" *Globalizations* 13(4): 440–453.

Koo, H. (forthcoming). "Rising Inequality and Shifting Class Boundaries in South Korea in the Neo-Liberal Era." *Journal of Contemporary Asia*: 1–19.

Krug, B., and J. Mehta (2001). "Entrepreneurship by Alliance." *No. ERS-2001-85-ORG.* Rotterdam, the Netherlands: Erasmus Research Institute of Management.

Lan, P. C. (2011). "White Privilege, Language Capital and Cultural Ghettoisation: Western High-skilled Migrants in Taiwan." *Journal of Ethnic and Migration Studies* 37(10): 1669–1693.

Lee, C. J. (1986). *China's Korean Minority: The Politics of Ethnic Education.* Boulder, CO: Westview Press.

Lee, C. J. (1996). *China and Korea: Dynamic Relations.* Stanford, CA: Hoover Institution Press.

Lee, C. K. (2017). *The Spectre of Global China: Politics, Labor, and Foreign Investment in Africa.* Chicago: University of Chicago Press.

Lee, H. K. (1932). "Korean Migrants in Manchuria." *Geographical Review* 22(2): 196–204.

Lee, H. K. (2013). "Employment and Life Satisfaction among Female Marriage Migrants in South Korea." *Asian and Pacific Migration Journal* 22(2): 199–230.

Lee, H. K. (2018). *Between Foreign and Family: Return Migration and Identity Construction among Korean Americans and Korean Chinese.* New Brunswick, NJ: Rutgers University Press.

Lee, H. S. (2003). *Korean Dream: A Report on its Hope and Struggle* (in Korean). Seoul: I-Field.

Lee, T. S. (2010). *Born Again: Evangelicalism in Korea.* Honolulu: University of Hawaii Press.

Lee, Y. (2015). "Labor after Neoliberalism: The Birth of the Insecure Class in South Korea." *Globalizations* 12(2): 184–202.

Levitt, P., and B. N. Jaworsky. (2007). "Transnational Migration Studies: Past Developments and Future Trends." *Annual Review of Sociology* 33: 129–156.

Lie, J. (2008). *Zainichi (Koreans in Japan): Diasporic Nationalism and Postcolonial Identity* (Vol. 8). Berkeley: University of California Press.

Lie, J. (ed.) (2014). *Multiethnic Korea? Multiculturalism, Migration, and Peoplehood Diversity in Contemporary South Korea.* Berkeley: Institute of East Asian Studies, University of California Press.

Light, I., and Bonacich, E. (1988). *Immigrant Entrepreneurs: Koreans in Los Angeles, 1965–1982.* Berkeley: University of California Press.

Light, I., G. Sabagh, M. Bozorgmehr, and C. Der-Martirosian (1994). "Beyond the Ethnic Enclave Economy." *Social Problems* 41(1): 65–80.

Lim, H. C., and J. H. Jang. (2006). "Between Neoliberalism and Democracy: The Transformation of the Developmental State in South Korea." *Development and Society* 35(1): 1–28.

Lim, T. (2002). "The Changing Face of South Korea: The Emergence of Korea as a 'Land of Immigration.'" *Korea Society Quarterly* 3(2–3): 16–21.

Ma, L. J., and B. Xiang. (1998). "Native Place, Migration and the Emergence of Peasant Enclaves in Beijing." *China Quarterly* 155: 546–581.

Morrison, A. M., R. P. White, and E. Van Velsor. (1987). *Breaking the Glass Ceiling: Can Women Reach the Top of America's Largest Corporations?* London: Pearson Education.

National Bureau of Statistics of China. (2005). *China Statistical Yearbook.* Beijing: China Statistical Press.

Oliver, R. T. (1993). *A History of the Korean People in Modern Times: 1800 to the Present.* Newark: University of Delaware Press.

Paik, W., and M. Ham (2011). "From Autonomous Areas to Non-Autonomous Areas: The Politics of Korean Minority Migration in Contemporary China." *Modern China* 38(1): 110–133.

Parish, W. L. (1984). "Destratification in China." In *Class and Social Stratification in Post Revolution China,* edited by J. Watson, 84–120. Cambridge: Cambridge University Press.

Park, A. M. (2019). *Sovereignty Experiments: Korean Migrants and the Building of Borders in Northeast Asia, 1860–1945.* Ithaca, NY: Cornell University Press.

Park, H. O. (2015). *The Capitalist Unconscious: From Korean Unification to Transnational Korea*. New York: Columbia University Press.

Park, H. R. (1996). "Narratives of Migration: From the Formation of Korean Chinese Nationality in the PRC to the Emergence of Korean Chinese Migrants in South Korea." PhD dissertation, University of Washington.

Park, J. S., and P. Y. Chang (2005). "Contention in the Construction of a Global Korean Community: The Case of the Overseas Korean Act." *Journal of Korean Studies* 10(1): 1–27.

Park, K. (1997). *The Korean American Dream: Immigrants and Small Business in New York City*. Ithaca, NY: Cornell University Press.

Park, S. J. (2009). "Ms. C's Tears of Bitterness in Her 13th Year of Living in Beijing" (in Korean). *Monthly Chosun*, 30(4).

Park Matthews, N. Y. (2005). "Development, Culture and Gender in Korea: A Sociological Study of Female Office Employees in Chaebol." PhD dissertation, London School of Economics and Political Science.

Piao, C. (1990). "The History of Koreans in China and the Yanbian Autonomous Prefecture." In *Koreans in China*, edited by D. Suh and E. Shultz, 44–77. Honolulu: University of Hawaii Center for Korean Studies.

Portes, A. (1987). "The Social Origins of the Cuban enclave of Miami." *Sociological Perspectives* 30(4): 340–372.

Portes, A. (1997). "Immigration Theory for a New Century: Some Problems and Opportunities." *International Migration Review* 31(4): 799–825.

Portes, A., and R. Rumbaut (2001). *Legacies: The Story of the Immigrant Second Generation*. Berkeley: University of California Press.

Rohlen, T. P. (1979). *For Harmony and Strength: Japanese White-Collar Organization in Anthropological Perspective*. Berkeley: University of California Press.

Ropp, S. M. (2000). "Secondary Migration and the Politics of Identity for Asian Latinos in Los Angeles." *Journal of Asian American Studies* 3(2): 219–229.

Ryang, S. (2008). *Writing Selves in Diaspora: Ethnography of Autobiographics of Korean Women in Japan and the United States*. Lanham, MD: Rowman & Littlefield Publishers.

Sanders, J., and V. Nee (1992). "Problems in Resolving the Enclave Economy Debate." *American Sociological Review* 57(3): 415–418.

Sayer, A. (2005). "Class, Worth and Recognition." *Sociology* 39(5): 947–963.

Seo, J. (2007). "Interpreting Wangjing: Ordinary Foreigners in a Globalizing Town." *Korea Observer* 38(3): 469–500.

Seol, D. H., and J. D. Skrentny (2009). "Ethnic Return Migration and Hierarchical Nationhood: Korean Chinese Foreign Workers in South Korea." *Ethnicities* 9(2): 147–174.

Sklair, L. (2002). "The Transnational Capitalist Class and Global Politics: Deconstructing the Corporate-State Connection." *International Political Science Review* 23(2): 159–174.

Snyder, S. (2009). *China's Rise and the Two Koreas: Politics, Economics, and Security*. Boulder, CO: Lynne Rienner Publishers.

Solinger, D. J. (1999). *Contesting Citizenship in Urban China: Peasant Migrants, the State and the Logic of the Market*. Berkeley: University of California Press.

Song, C. (2009). "Brothers Only in Name: The Alienation and Identity Transformation of Korean Chinese Return Migrants in South Korea." In *Diasporic Homecomings: Ethnic Return Migration in Comparative Perspective*, edited by T. Tsuda, 281–304. Stanford, CA: Stanford University Press, 281–304.

Song, J. (2009). *South Koreans in the Debt Crisis: The Creation of a Neoliberal Welfare Society*. Durham, NC: Duke University Press.

Spencer, J. H., P. R. Flowers, and J. Seo (2012). "Post-1980s Multicultural Immigrant Neighbourhoods: Koreatowns, Spatial Identities and Host Regions in the Pacific Rim." *Journal of Ethnic and Migration Studies* 38(3): 437–461.

Stovel, K., and L. Shaw (2012). "Brokerage." *Annual Review of Sociology* 38: 139–158.

Walder, A. (1986). *Communist Neo-Traditionalism: Work and Authority in Chinese Industry*. Berkeley: University of California Press.

Wang, Y. P. (2004). *Urban Poverty, Housing and Social Change in China*. New York: Routledge.

Whyte, M. K. (2012). "China's Post-Socialist Inequality." *Current History* 111(746): 229–234.

Wong, D., Y. L. Chang, and X. S. He (2007). "Rural Migrant Workers in Urban China: Living a Marginalized Life." *International Journal of Social Welfare* 16(1): 32–40.

Wu, F., and K. Webber (2004). "The Rise of 'Foreign Gated Communities' in Beijing: Between Economic Globalization and Local Institutions." *Cities* 21(3): 203–213.

Yang, E. K. (2010). "Ethnic Return Migration and the Discursive Construction of Hierarchical Nationhood: The Case of 'Korean-Chinese' Discourse on Chosun-Ilbo." *Korean Journal of Broadcasting and Telecommunication Studies* 24(5): 194–237.

Yang, M. (1994). *Gifts, Favors, and Banquets: The Art of Social Relationships in China*. Ithaca, NY: Cornell University Press.

Yang, M. (2018). *From Miracle to Mirage: The Making and Unmaking of the Korean Middle Class, 1960–2015*. Ithaca, NY: Cornell University Press.

Yi, J., and G. Jung (2015). "Debating Multicultural Korea: Media Discourse on Migrants Minorities in South Korea." *Journal of Ethnic and Migration Studies* 41(6): 985–1013.

Yoon, I. J. (2012). "Migration and the Korean Diaspora." *Journal of Ethnic and Migration Studies* 38(3): 413–435.

Yoon, S. J. (2020). "The Split Enclave: Transnationalism and Co-ethnic Conflict in the Koreatown in Beijing." In *Koreatowns: Exploring the Economics, Politics and*

Identities of Korean Spatial Formations, edited by S. M. Kim, J. Kim, and S. Suh. Lanham, MD: Lexington Books.

Zelizer, V. A. (2011). *Economic Lives: How Culture Shapes the Economy*. Princeton, NJ: Princeton University Press.

Zerubavel, E. (1991). *The Fine Line*. Chicago: University of Chicago Press.

Zerubavel, E. (2012). *Ancestors and Relatives: Genealogy, Identity, and Community*. Oxford: Oxford University Press.

Zhan, X. (2004). "Analysis of South Korea's Direct Investment in China." *Journal of International Logistics and Trade*, 2(2): 125–132.

INDEX
....

Figures are indicated by *f* following the page number.

V

Van Velsor, E., 95
vulnerability, church members
  church group environment, 134–136
  emotional, 126, 127
  Korean Christians, early, 125
vulnerable ethnography method, 24–27

W

Wangjing enclave, 1, 59–79. *See also specific topics*
  foreign investment, 59–60
  history and sudden growth, 59–60
  Koreatown, 1–2
  maps, 64*f*, 65*f*
  South Koreans, higher status, 10–11
  technology park, 59–60
  transnational resources, 5
  types of Koreans, 1–2
Wangjing enclave, everyday life, 60–61
  coethnic relations, interaction spaces, 61–62
  cultural hybridity, 69–70
  discrimination, Korean Chinese and South Korean migrants coethnic, 68–74
  Fleischer ethnographic study, 60–61
  good intentions, limits of, 74–78
  Han Chinese, 60–61
  housing and rent, 60, 65*f*, 66–68, 72–73
  Korean Chinese, intimacy and familiar routines, 61, 62*f*, 63*f*
  Korean Chinese, minorities, 10, 68–74
  perceptions of reality, questioning, 78–79
  rise of, 62–68

South Korean migrants, stages of migration, 63–66
  surface appearance, 60
White, R. P., 95
women
  gendered dynamics, 94
  Korean Chinese, cost-benefit analysis, 47–48
  Korean Chinese, guilt, leaving *gohyang*, 47–48
  Korean Chinese wives and paper marriages, 44–46
  roles, *chaebol* on, 21
  South Korean, young, migration and remittances, 44–45
working overtime, significance, 98–101
workplace. *See also chaebol*
  ethnic boundaries, 19, 83, 88–89
worthiness, masculinized, 21

Y

yaban doju, 3 *See also* fleeing by night
Yanbian University of Science and Technology (YUST), 22–23
Yellow Sea, 53
Yim, D., 84, 94
youth, South Korean, 168–173
  faith, as direction, 168–169
  middle class, precariousness, 169–172
  neoliberal reform and ethnic enclave, 172–173
  unemployment and *sampo* generation, 170–171

Z

Zerubavel, E., 69, 72